GETTING AWAY
with
MURDER

Weapons for the War
Against Domestic Violence

Raoul Felder

and

Barbara Victor

SIMON & SCHUSTER

NEW YORK   LONDON   TORONTO
SYDNEY   TOKYO   SINGAPORE

SIMON & SCHUSTER
Rockefeller Center
1230 Avenue of the Americas
New York, NY 10020

Designed by Edith Fowler
Manufactured in the United States of America

10   9   8   7   6   5   4   3   2   1

Library of Congress Cataloging-in-Publication Data

Felder, Raoul Lionel, 1934–
    Getting away with murder : weapons for the war
against domestic violence / Raoul Felder and
Barbara Victor.
        p.   cm.
    Includes index.
    1. Family violence—United States—Prevention.
2. Victims of family violence—United States.
3. Abused women—United States. I.   Victor,
Barbara.   II. Title.
HQ809.3.U5F45   1996
362.82' 92—dc20   95-53993   CIP
ISBN 0-684-81362-9

This is a work of nonfiction. The names and certain
identifying characteristics of some of the individuals
discussed have been changed.

ACKNOWLEDGMENTS

Thanks to Robert Mecoy for his steadfast commitment to this project, his bottomless bag of ideas, and his profound desire to change the world. Thanks also goes to Brian McSharry for his remarkable ability to practice grace under pressure. And for everyone cited and not cited in this book who shared their experiences, opinions, and pain, we are deeply grateful.

FOR ALL OF THOSE
WHO DID NOT SURVIVE
THIS CRIME OF VIOLENCE

CONTENTS

ONE

"Why Didn't She Just Leave?"

CHARLES AND TRACEY THURMAN had been married only long enough to have a child when she left him. The reason: he was abusive. For the next eight months, Tracey, with her infant son, lived in constant fear. Thurman made harassing phone calls. He followed her when she left the house, abused her, and on several occasions even publicly threatened to kill her. But it wasn't until Tracey was sitting in her car one afternoon and Thurman came along and smashed the windshield in view of a policeman that he finally was arrested. After his conviction the court suspended his six-month sentence and put him on probation, but the probation order nonetheless prohibited Thurman from assaulting or harassing her.

Within days, Thurman violated his probation by showing up at Tracey's house, brandishing a gun and threatening to shoot her and their baby. Tracey called the police. The police, however, refused to make an arrest. Instead, they told Tracey to call back in three weeks, and in the interim, if she was "really afraid," to seek help from the Family Relations Office there in Torrington, Connecticut. Tracey begged the police to help her, arguing that a violation of probation was police business, not the problem of a local social service agency. The police remained adamant.

With no other option available, Tracey went to the social

service office and, as she suspected, was told that her problem was a police matter. Returning to court and explaining what the police and the social service office had told her, she was finally able to convince the judge to issue a restraining order against her estranged husband, barring him not only from assaulting or threatening her, but also from coming within two miles of her house.

During the next three weeks, Charles Thurman continued to harass and threaten his ex-wife, and on several occasions showed up at her house, followed her, and publicly abused her. Three weeks later, and armed with that order of protection, Tracey returned to the police and demanded once again that they arrest her estranged husband for having violated the order on numerous occasions since it had been issued. The excuse that the police gave Tracey on that occasion was that they couldn't make an arrest until after the Thanksgiving weekend. Again, Tracey went away without police protection but returned first thing on Monday morning, demanding Charles Thurman's arrest for violation of the restraining order. Once again, the police refused to act, informing her that the only officer who could help her happened to be on vacation and was not due back for several weeks. And so, yet another time, Tracey went away empty handed, but not without putting it on record that she was in constant fear for her life and the life of her baby.

In fact, Tracey's family and friends also reported Thurman's threats to the police. It was clear to everyone except the police that Thurman was making it impossible for Tracey to leave the house or lead a normal life. As Tracey told CBS-TV's Dan Rather in a television interview long after the fact, "I went as far as I could go; if my ex-husband would call me on the telephone and threaten me, I would call the police immediately. 'I want this put down on record,' I would tell them, because I figured that if they heard his name enough times, they would finally pick him up." But Tracey figured wrong. It took much more before the police would finally respond.

On June 10, 1983, Charles Thurman showed up in front

of Tracey's house shouting, threatening, and demanding to see her and their baby. Tracey called the police. By now, the police were well aware of the name "Thurman." For eight months, they had taken numerous calls about incidents of violence, neighbors' complaints, and violations of court orders, all concerning Tracey and against Charles. Yet, despite all that, plus the fact that the police knew that Charles Thurman had a history of battering his wife and threatening to kill both her and their infant child, the officer who took the call apparently considered it more important to stop by the station to urinate before speeding off to protect Tracey Thurman from what was a potentially lethal attack.

According to testimony by neighbors, the policeman arrived twenty-five minutes later but remained across the street from Tracey's house in his car. In fact, according to those same witnesses, the police officer stayed in his car and watched while Charles Thurman chased Tracey to the backyard with a knife, grabbed her by the hair, slashed her cheek, stabbed her in the neck, knocked her down, and stabbed her twelve more times. Though the policeman saw Charles Thurman run behind the house and heard a scream, when he finally got out of his car, he went to knock on the front door first. When he got to the backyard, he persuaded Thurman to turn over the bloody knife, but still did not either subdue him or arrest him. The officer later said he had not seen Tracey's body and could not tell whether Charles Thurman had stabbed a person or a chicken or a dog, though he had heard Tracey's scream. While the policeman went to lock the knife in his trunk, Thurman, now unarmed, attacked Tracey again as she lay there, injured and bleeding. Kicking her in the base of the skull, Thurman broke her neck before he ran upstairs and grabbed the baby, dropping him on Tracey's limp body before kicking her one final time in the head. Apparently, while that first officer on the scene was still inside his car, he had summoned backup help, because suddenly everywhere were flashing lights and sirens. An ambulance along with several police cars arrived on the scene, uniformed reinforcements spilling out of the cars and gathering on Tracey's front lawn. But it wasn't until Tracey was being lifted into the ambulance and Thurman rushed forward to attack her again that the police finally restrained him and took him into custody.

The question that comes to mind, even before the obvious one about why the police didn't interfere earlier, is, what exactly was Charles Thurman thinking at the time, knowing that he was able to assault his wife again and again in front of the police without being stopped? Here is what Charles Thurman said: "I wasn't thinking. I don't even remember being there or what happened. All I saw was this blinding white light, nothing else. I don't remember anything else." But Tracey remembers, and so do a lot of other people, including the Torrington police.

In 1988, after Charles Thurman was sentenced to jail for twenty years for the attempted murder of Tracey Thurman and had served four years of his sentence, Dan Rather came to Torrington, Connecticut, to interview Tracey for the CBS television program *48 Hours.* The subject of Rather's show was Tracey's feelings about the fact that her ex-husband would be eligible for parole in 1990. "I know he's going to come back after me," Tracey told Rather, "and that frightens me. And it scares me to think that I'm going to have to live like I lived for eight months, when I was going through the separation ... And I know I'm going to have to go through it all again ... Hopefully they [the police] will be there on time, and they'll be able to protect me ... but I know he [Charles Thurman] is determined ... He stated several times that both of us can't live in this world and he's not going to be the one to go. But if he was ever to get to me again, I would rather that he finish the job, because I could never deal with another beating like this ... How much more handicapped could I be?"

In response to Tracey's fears concerning Thurman's possible parole, Dan Rather posed the following question: "Why not move away?" he asked, "Why not get a long, long way away?" It was an interesting variation on the more familiar question "Why didn't she just leave?" In the case of Tracey Thurman, "leaving" had not been enough, since she had tried that and still suffered dire consequences. In fact, not only had Tracey left her abusive and violent husband and filed for divorce, but she had followed all the rules, utilized every service available to her within the community, called the police, reported her estranged husband's abuse and threatening behavior, went to court, signed a complaint that resulted in Charles Thurman being placed on probation, reported that he violated his probation, went back to court and swore out a restraining order against him, called the police to report that he violated the restraining order —and still ended up partially paralyzed and permanently disfigured because the system failed her each and every time. Even on that very last day, when Tracey sustained her most serious injuries, it was because the police remained consistent in their policy of not taking Tracey's pleas seriously and because the police officer who took that final emergency call evidently judged it more effective to remain in his car yards away from a woman who was being beaten almost to death.

In fairness to Dan Rather, however, and to everyone else who asks that question or any variation of it, there is a history worth citing.

According to historian Elizabeth Peck, the question "Why didn't she just leave?" was first asked in the 1920s. Back then, sociologists believed that battered women stayed in abusive relationships because they were of low intelligence or mentally retarded. During the 1940s, sociologists changed their minds and assumed that battered women remained with their battering mates because they were masochistic and enjoyed being beaten. By the 1970s, the victim was thought to stay with her abuser because, as a married woman, she was isolated from her friends, family, and neighbors, had few economic or educational resources, and had been terrorized into a state of "learned helplessness"* resulting from repeated beatings.

* Years of studies conducted by Lenore Walker and described in her book *The Battered Woman* reveal that "traumatic psychological infantilism," which is seen in hostages or political prisoners, is comparable to what she calls "learned helplessness," a condition that, according to Walker, has "three basic components: information about what will

But the truth was, even then, that the victim frequently had, indeed, tried to use the medical, social service, and legal systems to protect her: she *did* call the police, she *did* seek medical attention, and she *did* tell friends and family and doctors that one day her partner would kill her. In too many cases, all these cries for help went unheard and the woman ended up predicting her own murder. While the experts' rationalizations have changed from the 1920s to the present as to why victims don't leave their assailants, one thing hasn't changed: in most states assaults against wives and girlfriends are still considered misdemeanors. This is true even in states where an identical assault against a stranger is a felony.

Another thing that hasn't—and won't—change is that *the* question, "Why didn't she just leave?" (or any variation of it) is rhetorical. It is not only rhetorical but, more important, it is life threatening as it pertains to Tracey Thurman and every other woman who suffers abuse, terrorization, or attempted murder at the hands of an intimate partner. In fact, the real problem with that question, however phrased, is that it isn't really a question at all. Rather, it is a statement that, while often made unknowingly by those who think they are asking a question, tells everything that is wrong with society's response to the crime of domestic violence. By the mere asking of that question, the victim of this type of crime is automatically blamed for not taking action, either by leaving or moving away—an action or reaction to violence that is supposed to protect her from her assailant.

The reality is that women leave all the time. Often they give up their homes, friends, family, and jobs, all in an at-

---

happen; thinking or cognitive representation about what will happen (learning, speculation, belief, perception); and behavior toward what does happen." That concept, Walker believes, is important for understanding why battered women do not attempt to free themselves from a battering relationship. "Once the women are operating from a belief of helplessness," Walker says, "the perception becomes reality and they become passive, submissive, and helpless."

tempt to be safe and far from their abusers. And most of the time, as in the case of Tracey Thurman, leaving doesn't protect them or make them safe. There are many other cases, especially if children are involved, when the courts actually make it possible for the abuser to find the victim: when they force her to give the court and the lawyer for the accused her address and phone number so that the accused is not deprived of his parental rights, and can keep in touch with, or even visit, his children.

There are millions of women, including Tracey Thurman, from many different social, racial, ethnic, religious, economic, and intellectual backgrounds, who call the police, testify in court, swear out orders of protection, seek care at hospitals or at the offices of private physicians, detail their injuries, allow their injuries to be photographed, flee to shelters, to friends or family, and even, trusting of the system, bravely name and identify their abusers for police to arrest, prosecutors to prosecute, and judges to sentence. These are the same women who depend on the system to protect them, rely on the good advice and instructions of law enforcement officers and on the judicial process, and in the end are brutally and violently disappointed, if not brutally and violently injured or killed.

And then there are the battered women who don't leave, who have no family, money, or support system to help them escape a violent situation. Some of these women remain silent about their abuse because they are ashamed that society will judge them to be mentally ill or unable to control their own lives. Occasionally, these are the same women who finally muster up the courage to tell their priest, rabbi, or pastor about the abuse they suffer, and instead of receiving help and understanding, are ultimately blamed for provoking the abuse or being less than perfect wives.

There are still other victims of this crime, women who happen to be married to rich men, famous men, pillars of the community, men who control their every financial decision and monetary expenditure, men who are in a position to finance a long, drawn-out divorce case and mobilize public opinion—actions that might result in these women losing their children or ending up homeless and destitute. The reality is that, rich or poor, most of the battered women who hide their agony are so beaten down emotionally and physically that they are unable to make decisions, plan escapes, or even feed themselves or their children without depending solely on their abusers.

There are no guaranteed outcomes for victims of domestic violence, whether they leave or stay, whether they tell the world about the abuse they suffer or hide it even from their closest friends and family. These are the innocent victims of crime who risk losing their children in either case, just because they can neither stop the abuse in their homes nor stop their abusers from finding them. These are the same women who, even when they flee to shelters to escape and give up their homes and all their possessions, are still at risk. These are the innocent crime victims who, often employed and even highly successful in their professions, lose their jobs either because their abusers harass them at work or because bruises, injuries, or emotional trauma force them to call in sick one time too many. These are the battered women who are afraid to report their abusers for fear that they will retaliate either physically or financially, or who are afraid that even if their abusers are arrested and incarcerated, they themselves will lose everything in the process.

Although each of the above-cited eventualities and fears is well known, they have never provoked adequate response throughout society to deal with the problem from the beginning. For example, whose responsibility is it to see that all women and children at risk are protected under the law, are given adequate medical care, are offered viable options to start new lives, and are assured that they can keep their children and care for them in a happy and healthy atmosphere? Whose obligation is it to protect these women when they finally do report their injuries and press charges against their abusers? Whose obligation is it to insure these women their rights in every sense of the word so they are not forced to pay over and over again an inordinate and inhuman price for having once made a bad choice of a life partner? Or twice, or however many times it happens to them. Whose responsibility is it to lead them to safety?

According to a survey done in 1995 by the Federal Bureau of Investigation, somewhere in the United States a woman is battered every seven seconds. The problem is that every time a woman suffers this kind of abuse, there are very few people—even among those who are otherwise enlightened, respectable, intelligent, and sane and who consider themselves politically correct and nonviolent—whose first question when they hear about a case of spousal assault or murder is not, "Why didn't she just leave?" Tragically, what this particular type of violent crime usually does *not* provoke is questions that are far more relevant and lucid and that would provide much more useful and concrete solutions to stopping it, questions such as

"How can that man get away with that?"
"Where were the police?"
"Was he arrested?"
"Was he thrown out of his house?"
"Will he stand trial and be convicted and serve a stiff
    jail sentence?"
"Will the victim get police protection, financial aid,
    medical care, legal advice, child support?"
"How will that woman and her children survive,
    financially and emotionally?"

Instead, by asking the question "Why didn't she just leave?" society makes an immediate judgment about the victim's part in a crime that was committed against her—a crime, by the way, that is covered under every single criminal statute throughout the United States, whether that crime is assault, battery, harassment, or, in the extreme, murder. In every instance, the only possible outcome of that question is that it automatically blames the victim of the crime for inciting, tolerating, or even enjoying the abuse. What usually follows is the assumption that in some kind of macabre and inexplicable way, the victim of spousal violence cooperated or acted in complicity with her assailant, allowing him or enabling him to carry out his assault. This in turn exonerates the police, health care providers, social service workers, prosecutors, and judges from acting on the victim's behalf. Consciously or unconsciously, inadvertently or on purpose, the effect of that question is to separate crime victims assaulted by intimate partners from crime victims assaulted by strangers.

The implications of that question are not unlike a remark made by the former French prime minister, Raymond Barre, after a terrorist bombing by Palestinian Arabs of Goldenberg's Restaurant in the Jewish quarter of Paris. Condemning the act on national television, Prime Minister Barre said, "There were sixteen Jews killed and twenty-four innocent victims." Now, what Raymond Barre meant to say was that there were sixteen specifically targeted victims—Jews—who lost their lives and twenty-four non-Jews who also died, because they just happened to be passing by when the bomb exploded. As they concerned the terrorist attack in Paris, the prime minister's words were an unfortunate error in judgment.

As they concern domestic violence, judgments about which victim is innocent or guilty based on her relationship with the assailant or whether or not she was the only intended target are the result of an inherent prejudice throughout society regarding this particular crime. To put it another way, if the public stopped and considered the following questions before asking *the* question—"Why didn't she just leave?"—they might find that they wouldn't have to ask it at all:

> Should the crime of domestic violence be ignored by the system, and the perpetrator of that crime go unpunished, if he manages to injure or kill only his intended target?
>
> Should the crime of domestic violence be punished, and the perpetrator of that crime be convicted,

only if, in the course of his committing that
crime, "innocent" people were also harmed?

Should criminals be convicted on the basis of the law
and not on the basis of whether or not they successfully isolate their intended target?

Should criminals be convicted of a crime regardless
of their relationship to their victim?

Should any victim of a crime be judged innocent or
guilty on the basis of whether the victim facili-
tated the crime that was committed against him
or her?

Or, should the accused be the only one forced to
stand trial for a specific crime, to be judged innocent or guilty by a jury of his peers in a court of
law?

The answers to these questions seem obvious, at least on
the surface, as long as crimes are not broken down into
specific categories depending on whether victims and perpetrators happen to have, or have had, a relationship. The
immediate and correct response should be that there are
only innocent victims of crime; accused criminals, when convicted, must be punished under the law regardless of what
their relationship is to the victim, regardless of what the
victim did or did not do to prevent the crime from occurring
in the first place, regardless of whether the intended victim
was the only one who was injured or killed. Most people, if
they think about it, might even add that there should be no
exceptions to the law, or extenuating circumstances based
on social, emotional, familial, or economic reasons when it
comes to arresting and convicting criminals of assault, rape,
or murder. Considerations such as personal feelings and
opinions on the part of the police concerning the crime
itself, the victim, or the perpetrator should not be a factor in
the arrest. Concern on the part of prosecutors or judges that
the perpetrator may lose his job if he is convicted or that
legal action against him will break up the family—or doubts
about whether the victim will carry through to press charges

and testify down the line—should not influence the legal process. Assumptions on the part of the police, prosecutors, judges, or health care providers that the couple will work things out themselves, a belief that what happens behind closed doors is a private matter, suspicion that the victim is lying to get a better financial settlement in a divorce, concern about false-arrest lawsuits, or a belief that the victim has the right to conceal her injuries and protect the person who inflicted them should all be irrelevant to the crime that was committed.

When the police arrive on the scene of a crime and determine that an individual's life is at risk, all other issues —social, emotional, or financial—should be dealt with only after measures are taken to separate the victim from her assailant. Tracey Thurman is one of the best examples of a woman who not only left, but also considered it her right to use the system to protect her from harm. Yet in the end, she was a victim not only of her husband, but also of a system that failed her by its blatant lack of response.

In quite another way, and with all good intentions, advocates for battered women, while the most effective voices for making society aware of this crime, are also guilty of compromising the safety of victims. Their support of "empowerment," that is, the right of women to choose whether or not to report their injuries at hospitals or offices of private physicians, to press charges against their assailants, to testify in court, to return home to their abuser to try and calm things down, to work things out—at the moment when they are terrorized, traumatized, or badly injured—puts victims in continued jeopardy. As they pertain to "stranger crime," these same so-called rights are not considered, which might account for the fact that perpetrators of stranger crime are arrested and prosecuted far more often and far more successfully than men who assault women with whom they share or have shared an emotional history.

Regardless of whether the intentions are good or bad, it is the victim who pays the ultimate price because the system does not respond or because the system does not take the initiative to protect her without her consent. The crime of domestic violence, therefore, risks becoming a secondary issue, while the rights of the victim are put before the wrong that has been committed—or the rights of the perpetrator are put before the most important rights of the victim, which are to live without fear and free from harm. Even more detrimental to the victim is this: that encouraging her to make her own decisions precisely at a point in her life when she needs others to take over for her only provokes the question "Why didn't she just leave?"

The answer to the question of when to arrest a batterer is suddenly not so obvious. On some very visceral level, society judges that if a victim knows her assailant, she should somehow be able to prevent the assault, while at the same time, society also judges that a victim who is assaulted by a stranger has no way of avoiding what is considered to be a random attack. In other words, when it comes to crimes of domestic violence as opposed to stranger crimes, society differentiates, just as Prime Minister Barre did in Paris, between victims who are innocent and victims who are guilty.

While judging any victim of a crime carries serious moral consequences in our system of justice, judging the guilt or innocence of a victim of domestic violence creates an even more dangerous consequence. Sending a message to men—specifically husbands, ex-husbands, boyfriends, or ex-boyfriends—that battering women they know is treated less severely under the law than battering strangers makes all women more vulnerable. Instead, given the proximity of victim and assailant in crimes of domestic violence, not only should the victim be overprotected, but every crime should be treated as a potential homicide. That would not only insure greater protection to all women, but also, as a secondary gain, send a new message to men: that the crime of domestic violence is considered more serious than stranger crime.

Tracey Thurman answered Dan Rather's question on television that evening—"Why don't you move a long, long way away?"—by saying, "Why should I leave? I grew up here, my family is here, my support is here . . . and even if I did run away, he'd find me."

Tracey Thurman could have added that, at least the next time, if Charles Thurman went after her again, when and if he was released on parole, the Torrington Police Department would think twice about ignoring her pleas for help, not think twice about arresting him, and certainly take appropriate measures against any member of their police force who stopped to urinate before speeding over to a possible homicide in progress, or worse, remained inside a police car, watching an attempted homicide in progress.

While Tracey Thurman is by no means an exception to what can and often does happen to any victim of domestic assault, she is an exception when it comes to the judicial outcome of her case. Under the circumstances, however, she paid an enormous price for her victory.

Suing the city of Torrington as well as twenty-nine individual police officers, Tracey Thurman claimed a violation of her constitutional rights set forth in the Fourteenth Amendment to the United States Constitution, which says, "nor shall any State . . . deny to any person within its jurisdiction the equal protection of the laws." Originally, the equal protection clause was applied only to cases of race discrimination, but in 1961, the Supreme Court held that Section 1982 of the U.S. Code afforded a more general "federal right in federal courts because, by reason of prejudice, passion, neglect, intolerance or otherwise, state laws might not be enforced and the . . . rights guaranteed by the Fourteenth Amendment might be denied by state agencies."

A federal court jury heard the case in 1985, found twenty-four of the officers liable, and awarded Tracey Thurman $2.3 million in compensatory damages.

Tracey Thurman was fortunate in that an extraordinary man came forward and offered to represent her. Burton Weinstein was not only a good lawyer but a genuinely good human being who believed that a major injustice had been done and that Tracey Thurman had the right to be heard in a court of law to rectify that injustice. But what about all the other battered women who are failed by the system and who aren't able to sue the police for violating their civil rights? What about the women who don't have a Burton Weinstein to stand up for them?

Ideally, the answer should be found within each system already in place within society—medical, legal, judicial, and social service—but for that to happen, concrete changes must be made within each system and under the law to insure that not one woman or child slips by untreated or unprotected. Only then is it possible to save victims of this crime before they become statistics in another book, article, or government study on domestic violence.

Success depends on a unified effort. As in the case of Tracey Thurman and millions of other victims of this crime, all it takes is one part of one system to fail along the way, and all systems fail; that gives the abuser blanket permission to continue his abuse until it can (as it often does) escalate into murder. If one doctor or nurse, one social worker or police officer, one prosecuting attorney or judge fails in his or her job to treat, diagnose, record, report, and advise concerning injuries or traumas suffered by the victim, to arrest, prosecute, and sentence a batterer, it is tantamount to handing down a guilty verdict against the victim, sentencing her to life in prison or even death.

To those of us who followed the O. J. Simpson murder trial, one of the most chilling reports was the one that described Nicole Brown Simpson, after she was already divorced, cowering behind hedges on her own property, beaten and bruised, bloodied and terrorized, clad only in a bra and sweatpants, waiting for the police to arrive after her ex-husband broke into her house, beat her, and threatened to kill her. Nicole's words to the police when they finally showed up sum up perfectly the failure of the system—and our failure as citizens of a democracy dedicated to protecting the rights and well-being of everyone, including women harassed by the men they love, trust, honor, and even divorce. "You never do anything," Nicole cried. "You always come here and you never arrest him."

Perhaps an even more chilling commentary on society, however, is the typical response given by men who batter their partners or ex-partners when they are confronted by the authorities.

According to police reports, on another occasion, years before Nicole Brown Simpson was divorced, when she was still living with her husband and their children, in the early morning hours of a New Year's Day, her husband came to the door of their house after he had just blackened her eye, split her lip, and choked her, to tell police, "This is a family matter. Why do you want to make a big deal out of it?"

Similarly, two years before the bloody end of the Steinberg/Nussbaum case in New York City, while Hedda Nussbaum huddled in a corner, bloodied and beaten, Joel Steinberg came to the door of their Greenwich Village apartment to tell the police, "Interfering in a private discussion in my home is a violation of my civil rights."

Both men spoke for thousands of others who think it unworthy of public notice when they assault the women they live with, bully them with words, silence them with fists, and finally shut them up permanently with knives or guns.

Domestic violence is a crime. The confusion about this crime begins when it is assumed that, given its private nature, it presents less of a threat to society at large. Police and the judicial system often share the belief that crimes involving family members or crimes that occur within the privacy of the home are less of a threat to the general public. After all, the man who beats, rapes, or kills his partner is not likely to stalk strange women on the street, mug the elderly, or molest random children. As a result, the system tends to justify its nonintervention by reason of quantity, the number of those at potential risk, rather than quality, the seriousness of the crime committed. Only when domestic violence ends in murder does the quantitative aspect of the crime cease to be an issue. What was once considered a private matter changes, and the horror of private lives becomes grist for the tabloids and confessional talk shows, when television cameras appear in courtrooms, making the public privy to every last gruesome detail of what was once considered to be the personal hell of one dysfunctional family. Tragically, what society chooses *not* to do is to penetrate those walls and doors and interfere in that private violence before it becomes a public funeral.

To go from one extreme to the other in order to achieve the norm is not unlike what the Japanese and the Germans did after World War II. Both countries adopted an official policy that dissolved and prohibited the rebuilding of their armed forces. With the exclusion of an armed police force, laws were written into their constitutions that forbade any military intervention or involvement anywhere in the world.

In order to achieve the norm concerning a response to domestic violence, taking action in the extreme might be the appropriate way to begin. Only when there are no automatic judgments made about victims, or opinions about extenuating circumstances for men who abuse, beat, rape, or terrorize women they know, will this crime eventually be viewed, judged, and punished the same as stranger crime. Actions against batterers such as must-arrest laws, no bail, mandatory jail sentences, and participation in batterers' intervention programs are all possible solutions.

The problem of domestic violence has itself become so extreme that it isn't necessary to recount the details of certain cases. The names of the victims are enough to conjure up immediately what these women went through at the hands of their intimate partners. But what does it take for those names to become synonymous with public apathy and nonintervention regarding domestic crime, in the same way that Kitty Genovese has become a byword for public apathy and nonintervention regarding stranger crime? Just the name "Kitty Genovese" forces us to remember the tragedy when neighbors listened to her cries for help and did nothing while someone brutally murdered her on a Queens street in front of her own house. If public apathy concerning random crime in the streets has as its symbol of shame the name of Kitty Genovese, domestic violence certainly has enough names to choose from, beginning with Tracey, Hedda, or

Nicole, to provoke shame throughout society for ignoring their cries for help.

There are social issues related to every crime, and they must not be forgotten as part of society's obligation to each member; but in criminal cases involving strangers, those issues do not interfere with, trivialize, influence, or ignore the due process of the law. If an individual holds up a 7-Eleven and it is later learned that he was unemployed and hungry, society does not create a social issue, calling for long-term goals (such as wiping out unemployment, illiteracy, hunger, and prejudice) in lieu of the short-term solution of incarcerating the criminal. To achieve a crime-free society means upholding the law in the short term; to create better social conditions vital to a crime-free society in the long term means instituting social programs to wipe out prejudice, illiteracy, poverty, and unemployment.

While long-term programs, such as teaching children and adults new attitudes and behavior about respect, equality, and alternative ways to work out disagreements, are critical in changing fundamental attitudes and prejudice within society about women, the crime of domestic violence remains a crime regardless of any concurrent sociopolitical, gender-related, or social programs that are put in place in schools, churches, synagogues, or corporations. Robbery is a crime, just as assault and battery are crimes, just as rape and murder are crimes. Relationships between victims and assailants, under all circumstances, must remain irrelevant under the law. In the case of any crime, short-term programs should not preclude long-term goals, nor should long-term goals replace short-term solutions.

If there is one long-term program that should be instituted in conjunction with these short-term changes across the board regarding the law, it is a total revision of the standards that have been applied in our criminal justice system and throughout society over the last two hundred years concerning men and women who are or have been in a relationship. In other words, anyone has the potential to become a victim or perpetrator.

The response to change in so many cases has always come down to financial—that it costs money, tax dollars, to make changes or implement new programs within any system in society, whether it is the medical, legal, judicial, or social service system. For every proposed change and program, this book will show that it costs less money than financing one trial of a man accused of murdering his wife, ex-wife, girlfriend, or ex-girlfriend—less money than mounting another case against the accused should he decide to appeal his conviction.

There are a limited number of case histories in this book, mainly because, just like that question "Why didn't she just leave?" they have become redundant. We all know the stories. We can't avoid knowing them, because we read the printed press or watch television, or because we know people who are involved in this crime either as victims or perpetrators, or because we have personal experience—we have suffered in the past, or continue to suffer, or are making or have made others suffer. By and large, the stories do not differ. The names are different, as are the circumstances and the reactions, but not the methods of abuse, or the injuries that result, or the permanent psychological damage, or the legal outcomes in most cases.

Rather than giving only details of isolated cases of abuse, we have set out the situation as society currently deals with the problem of domestic violence. The only examples given of specific cases of criminal assault or murder are provided to underline failures in each system throughout our society. By citing case studies to underline those failures, we offer alternatives and solutions that will best deal with this crime, protect its victims, and punish the perpetrators.

Nearly a century ago, in one of the first essays ever written in English about domestic violence, Frances Power Cobbe told horror stories about wife abuse. In the process, she appealed to the essential and basic fairness of good and true Englishmen to right these wrongs. This book is written with that same intention, to appeal to the essential and basic fairness of good and true Americans to right these wrongs throughout our society. We have overcome so many examples of injustice since America was founded, beginning with slavery and segregation; and changed so much antisocial behavior, the least of which was a successful campaign to stop secondary-smoke poisoning in public places.

Domestic violence is a crime committed by one human being against another. For this reason alone, it must be stopped. To stop it, however, takes courage, not only courage on the part of victims to report it, but courage on the part of every one of us to condemn it for what it is—a crime. Only by speaking out can we stop it from happening again and again until there is nothing left but shattered lives. Only with change, cooperation, and communication within every system throughout society and within every family and neighborhood can we stop it from affecting generation after generation of innocent women and children.

In this effort, we have approached this issue as a journey, taking everyone—victims and batterers, as well as men and women who believe they have never suffered abuse at the hands of an intimate partner or have never inflicted it— through the process of this crime step by step, before, during, and after it has been committed: from the beginning of a relationship to the beginning of abuse, to the actual physical assaults, to the police, hospitals, social service agencies, shelters, batterers' intervention programs, offices of lawyers and prosecutors, judges, and into the private lives of the victims and their children. The hope is that eventually we will all be able to judge the successes, condemn the failures, and, above all, identify and recognize this crime in all its different forms. Instead of asking the question "Why didn't she just leave?" we propose three crucial words: change, cooperation, and communication.

TWO

Last Rights

On August 8, 1993, United States Attorney General Janet Reno spoke at the Women Lawyers of Achievement Awards Luncheon. Her speech began, "There is a lot of discussion about whether domestic violence is a public health problem. There should be none. Of course it is. If doctors and lawyers work together, focusing on it as a true public health problem, [in] a criminal justice system that cares, we can make a difference."

Domestic violence is not a public health problem, nor is it a disease, preexisting condition, or accidental injury. Domestic violence is a crime. It becomes a public health problem only after the crime is committed, when physical injury and psychological trauma (if they don't result in death) are seen and treated by health care providers in hospitals and private offices. Any cooperation between doctors and lawyers to "make a difference," as Attorney General Reno stated, will matter only when doctors and lawyers cooperate within a criminal justice system and understand that domestic violence is a crime that causes, just as stranger crime does, physical and emotional injuries.

At the same moment that Attorney General Reno was addressing the Women Lawyers of Achievement Awards Luncheon, paramedics from the Hatzoaluth emergency service in the Crown Heights section of Brooklyn alerted the Brook-

dale Medical Center in East New York that they were bringing in a white female, age twenty-four, who had been hit by
a car.

The paramedics advised the emergency room staff that
Emily Goldenberg was stable and conscious, with a steady
blood pressure, and at first glance appeared not to have
suffered any fractures or head trauma. An IV had already
been started as a precaution against blood loss, as there
was every reason to assume that she had sustained internal
injuries. A bed in the emergency room had been cleared for
Emily, and the trauma surgeon on duty had been alerted
that an accident victim was coming in with possible internal
hemorrhaging. An operating room had also been prepared,
and a team of trauma nurses, an anesthesiologist, and two
surgical residents were standing by.

Emily was still conscious when she arrived at the hospital. After the trauma surgeon palpated her abdomen, he
announced that there was significant tenderness over the
patient's liver, which suggested that she was sustaining abdominal bleeding. While two nurses removed Emily's clothes
and put a blood pressure cuff on one arm, a technician
placed electrodes on her chest, arms, and legs and a resident
hooked up another IV bag to make sure she was getting
sufficient fluid to maintain her blood pressure. Emily's condition remained stable while yet another resident drew blood
to cross-match in the event a transfusion was indicated, before he began prepping her for further diagnostic studies.

As the team worked on Emily, the surgeon questioned
her, more in an effort to keep her alert than to solicit information. He considered it encouraging that she was sufficiently oriented to recite her mother's telephone number as
well as request that someone call the insurance company
where she worked as an executive secretary to explain what
had happened. When a nurse appeared with a set of hospital
release forms, Emily had no trouble signing her name, giving
the hospital permission to operate if necessary.

In response to the surgeon's questions about the accident, Emily explained that her fiancé had accidentally run

her over as she stepped off the curb to get into the passenger side of his car. According to Emily, he had stepped on the accelerator instead of the brake. The doctor later remembered thinking at that point how guilty and anguished the young man must be feeling, knowing he had inadvertently caused the woman he loved to go through such an ordeal.

After Emily had been hooked up to the monitoring equipment and preliminary examinations were finished, the doctor announced to the others that, in his opinion, a vein or small artery had been nicked or torn as a result of the patient's impact with the car. Given Emily's vital signs, he remained optimistic that any blood loss was due to a slow leak; that made it possible to repair before her condition became life threatening. Within twenty seconds of the surgeon's observation, however, Emily's blood pressure dropped and her abdomen distended markedly. What had been a controlled situation had suddenly turned critical, with all the signs pointing to massive hemorrhaging in the abdominal cavity. There was no time for further diagnostic tests or X rays. Rallying in response to her rapidly failing condition, the trauma team prepared Emily for emergency surgery. Wrapped in an antishock garment with only her pale face visible, Emily Goldenberg was rushed upstairs to the operating room. As she was being wheeled through the corridors, she clutched the surgeon's hand tightly, pleading with him not to let her die.

By the time Emily was anesthetized and her abdominal cavity opened, her medical condition had deteriorated even more. What became immediately evident was that the source of blood leaking into her abdomen was due to a tear in the inferior vena cava, the main vein that drains blood from the lower half of the body, filtering it through the liver before it runs back into the heart. Tragically, what the doctors had no way of knowing until Emily was on the table was that her liver had been literally severed from her heart. Precisely, the medical report would read that "patient's condition passed the critical point by the time she was opened up due to hemorrhagic shock which led to refractory cardiac arrest."

Emily Goldenberg died on the operating table a little more than sixteen minutes after she arrived at the hospital.

Emily's final visit to a hospital emergency room was by no means her first. During the previous year, she had sought medical treatment at hospital emergency rooms in Brooklyn, Queens, and Manhattan on three separate occasions. According to records uncovered during the investigation following Emily's death, she had presented ailments that included a split lip, black eyes, a fractured shoulder, and cigarette burns on her breasts; and not more than three months earlier, she had barely been conscious when she was brought into an emergency room by her fiancé. According to the hospital report on that occasion, Emily claimed that she had accidentally taken an overdose of barbiturates for a toothache. Concerning Emily's accidental overdose, her mother remembered calling her daughter at her fiancé's to see if her toothache was better and was surprised to hear that the couple was in the middle of an argument. Tearfully, Emily's mother also admitted that she had encouraged her daughter to work things out since invitations for the wedding had already been mailed. After all, most couples experienced tension just prior to getting married. What Emily's mother never knew until after her daughter's death was that the argument had escalated until, sometime in the early morning hours, Emily had swallowed a handful of pills. According to a close friend in whom Emily confided after the incident and who came forward after the funeral, it apparently wasn't until daybreak, when Emily was curled up on the bathroom floor, barely conscious, that her fiancé became alarmed enough to take her to a hospital emergency room somewhere in Queens.

Further examination of all the hospital records indicated that while Emily appeared to be a healthy young woman, she seemed to be accident prone. But doctors, investigators, and prosecutors soon suspected that Emily wasn't accident prone at all, nor had she ever been suicidal or depressed. What the hospital records did not indicate, and what family and friends of the dead woman did not realize until it was too late, was that Emily had become very skilled at covering up the truth about the pain and anguish she was going through in her life. What Emily never chose to mention during any one of those hospital visits, or talk about to the people who loved her, was that none of her injuries had been the result of accidents at all but rather the result of abuse at the hands of her boyfriend. Even when Emily lay dying on the gurney in the emergency room at Brookdale, she continued to lie when she claimed that her fiancé had *accidentally* run her over by accelerating instead of braking.

In the weeks that followed Emily's death, the district attorney who was investigating the case interrogated several witnesses to the accident. They all confirmed what Emily had said and what Asher Fram, her fiancé, claimed as well, that had he not made that fatal error of accelerating instead of braking, the accident would never have happened. The only discrepancy, however, was that those same witnesses claimed that Fram, after running Emily over once, put the car in reverse and ran her over a second time. When questioned, Fram insisted that after he realized that he had hit Emily, he became so distraught that instead of accelerating or turning off the motor, he put the car in reverse and accidentally hit her a second time.

In addition to interviewing witnesses to the accident and talking to Emily's mother, the D.A. also questioned Emily's friends and coworkers, all of whom reluctantly admitted that they had suspected that the couple's two-year relationship had been troubled. Notwithstanding their testimony about the nature of the relationship, however, and despite witnesses who testified before the grand jury as to what they saw happen, the district attorney was unable to get an indictment against Asher Fram for murder.

The grand jury judged Emily's death to be an accident and did not even implicate Fram for vehicular homicide, as he had not been under the influence of either drugs or alcohol when the accident occurred. Ironically, the most damaging witness to the prosecution's case was the surgeon who testified that Emily herself had told him that Fram had accidentally accelerated instead of backing up.

As for the apparent history of prior abuse, had Emily

reported it during her three previous hospital visits, or had any of the hospitals where she sought treatment, at the very least, recorded her injuries in her official medical record, the state of New York would have had the evidence to construct a case of premeditation or predisposition of violence on the part of Asher Fram, ultimately resulting in Emily Goldenberg's death. But there was no record of Emily ever having been the victim of domestic abuse. On only one occasion, at New York University Medical Center in New York City, had any reference been made of suspected abuse, and that was because a nurse didn't believe Emily's story that the burns on her breasts were caused by an electric heater. During the investigation, the nurse testified that she had considered contacting the hospital's advocate for battered women, a staff member, but Emily had come into the emergency room at two o'clock on a Saturday morning, and the advocate was there only on weekdays between nine and five. And, anyway, the nurse added, Emily vehemently denied that her injuries were the result of abuse.

What is certain is that because of a society whose consciousness has been sufficiently "raised" to consider that abused adult women should not be treated the same as abused children, Emily Goldenberg had the right to make her own choices in her own time about her own life concerning criminal actions that had been committed against her by an intimate partner. The result was tragic. Not only was Emily Goldenberg the victim of her abusive fiancé, but she was also the victim of laws and regulations within the medical, legal, and social service systems in New York State that (just as in most other states) do not mandate hospital personnel to report or even record suspicious injuries, ailments, or vague psychological symptoms that might be the result of domestic abuse. As the product of a social, medical, and legal system that strives to be politically correct, Emily Goldenberg died an "empowered" woman at the age of twenty-four.

THREE

America's Dirty Little Secret

THERE ARE highly qualified people within the health care profession who are concerned about the increasingly widespread problem of domestic violence. These health care professionals are very aware that in order to save lives, changes must be made, new laws put into effect, and better programs adopted throughout all medical facilities. Yet when it comes to implementing those changes or translating their concerns into practical laws, protocols, and programs, doctors and nurses find reasons—subtle, social, and medical—for not taking action.

The hospital team who worked on Emily Goldenberg did everything possible to save her life, and failed. They failed not because mistakes were made either in diagnosing or treating her injuries, but because her condition was just too serious to reverse. The real tragedy about Emily is that she did not have to die, not because she wasn't brought into the emergency room fast enough or because the professionals on duty didn't have the knowledge or equipment to save her. Emily died because on all those other occasions when she sought medical help for injuries that were not life threatening, doctors and nurses accepted her explanations for how her injuries occurred and dealt with her only superficially. Had they investigated or practiced better preventive medicine, that final outcome perhaps could have been avoided.

When a patient suffers from a curable illness, the duty of the doctor is to cure. In cases where an illness can be prevented either by vaccination or prophylactic treatment, the responsibility of the doctor is to effect those measures. If an injury, illness, or trauma is caused by a criminal action, the doctor is expected to *record* any visible injury, trauma, or illness as possible evidence. To prevent recidivism, the doctor is also required to *report* any injuries that might be the result of possible criminal assault. The same is true of diseases perceived to be contagious. Often doctors are forced to act as detectives, searching for clues and cures for a mysterious virus or illness with only vague or nonspecific symptoms to guide them.

Why are victims of domestic violence, women and children who suffer injuries, illnesses, traumas, and syndromes resulting from a crime, treated differently? Why do doctors fail to persist when they question victims of this crime about plausible explanations for those symptoms, injuries, or traumas? What makes the medical response to the physical and emotional symptoms of battered women different from their response to other patients who suffer the same symptoms because of stranger crime, epidemics, or accidents?

The answers to those questions are usually so varied that they only confuse the issues even more.

In 1985, then surgeon general C. Everett Koop declared that domestic violence was a public health menace with which police alone could not cope. He suggested that hospitals and trauma centers might prevent further violence inflicted on women by intervening, especially since the same women appeared repeatedly with similar symptoms and injuries. Surgeon General Koop called for specific guidelines to be put into effect throughout the medical system, requiring hospitals and private physicians, as a matter of routine, to question women whose injuries, illnesses, or traumas are suspected to have been caused by abuse. The reaction was disappointing.

Health care providers said there was too little time in busy emergency rooms, too little staff in physicians' private offices, and too many budget cuts in most city-run hospitals for anyone to question every patient who presented symptoms of abuse. And if time and money don't make things difficult enough, patients themselves are often reluctant to discuss their private lives; and even if they are willing, there's rarely support or facilities where they could be referred. Further, doctors and nurses also claimed that any woman who was in jeopardy would not only eventually seek medical help on her own, but also report the crime that had been committed against her. In other words, "It's not my job."

The reality is that the victim of domestic violence often waits to report the crime and her injuries, usually because her assailant is someone whom she knows or has known intimately and with whom she may even have children in common. Rather than come forward when "things get bad enough," victims of this crime often appear at hospitals and doctors' offices with symptoms and injuries that are the least serious that they have suffered at the hands of their batterer. Unlike a victim of stranger crime, the battered woman is reluctant to report the cause of her injuries because she is afraid of reprisal by her abuser, either physical or financial; afraid that the system will take away her children, who are witness to or victims of that abuse; or embarrassed that she has lost control of her own life. The fact that a victim of this crime often waits to report the crime or her injuries is precisely one of the best arguments for stepping in and taking action. In so many cases, the victim appears for care and treatment at the last and only opportunity for the system to reach her.

According to doctors and nurses, even when the battered woman seeks medical advice she gives a variety of evasive and embarrassed responses, typical for someone as stressed and frightened as she is. In many cases, the patient even believes that she provoked the abuse, because that's what her husband or boyfriend told her every time he assaulted her. She may even choose to take responsibility for the abuse, if only to convince herself that she has some control over her own life. In other words, while health care

providers are not always thorough enough in their evaluation of the victim, the victim does not always make it easy for
them to make an accurate diagnosis.

The obvious answer would be for health care providers
to encourage the battered woman to seek treatment rather
than to create obstacles that would only make her more
afraid of being truthful either about her injuries or how she
sustained them. Encouraging the victim of this crime to
come forward, however, can be done in several different
ways, either negatively, so that she is even more apprehen-
sive, or positively, so that she understands she won't suffer
additional repercussions.

Emily Goldenberg, before her final visit to the hospital,
sought treatment on several occasions for injuries that were
not consistent with the reasons she gave. Yet she was neither
pressured nor forced to tell the truth about how she was
injured. Another obstacle was Asher Fram, Emily's fiancé.
Each time she was hurt, he took her to a different hospital
emergency room. That way there was no previous record of
other suspicious injuries.

What if the doctors or nurses who treated Emily had
presented her with a form that was routinely given to every
female patient, questioning her about domestic violence?
What if an advocate for battered women had been on duty
twenty-four hours a day, seven days a week, to be able to talk
alone with Emily? What if there had been a computerized
system between hospitals that would have signaled that Emily
Goldenberg was a frequent patient, seeking medical care
for injuries or symptoms that were indicative of a victim of
abuse?

The ideal would be a system in which battered women
could feel safe and secure, one that protected them from
their abusers, guaranteed them that they would not lose their
children, assured them that the assault and violence they
endured was not their fault, and treated their medical and
psychological injuries and traumas. Unfortunately, the reality is far from this ideal. Battered women are encouraged to
come forward for medical treatment, criticized when they

are less than truthful, assured that they can make their own decisions, legally and medically, when it comes to pressing charges against their assailants—but are given no guarantees that by taking those actions, they will be safe.

In 1989, Koop again tried to initiate a campaign calling for medical intervention on behalf of battered women. And again his efforts met with little enthusiasm or support from the medical community.

Dr. Antonia Novello, Koop's successor, went even further when she recommended that medical personnel be required to report domestic violence under the same laws and guidelines that were already in place to report child abuse. What that meant was that health care workers would be mandated by law to report all cases in which women seeking medical care presented symptoms of having been assaulted or abused by their partners. Under certain specific conditions, cases of suspected violent crime, albeit domestic violent crime, would be reported to the authorities without the cooperation or permission of the patients.

Mandated reporting throughout the medical system is not a new concept, and not only as it applies to child abuse. The law requires health care providers to report every criminal act of abuse inflicted on people over the age of sixty-five, all cases of gunshot wounds, muggings, stabbings, hit-and-run accidents, certain contagious diseases, and even animal bites. Surgeon General Novello's suggestion of mandated reporting of battered women was not especially innovative, since it meant only including another type of violent crime under a regulation that already existed throughout the medical profession. This time, however, the reaction to the proposal was overwhelmingly negative, especially among advocates for battered women and among feminists, but even within the medical profession itself.

Advocates for battered women claimed that mandated reporting of domestic violence disempowered women by treating them like minor children, especially women who had already been disempowered by their abusers. They presented a strong argument against mandated reporting, also claiming that often the victim herself knows how best to avoid another attack—which is not necessarily by pressing charges against her assailant. In fact, they argued, arresting a batterer only enraged him, so that when he was freed several hours later, he would assault his partner even more severely.

Opposing mandated *reporting* in a hospital setting under certain circumstances and mandated *recording* under all circumstances does nothing to empower the victim of this crime and everything to empower her batterer. The only way a victim of domestic violence can be empowered is to disempower her assailant from committing continued acts of violence against her. Until the system intervenes to prevent domestic crime and injury, there will always be open season on women at the hands of men they know, trust, and love. Further, the rate of recidivism is too high to believe that empowering victims of spousal assault should go before victim safety. The reality is that the system is programmed to fail the victim, albeit by good intentions, by creating impediments to rescuing innocent women and children from abusive partners and to preventing more serious crimes from occurring. It happened to Tracey Thurman when the police failed to protect her, and to Emily Goldenberg when doctors and nurses accepted her explanations for her injuries. They were unable to save her, and it happens to thousands of other women every day.

In an effort to be politically correct at all costs, advocates for battered women have created a hands-off policy. This, in turn, influences attitudes within the medical, legal, social service, and judicial systems. Curiously, the only person who does not share that hands-off policy when it comes to the victim's rights or person is her assailant. And as long as he goes unpunished, unprosecuted, and free, chances are that he will not only continue his abuse but escalate it in its lethality.

The irony is that, under present conditions, the argument presented by advocates for battered women or by those within the medical profession who oppose mandated reporting is not wrong. Specifically, men who are arrested for battering and who are released several hours later do, in fact, often return and batter their partners even more severely. And even if health care providers questioned patients they suspected of having been battered, and even if they were successful in gaining their trust, it would serve no purpose unless there were appropriate backup facilities within other systems or within each hospital to which these women could be referred. But before alternative solutions are given, it is important to hear the rest of the debate.

Advocates for battered women acknowledge that during a crisis situation, victims of this crime, given their injuries, traumas, fear, or emotional paralysis, are rendered incapable of making decisions that would protect them from ongoing abuse or, in extreme cases, death. Those same advocates also maintain that given the victim's weakened emotional and physical state, she should not be held responsible for remaining in an abusive relationship. In support of their argument, they also point out that Amnesty International provides a list of methods used to brainwash and torture combat soldiers, prisoners of war, disaster victims, and hostages that match almost exactly the methods used against victims of domestic violence by their abusers. Those methods, listed by Amnesty International, include isolation, monopolization, induced debility, threats, occasional indulgences, demonstration of omnipotence, degradation, and enforcement of trivial demands.

The most apparent difference between a hostage and a battered woman, however, is that a hostage experiences those tactics while chained to a radiator in a bare room or held in an isolated cell in a foreign country, while a victim of domestic violence experiences those same deprivations and tortures in her own home. As a result, hostages and political prisoners are more easily identified than battered women, first, because hostages are held in a hostile environment, and, second, because battered women appear to be functioning on a normal level, walking, talking, performing household or professional tasks, and caring for their children. Yet both sets of victims are concentrating on surviving from day to day in a situation where violence can erupt without warning at any moment. It is that instability which terrorizes the battered woman to the same degree as it does the political hostage or prisoner.

All similarities between hostages and battered women end, however, when it comes to rescuing those who are held hostage (or are otherwise victims of psychological or physical oppression) and rescuing battered women. Society does not see it as an act of disempowering hostages when measures are taken to extricate them, but rather as a heroic deed on the part of their rescuers. This provokes the logical questions: How can those opposed to mandated reporting consider methods listed in Amnesty International guidelines as similar to those used on victims of domestic violence, yet set different rules and conditions for response? If victims of domestic violence are suffering the same psychological and physical abuse as hostages, why would identical measures taken for rescue be perceived as disempowering one group and not the other? If protocols and procedures are successfully implemented to save those who are taken hostage by foreign powers or by random criminals, why are those same techniques not justified to save women who are taken hostage in their own homes and in their private lives? Statistically, it is far more likely for a woman to be a victim of domestic violence than to be taken hostage and chained to a radiator or be thrown into a cell in a foreign country.

If lives are to be saved, it is crucial to differentiate between a woman who is permanently disempowered by her abuser and a woman who is temporarily disempowered by health care providers acting on her behalf to guarantee, in the long term, that she will be able to take back control of her own life. Yet in what appears to be an even more confused response to abuse, those who oppose mandated reporting also maintain that *the* question—"Why doesn't she just leave?"—should be replaced in every instance by the question "Why was the batterer allowed to stay?"

If logic governed all decisions and dialogue pertaining

to domestic violence—which it does not—the responsibility to answer either question would clearly be up to those who oppose mandated reporting and mandated recording in any medical setting. Precisely, the batterer *stays* because he is allowed to stay. He batters because he can, without the threat of reprisal or judicial repercussion that would follow if he battered a stranger in a barroom brawl or his secretary because she was a bad typist. The answer to the original question is that the victim doesn't leave because society fails to offer her the appropriate support, or she is unable to leave because she is terrified that she has no place to go. Ironically, advocates for battered women who understand the injustice and inequity that are inherent in society when it comes to an appropriate response to crimes of domestic violence are the same people who oppose changing certain protocols and procedures that will help victims. As a result, battered women are *left* without adequate support and resources. Before any battered woman is empowered, or is offered privacy, or has her rights upheld so that she is able to make all legal decisions concerning a crime that was committed against her, the following questions must be asked: Which takes precedence, privacy or prevention? And is it society's responsibility to protect victims of criminal violence who are rendered temporarily unable to protect themselves?

Judging by the situations in which society acts for other victims of violence, the answers should be: Prevention takes precedence over privacy. And *yes*, it is society's responsibility to protect those victims of criminal violence who are rendered temporarily unable to protect themselves. Perhaps a more persuasive argument for protection and prevention would be that if there were advocates for batterers and those advocates gave them the choice between privacy and prevention, batterers would choose privacy over prevention every time.

Advocates for battered women who work tirelessly to stop domestic violence and who fight for more social programs for victims are often the same group who are responsible for putting protocols in place and people on staff to deal with this problem in hospitals throughout the country. Yet in what is probably the most damaging contradiction, given their position and influence, these men and women are also responsible for putting obstacles in the way of all health care providers to utilize those programs and protocols in a way that would guarantee their success.

By insisting on upholding the rights of the victim of this crime, those opposed to mandated reporting and recording have provided health care workers with a ready excuse not to act on behalf of the victim. Forcing empowerment on a woman who is suffering in a *temporary* state of crisis or confusion because of physical or emotional trauma is tantamount to putting an unarmed person in a lion cage with neither weapon nor tamer to protect that person from injury or eventual death. Society cannot afford to put social and political rights of citizens before emergency medical measures which must include mandated recording and reporting until social and political habits, morals, and values guarantee the equal treatment of all people under the law. Only when it becomes socially and politically unacceptable for men to batter their intimate partners can society require medical personnel to put empowerment before saving lives.

In fact, words such as "disempower" and "disenfranchise" are relevant in this situation only if they describe long-term goals of prescribed acceptable behavior between all men and women, boys and girls, in and out of relationships. These words have neither a place in nor a bearing on short-term solutions meant to save lives, to prevent recurring injuries, suicides, or homicides.

Mandated reporting and mandated recording can only be short-term solutions, solutions that take the form of laws that protect women who are in situations of constant danger. When these protocols are implemented, guarantees are automatically given to battered women so they can count on others when they are either so afraid or so injured that they are unable to take action to protect themselves.

From a practical viewpoint, mandated recording of injuries provides the victim with the necessary proof when and if she decides to take legal action; in the case of her death, it provides the judicial system with the necessary proof to prosecute her assailant. This is the barest possible minimum response available to us. From a legal viewpoint, mandated reporting allows the judicial system to take over, arrest, and prosecute a criminal who has assaulted his partner (and in all probability will assault her again, if not kill her) or, if left unpunished, will go on to assault and possibly kill other women.

In response to the points made by advocates for battered women—specifically, that holding a batterer for several hours almost insures that he will return and batter his victim even more severely and that there are inadequate systems in place for health care providers to refer victims of domestic violence, even if they are successful in eliciting the truth about their injuries—the following questions might be considered.

What if there were a legal system in place that would detain the batterer for more than just several hours? What if he were held without bail until his hearing, even if that meant his being held overnight or over a weekend? And what if, whether he was incarcerated, released with a warning, fined, or given probation, he were obliged, under the terms of his release or incarceration, to enter into a batterers' treatment program, as well as wear an electronic bracelet or other monitoring device?

What if, after the victim reported the assault or her doctors reported her injuries, her assailant would forever be a name and number in a computerized system that would track his behavior? And what if there were appropriate backup facilities within the medical and other systems to refer battered women to after they were truthful about their injuries and the crimes committed against them?

Clearly, if those protocols, laws, and programs were put into effect, advocates for battered women would no longer be responsible for either of those pejorative questions: "Why doesn't she just leave?" and "Why is the batterer allowed to stay?"

The medical profession knows that these kinds of solutions are possible, just as the police, prosecutors, judges, social workers, and even the advocates for battered women know. So, why aren't these solutions put into effect?

Health care providers have a problem with delving into the private lives of their patients. Specifically, a survey taken by the National Institutes of Health in 1994 revealed that physicians are reluctant to intervene on behalf of the battered woman. As a result, health care providers have not put pressure on the American Medical Association to implement training programs that would help them know how to ask delicate questions or guide them in responding to the patient's painful confessions. While physicians are required to participate annually in a training program concerning mandated reporting of child abuse, there are no required training programs for domestic violence against adult women. According to Dr. Carol Warshaw, a primary care physician at Cook County and Michael Reese Hospitals in Chicago and a prominent advocate for battered women, "In most cases, physicians are uncomfortable acting as police, judge, or jury. Most admit that they are barely comfortable with mandated reporting of child abuse."

Everyone agrees that victims of this crime have very different emotional reactions and, therefore, different medical needs than victims of stranger crime. Yet there is no separate set of medical responses specifically targeted to serve these needs. This often results in women receiving inadequate medical care.

Neither Surgeon General Novello's nor Surgeon General Koop's recommendations can be taken out of context, nor can they stand alone. Success depends on how the victim is approached and treated and, above all, on *mandated* cooperation between all the systems, which is the only way to eliminate the victim's fear and resistance by proving to her that there are people and facilities able to take over. The most important method of treating victims of this crime is to gain their trust and confidence. Promises must be kept. Concrete solutions must be delivered.

While neither surgeon general succeeded in mobilizing the medical profession to include mandated recording and reporting of domestic violence, they were successful in making this issue a priority with the American Medical Association. In response, the AMA in 1991 announced the beginning of a campaign to combat what they termed a "public health epidemic." At a press conference in Chicago, AMA leaders provided doctors with an information packet identifying family violence as "America's dirty little secret." It was a bad beginning. Domestic violence was no secret. If anything, domestic violence was America's tacit little agreement.

The reality remains that most health care providers neither insist nor investigate when patients give less than truthful reasons for the causes of physical or emotional injuries. The policy was and remains nothing more than "Don't ask, don't tell." The most dangerous ramification of this is that any doctor who knowingly accepts invented stories of accidental injuries inadvertently cements a complicity with the victim's abuser. In cases of stranger crime, acting in complicity with the perpetrator might be construed as aiding and abetting, which is a criminal offense. Yet despite all the ambiguities in defining what exactly is domestic violence, in deciding whether it is a health problem, social dysfunction, or crime, and despite all the debate concerning just how involved physicians should be, the AMA also came out with statistics showing that while symptoms and effects of domestic violence are health related, the cause is criminal. That was a good beginning.

Statistics compiled by the AMA prove that domestic violence causes more injury to women than auto accidents, muggings, and rapes combined. The public health impact of domestic violence is compounded in that incidents of violence often escalate in frequency and severity. Three-fourths of women who are injured once experience ongoing abuse, and one in three cases of reported assaults involves the use of a weapon. Further, between 30 and 46 percent of women who suffer domestic abuse are also raped by their partners.

Without appropriate interventions, health care providers claim, every one of these women is at high risk of developing serious and complex medical and psychological problems, including alcoholism and damage sustained from repeated suicide attempts. In fact, further statistics compiled by the AMA between 1992 and 1994 indicate that one in four female suicide attempt victims had a history of battering; one in two black women who attempted suicide had experienced domestic violence. Battering is also recognized as a significant cause of complications during pregnancy, a period in which many battered women experience an escalation of violence.

As a result of those findings, the AMA maintained that domestic violence should be separated from and viewed differently than stranger crime. The danger was that "differently" might mean less efficiently, which would result in victims suffering additional repercussions, both physical and emotional. For instance, while doctors and emergency room staff pay attention to all injured patients, including crime victims, they tend to minimize the crime of spousal assault. Even in a medical setting, the victim who knows her assailant is considered the only one at risk, while her assailant is judged not to be a public menace.

Another dangerous misunderstanding about domestic violence in contrast to stranger crime often arises after the victim's physical symptoms or injuries are treated. It is then that victims of this crime suffer greater ongoing emotional trauma than victims of stranger crime, since the person they love and trust, or once loved and trusted, is the same person inflicting the abuse. Given the proximity of victim to assailant as well as an emotional, financial, and familial history that is not present in stranger crimes, women who suffer abuse at the hands of intimate partners should never, under any circumstances, regardless of how many times they seek medical care for the same injuries, be considered as being in part responsible for their medical condition.

While most people believe that it is wrong for a man to beat his wife or girlfriend, many also believe that under cer-

tain circumstances it is almost inevitable. Logically, those
sentiments are shared by physicians and nurses as well, since
it is difficult for anyone not to have his or her own personal
feelings about a crime, illness, or injury. In fact, moral judgments are made in emergency rooms and hospitals and in
doctors' offices all the time concerning accident victims who
speed or drive while intoxicated, smokers who suffer heart
attacks or cancer, and AIDS victims who are IV drug users or
homosexuals. Similarly, in almost every case of spousal
abuse, even if the victim is not blamed, health care providers
in the course of taking her history almost always ask *the* question, "Why didn't she just leave?"

If Tracey Thurman, Nicole Brown Simpson, or millions
of other women who have left abusive situations can serve as
examples, it becomes apparent that every excuse, rationaliza-
tion, reason, or justification given about why women stay is
judgmental and irrelevant. And for those women who do not
use the system to save their own lives, for whatever reasons,
the fault lies only with the system for not providing sufficient
protection and assurance so that they have the courage to
come forward. In every instance, if battered women conceal
their injuries or are failed by the system, the fault lies with
the system and never with the victims.

Even today, after all that we have learned about this
crime and after all the cases of battered women and children
that have been made public, experts in the fields of psychiatry, medicine, and sociology study not only why women stay
in violent and abusive relationships, but also which women
are most likely to enter into them in the first place. Funded
by government grants of hundreds of millions of dollars,
studies are conducted about the personalities of battered
women, their education level, family history, previous experiences with violence, physical and mental health, employment skills, use of alcohol or drugs, sexual preferences,
attitudes, religious beliefs, verbal and problem-solving skills,
and self-esteem.

Specifically, in medical findings concerning victims of
domestic violence, battered women have been described by

some psychiatrists as manifesting dysfunctional behavior or suffering from hallucinations or paranoic tendencies. They are often diagnosed by medical doctors as suffering from psychosomatic symptoms or hypochondria, nervous disorders, hysteria, or depression. Insurance companies often consider injuries sustained by domestic violence victims as preexisting conditions and, therefore, not covered under standard health policies. What all of this means, when applied to the battered woman in her daily life, is that those people who are trained medically to treat the physical or psychological ailments of all patients, along with those who are in the business of insuring everyone so they can afford medical care, view her as an unstable woman filled with conflict and fear whose injuries or illnesses are misunderstood and therefore not covered under standard insurance policies. Furthermore, misconceptions of the battered woman also fuel the assumption that it is a waste of time, effort, and money to take the necessary measures to help her, since she either rejects the help, refuses to help herself, or invents and imagines her symptoms. In other words, society judges that the battered woman does not merit the same care or consideration as anyone else, even if she does suffer from psychological and psychosomatic symptoms in addition to the physical consequences of abuse. There is no probing to find the cause of any psychological symptoms, and the argument for nonintervention becomes financial: time, money, and effort should be directed toward "real" criminals and more "cooperative" victims, or "real" patients who have "real" complaints. It is no mystery that given these attitudes, which are so prevalent throughout society, victims of this crime are afraid to come forward or cooperate with the system. It is also no surprise that batterers have a warped perception of what is considered a crime against a stranger as opposed to a crime against an intimate partner.

If changes are not made quickly within the medical system so that people view this crime in ways that are constructive to the victims, domestic violence will remain America's dirty little secret.

FOUR

The Brigade

MEN'S VIOLENCE is men's behavior. That behavior cannot be explained by allocating millions of dollars to conduct studies on why women, or which women, become victims of this crime. Studying the victim only perpetuates the myth that women are to blame, that it is up to the woman to leave rather than the responsibility of society by due process of law to stop her batterer from assaulting her. If studies and surveys are indicated, they should be focused on the criminal. If grants and money are spent on the victim, they should be to provide shelters, job-training programs, legal assistance, and medical treatment centers for her as well as for her children.

In 1992, the Joint Commission on Accreditation of Health Care Organizations (JCAHO, a quasi-public agency responsible for accreditation for all hospitals and nursing homes) implemented policies and procedures in emergency rooms and ambulatory care facilities for identifying, treating, and referring victims of domestic abuse to social workers or the police. Again, the response within the medical community was inadequate.

Contrary to these JCAHO policies, the AMA still did not put programs in place that would educate health care workers about domestic violence. There were no new guidelines for them to follow, nothing to teach them why it was critical to follow those policies or, more important, how to follow them. Even the AMA's definition of domestic violence remained abstract: "coercive behavior that may include repeated battery and injury, psychological abuse, sexual assault, progressive social isolation, deprivation, intimidation perpetrated by someone who is or was involved in an intimate relationship with the victim." Those words are meaningless unless they are accompanied by instructions, guidelines, and examples that would transform the abstract into reality, to make "someone" a real and flesh-and-blood man who was abusing a real flesh-and-blood woman, rather than a "victim."

In 1992, the American Medical Association made a tentative effort to establish official protocols that would define and identify domestic violence in all its forms. The AMA went on to provide diagnostic and treatment guidelines that covered identification of victims, intervention, barriers to identification, documentation of cases, legal issues, risk management, and trends in treatment and prevention. While those guidelines were encouraging when they recognized domestic violence to be prevalent enough and intervention important enough to justify the routine screening of any woman seeking emergency, surgical, primary, pediatric, prenatal, and psychiatric care, they also included the caveat that the patient had the right to refuse treatment as well as to refuse reporting her injuries to the proper authorities. Victims, once identified and treated medically, were given the right to make their own choices concerning their safety and well-being. After everything was said and done, the AMA took an official stand against mandated reporting. As a result, none of the guidelines or diagnostic standards were incorporated in any medical school curriculum to educate health care workers on their application.

According to Dr. Carol Warshaw, in only half of all medical schools is anything mentioned about family violence, and of those that do offer a course, it is usually limited to child abuse and listed as an elective. "In schools of psychology and family therapy," Warshaw contends, "there is even less attention paid to family violence as either an elective or required course than in medical schools.''

By not taking concrete measures to protect a victim of domestic assault, health care providers may be protecting her civil rights, but they are denying her the appropriate support and care that she needs when she finds herself unable to make the proper life-saving choices on her own. Prevention means going public and reporting the abuse as well as the person who causes it, which in cases of spousal assault is not difficult. There is no need to launch a costly investigation to catch the perpetrator of this crime. In most cases, either he is living with the victim or she knows where he is.

At the height of the debate over the medical profession's response to domestic violence, Senator Barbara Boxer, a Democrat from California, and Senator Bill Wyden, a Democrat from Delaware and the former cochair of the Judiciary Committee in the Senate, sponsored the Violence Against Women bill. One of the points cited in the bill was the need for mandated courses in medical schools on domestic violence. After much procrastination, it was finally passed as part of President Clinton's crime bill. On March 21, 1995, the president named Iowa attorney general Bonnie Campbell to head a new Justice Department office directed at curbing violence against women. The president also released a $26 million down payment on grants to help states protect women from crime.

This was a big step and a great accomplishment that is to the credit of so many advocates for battered women who fought and lobbied hard for this bill to pass. Unfortunately, given the medical profession's position on victims' rights, the result is not unlike Russian roulette.

If a hospital happens to have those diagnostic guidelines in place and a health care worker on duty happens to have the time, inclination, and training, he or she may implement them. In all other cases, when there are more urgent medical emergencies or when a doctor or nurse feels uncomfortable delving into the private life of a patient, these protocols are ignored and the victim is left on her own. Given an escalation of battering, advocates for battered women were those least satisfied with the progress being made throughout the medical system, judging that there was still insufficient effort to identify and treat these crime victims. Separating the problem into three distinct areas, advocates cited the American Medical Association's lack of comprehensive and connected protocols, a lack of training to identify and properly treat victims, and an absence of cooperation between the medical, social service, and judicial systems to punish offenders. Where the irony comes into play is that these advocates were the ones to set limits on intervention by insisting that victims had the right to decide on their own. On the one hand, advocates demand that guidelines to identify the battered woman be put in place throughout all hospitals, as well as protocols that provide for specific referrals to social service agencies and the legal system. On the other hand, they restrict health care workers from taking the initiative without the consent of the victim.

The Women's Forum is an international organization whose members are women who have achieved recognition and success in their respective fields. With the exception of the Equal Rights Amendment, the Women's Forum has not taken an official stand or engaged in national exploration of any particular women's issues. In 1993, however, the organization decided to open a Dialogue on Democracy program that would address issues vital to women.

The president of the Women's Forum, Susie Greenwood, suggested that domestic violence would be a timely and important subject for that dialogue, sending out announcements throughout the United States. The five affiliate groups of the Women's Forum who expressed interest in participating were those from New York, New Jersey, Michigan, Kansas, and Colorado. One of the initial points raised during the discussions was that the first place a battered woman seeks help is usually a hospital emergency room. "In the beginning, we focused on domestic violence as a crime, so we were looking for more appropriate responses from the legal system," Women's Forum member Charlotte Klein recalls, "when we realized that in order for the legal system to function properly, the American Medical Association had to set down specific guidelines to identify and treat battered women, record those findings so the legal system would have the means to punish their assailants."

The logical method of dealing with the problem would have been a process of intervention in which the victim, once identified and treated medically, was made aware of the options available to her by the social service system. Once safe, without the risk of ongoing violence, the victim would then be protected by the criminal justice system, which would proceed against her abuser under specific conditions, with or without her consent. In the event that the victim's injuries were not serious enough to warrant official response, protocols would be in place that allowed the victim, after recording her injuries, to consider other legal options available to her, while assured that her hospital record could eventually provide the necessary evidence to launch a criminal case. It would have been reasonable to assume, as well, that since the medical system was the first to respond, by treating the victim when she was in a state of extreme crisis, medical records would be kept detailing her injuries and traumas, and made available to the legal system as evidence in any future criminal proceeding. Left up to the victim, however, and without a policy of either mandated reporting or mandated recording, there is a curious absence of logic.

Charlotte Klein was appointed head of what was called the Hospital Brigade, a committee of women who had contacts within either the medical or the administrative levels of public and private hospitals throughout New York City.

The purpose of the Brigade was to meet with hospital and health care workers to convince them to create and implement a uniform set of guidelines to identify battered women before linking them up with the appropriate social service or legal system—all in a joint effort to combat what the AMA had already termed a "public health epidemic."

Klein and the others set out armed with optimism. They refused to believe that anyone in a position to make deci-

sions could offer a valid argument against establishing formal protocols in an organized hospital system to help
battered women and punish their abusers. Even if they
hadn't taken the high moral road to justify their mission, the
Brigade was also armed with real figures that showed the
monetary loss that resulted from domestic violence.

During 1994, for example, according to the American
Medical Association and several large insurance companies,
there were approximately one hundred thousand days of
hospitalization, thirty thousand emergency room visits, and
forty thousand visits to private physicians, with medical costs
due to domestic violence exceeding $100 million annually.

"We began targeting all the hospitals in the New York
area," Klein relates, "to convince them to hire a domestic
violence advocate on staff who would deal with battered
women. Our goal was that those advocates would implement
guidelines and develop multidisciplinary programs within
every hospital." According to Klein, the rationale behind
instituting a program that was multidisciplinary was that
every medical service would be obliged to utilize a uniform
set of guidelines to identify the battered woman, while being
assured that there was a program in place and an advocate
on staff to coordinate the appropriate support and treatment
for the victim. It was a valid mission to assure that not one
woman or child slipped through the system.

"Our idea," Klein explains, "was that every medical
service would receive training, from psychiatric to OB-GYN,
for identifying battered women, while at the same time they
would know that, once [she was] identified, there was a place
to refer the patient right there in the hospital."

Despite their citing monetary loss and moral obligation,
however, the group met with resistance. "Most of the resistance wasn't about the money that could be saved," Klein
admits. "It was about the money hospitals didn't have on
hand to implement the program and hire additional staff
people to run it."

There were several hospitals, however, that did agree to
respond to the Brigade's prepared questionnaire, indicating

what, if anything, was already in place in the form of a domestic violence program. The points addressed on the questionnaire were

> How do you help a victim of domestic violence who
> seeks help at your hospital?
> Is a domestic violence question included on your in-
> take questionnaire in the emergency room and
> on other services?
> Have you appointed a domestic violence advocate?
> Have you established treating domestic violence vic-
> tims as one of your priorities in the hospital?
> Do you have bulletins, posters, workshops, seminars
> on this subject?
> Do you continue to remind staff that every woman
> who seeks medical care is a potential victim of
> spousal abuse?

The Brigade's next step was to convince those hospitals
that had participated to make available a questionnaire,
which would be handed out to every female patient seeking
care in the emergency room, a physician's private office, or
a clinic, that would reveal if she was a victim of spousal
abuse. What was crucial was that health care workers learn
to identify the victim not only by her visible injuries but by
listening to the patient's answers to direct questions about
her relationship with her partner, her activities, habits, and
the general atmosphere in her home. Further, that questionnaire was designed so that the victim could identify the problem herself, since—either for cultural reasons or because
each victim has a different level of tolerance and different
criteria for defining what exactly is domestic violence—some
women are legitimately unaware that they are living in abusive relationships. Even the woman who seeks medical treatment after only one incident of violence is apt to have been
the victim of emotional or psychological abuse for months
or years until it finally escalated into a physical assault. Other
women, like Emily Goldenberg, while repeatedly seeking

medical attention for injuries resulting from domestic violence, were able to conceal a history of repeated abuse by rotating hospitals, since there is not as yet a computerized system that links hospitals even within the same city.

The questionnaire, targeted to female patients and provided to those hospitals that were receptive, was divided into two separate sections, covering emotional and physical or sexual abuse. It began as follows:

> *Does your partner:*
> constantly criticize you and your abilities as a wife or partner, mother, or employee?
> behave in an over-protective manner or become extremely jealous?
> prevent you from seeing family and friends?
> humiliate or embarrass you in front of others?
> deny you access to family assets such as bank accounts, credit cards, or car, or control all finances and force you to account for what you spend?
> use intimidation or manipulation to control you or your children?

The second section continued with the following questions:

> Are you in a relationship in which you have been physically hurt or threatened by your partner?
> Have you ever been in such a relationship?
> Are you or have you ever been in a relationship in which you felt you were treated badly? In what ways?
> What happens when you and your partner fight or disagree? Have you ever felt afraid of your partner?
> Has your partner ever prevented you from getting a job, or continuing your education?
> Has your partner ever destroyed things that you cared about?

Has your partner ever threatened or abused your children?

Has your partner ever forced you to have sex when you didn't want to?

Has he ever forced you to engage in sex that made you feel humiliated or uncomfortable?

How does your partner act when he is drinking or taking drugs?

Is he ever verbally or physically abusive?

Do you have guns in your home?

Has your partner ever threatened to use them when he was angry?

Has he ever hit, punched, slapped, kicked, shoved, or bit you?

The main objection to the questionnaires on the part of hospital staff was that women who entered the hospital for elective procedures, such as face-lifts, should not be subjected to such probing. The response is the same as the argument used by those opposed to the death penalty. Exceptions should not be made under any circumstance, regardless of the medical ailment or economic position of the patient. After all, it is far better to offend one plastic surgery patient or society matron than to let hundreds and thousands of battered women slip through the system undetected.

This process of taking a patient's history, while specifically targeted to battered women, is not in any way contradictory to usual medical treatment techniques. It is accepted policy that all health care workers, in order to identify a disease or ailment, question every patient before diagnosing an illness and prescribing appropriate medication.

According to guidelines set down by the AMA, if the patient answered in the affirmative to the majority of the questions listed above, doctors and nurses were to assume that she was a victim of spousal abuse, whereupon the advocate for battered women on staff at the hospital would be alerted. After meeting with the advocate and hearing what her options were medically, legally, and within the social service system, the victim would, according to those guidelines, still retain the right to choose what, if anything, she wanted to do to protect herself and her children from further violence.

"The key thing is that a woman has the right to make her own decisions when it comes to her personal safety," Klein reiterates. "Our only goal was to try and implement a program in every hospital to make health care workers aware of all potential victims and the widespread problem of domestic violence. We never advocated robbing women of their self-esteem." In conclusion, Klein expressed a contradictory statement in favor of empowering victims of domestic violence that is typically offered by the AMA, advocates for battered women, social workers, and feminists. "By the time the battered woman gets to the hospital," Klein maintains, "she is a shred, her confidence is gone, and she is in a helpless situation, unable to think or act rationally."

If the victim is a "shred" with her "confidence gone" and in a "helpless situation," it undoubtedly follows that she would also be suffering from severe psychological symptoms that would render her unable to make rational decisions to protect herself and her children. For this reason, any health care provider who treats a patient in this condition must be aware that any hysteria or psychosomatic symptoms she manifests are due to very real traumatic and violent events. What is missing in the well-meaning arguments of advocates is logic. Precisely because the victim has been beaten down and battered, professionals should be prepared to take over until she has healed, physically and emotionally.

In almost every case where a battered woman seeks care from a hospital or a private physician, she is adequately treated from a medical point of view, but she is often inadequately treated in the areas of preventive care and psychological therapy. In order to break the cycle of violence in her life, the victim needs a complete range of medical care. Without it, a domino effect results. Any failure within the medical system almost always reverberates into the legal system and all subsequent systems, ultimately resulting in both short-term and long-term failures that cost lives.

The danger from the medical standpoint in the short term is the inability to save lives, cure the sick, and prevent a reoccurrence of any medical problem; in the long term, it is the inability to change the perceptions that make victims of domestic violence the only group that suffers physical injuries and emotional traumas and at the same time is held responsible for the social dysfunction that led to their medical condition.

The danger from a legal standpoint is that, without mandated reporting and mandated recording, in the short term, medical personnel are not required to report injuries sustained through criminal acts, even though this is in the best interests of the patient; in the long term, they fail to create a record of evidence should the victim decide to press charges against her abuser in the future. Under extreme circumstances—in the event the victim is murdered after a history of abuse—there is nothing on record to provide the state with sufficient proof to indict and convict her murderer. It is as dangerous as the position of extremists in the right-to-life movement who justify the murder of health care workers who perform abortions by claiming that abortion is murder.

If the system is to work judiciously and efficiently in favor of the victim, it is not only the victim who must cooperate with the system, but advocates for the victim as well. These are the people who must reexamine their position concerning the rights of the battered woman by considering her both as a crime victim and as a patient who deserves the best possible medical care.

FIVE

Translating Medical Jargon

THE AMERICAN MEDICAL ASSOCIATION deserves credit for recognizing that the symptoms, injuries, traumas, and illnesses suffered by victims of domestic violence are caused by criminal activity. While change is essential throughout society to deal effectively with this crime, and cooperation between all the systems to make those changes work is vital, communication is what links people, programs, and emergency measures that will ultimately save lives. Health care providers must now learn to communicate the medical consequences of domestic violence in language that police, judges, and juries understand, so that the criminals who commit these crimes can be convicted. But above all, they must make the victim understand in order to inspire a relationship that is trusting and secure.

Every working system within society has its own language, words or phrases that have entirely different meanings or no meaning at all outside that profession. Certain key words or expressions are used almost as shorthand, not only to explain a situation quickly, but also to exclude those on the outside from understanding.

Medical jargon used by health care providers, which is usually incomprehensible to the average nonmedical person, automatically creates a distance between patient and physician. In any health care setting, doctors or nurses who use medical jargon to describe an illness, give a prognosis, or discuss a course of treatment with a patient only exacerbate an already fearful and tense situation. When people face an adverse medical problem or are just waiting for the results of a routine checkup—and certainly in the extreme, when they face a life-threatening illness—they need to have a clear understanding of the facts from their physicians. The goal of health care providers should be to make their patients comfortable in the knowledge that they are a team, striving together to make the best possible decisions for positive medical results.

The relationship between patient and doctor, by tacit agreement, is privileged, intimate, and at the same time un-equal, in that the patient is dependent upon the doctor for his or her knowledge, experience, and ability to heal. Those patients whose lives are saved by doctors, or the families of those who are saved, usually hold the physician above and apart from other professionals with whom they deal. It is not difficult to understand, given how others view them and the life-and-death nature of their job, that physicians also often hold themselves above and apart from the general lay popu-lation.

The average person has been known to repair a leak in his kitchen or bathroom to avoid calling a plumber, or re-place the spark plugs in his car instead of hiring a mechanic, or in certain cases even act as his own lawyer to save legal fees. There have not, however, been cases where a nonmedi-cal person has successfully operated on himself for a brain tumor, given himself a routine medical checkup, or done a root canal in his own mouth. Physicians, by virtue of their expertise, are part of an elite profession that is monitored under the law, which requires examinations and licenses for them to work.

From the beginning, therefore, before there is even any contact or relationship between patient and doctor, a certain distance has already been established, based precisely on the knowledge, expertise, and experience that the doctor has and the patient needs. It is for all these reasons that in many

medical schools throughout the country there is a movement
to teach doctors how to deal on a more human level with
their patients. Courses are given to make doctors more aware
of that distance by teaching them not only applicable methods to cure, but verbal skills to communicate in order not to
intimidate their patients. A successful combination of these
two skills also reinforces the goal of making patients more
involved and knowledgeable about all their medical problems. What is unfortunate but not surprising is that these
new outlooks on medical care have not yet included domestic violence, either in medical school courses or in hospital
training programs.

While it is a shock under any circumstances for a patient
to hear that he has cancer, even if the doctor says simply that
it has not spread and can be cured, the shock intensifies
when the patient hears the negative results of his tests described, for instance, as follows: "You have a Hodgkin's
lymphoma that is still supradiaphragmatic, indicating a
course of chemo and radiation therapy." The diagnosis is
not only terrifying, but the words themselves are so intimidating that often they discourage patients from asking vital and
important questions that will help them in their recovery. It
would have been just as easy if the doctor had said, instead
of "supradiaphragmatic," "a lymphoma that has not yet
spread." It is also important to note here that while the
physician used words that might have intimidated or confused the patient, neither the words used nor the physician
in any way implied that the patient was to be blamed for his
condition.

While medical jargon is used in all areas of medicine, as
it pertains to victims of domestic violence it tends to transform an already underestimated human condition into an
abstract medical problem. "Once the medical profession
learns to properly identify the battered woman," Dr. Carol
Warshaw says, "they must change the wording of their findings to make the patient's situation a human condition with
medical repercussions." Specifically, when doctors and
nurses use terms that only they can understand to describe

or record those injuries or traumas that battered women sustain, the words themselves tend to cast blame on the victims.

For example, the AMA recently issued a report that said, "Each year, 4 million women are battered in the United States." The impression that could be given by that statement is that each year, 4 million women are battered by the wind, or that 4 million women somehow keep running into invisible fists that batter them. Changing the wording even slightly would make a tremendous difference; the AMA might instead have stated, "Each year, men batter 4 million women."

The same type of error is often seen in newspaper advertisements or heard on television commercials concerning the medical consequences of domestic violence. The questions that are often raised are "How many injuries are sustained by women each year?" or "How much time do these women lose at work?" Seldom do these questions include any mention of or discussion about who causes those injuries or who is responsible for those women not showing up at work because they have bruises or black eyes or, worse, are in hospital or, in the extreme, are dead. According to Dr. Carol Warshaw, "It took years of struggle on the part of feminists and others to have domestic violence recognized as a sociopolitical issue rather than as a private family matter or as evidence of individual psychopathology."

Warshaw's observation is sound and clearly underscores the progress made when it comes to removing blame from any individual victim of domestic violence. The next question to be answered, however, is, how many more years before victims of domestic violence are not viewed separately from other crime victims?

Society must recognize domestic violence for what it is —a crime, and not only a sociopolitical issue or a medical condition. But in order for that to happen, doctors and nurses must understand that all symptoms and injuries that the battered woman suffers are the result of criminal acts that are committed against her. Dr. Warshaw cautions, however, that health care providers, because of their pivotal role in dealing with the victim of domestic violence, must also be aware of the "psychological dynamics of the relationship between the battered woman and her assailant." The potential for confusion still exists when health care providers, even when they do not blame the victim for her medical condition, are still unable to understand that the emotional problems she suffers account for her reluctance either to leave her abuser or report him to the authorities. In order for health care providers and society in general to stop differentiating in a prejudicial way between victims of spousal assault and victims of stranger crime, they must stop separating the battered woman's physical injuries from her emotional trauma. By recognizing that the emotional problems of the battered woman are a direct result both of her medical condition and of the crime and the criminal who caused that condition, doctors and nurses will be able to identify her more successfully and more often. "Not only should they [health care providers] be able to identify the battered woman by her physical symptoms," Warshaw contends, "but also by the specific syndromes, traumas, and certain types of injuries that she suffers, which are clues to the daily dose of violence and fear in which she exists."

According to Dr. Warshaw, there are specific medical clues to look for that signal when a woman is in a violent situation. Warshaw maintains that any woman seeking treatment for vague symptoms relating to fear, trauma, and shock could indicate spousal abuse. "Any woman who makes frequent visits to a hospital or private doctor complaining of vague symptoms without evidence of physiologic abnormality," Warshaw claims, "or any woman who admits to frequent use of prescribed minor tranquilizers or pain medication should be questioned thoroughly."

In a paper published in the *Journal of Women's Health*, Dr. Warshaw presents some of the most common psychological symptoms caused by the daily stress of living in an abusive relationship. They are chronic pain; psychogenic pain, or pain that has no basis of origin or visible explanation; physical symptoms related to stress; chronic posttraumatic stress disorder; other anxiety disorders or depression, such as sleep and appetite disturbances, fatigue, decreased concentration, sexual dysfunction, chronic headaches, abdominal and gastrointestinal complaints; palpitations; dizziness; paresthesia, or numbness and tingling in the hands or feet; dyspnea, or shortness of breath; and atypical chest pain.

Gynecologic problems relating to domestic or sexual abuse may include frequent vaginal and urinary tract infections; dyspareunia, which is pain during sexual intercourse; and general pelvic pain.

Physical injuries that are characteristic of victims of this crime are contusions, abrasions (cuts and bruises), and minor lacerations, as well as fractures or sprains; injuries to the head, neck, chest, breasts, and abdomen; injuries during pregnancy; multiple sites of injuries; and repeated or chronic injury.

Warshaw also suggests that physicians should suspect the possibility that a patient is the victim of partner assault when her explanation of how an injury occurred does not seem plausible, or if she has delayed seeking medical treatment.

The first step in treating victims of spousal abuse therefore is to identify them, and with a clear-cut array of symptoms, that should not be difficult. After that, all patients who enter hospital emergency rooms are taken to triage, where medical staff determine the extent and gravity of their injuries or assess the priority of their condition. In triage, patients are stabilized before they are sent to the appropriate services within the hospital, to continue with other diagnostic tests or X rays, or surgery, or care in the burn, cardiac, or intensive care units; or they are transferred back to the emergency room for further observation.

When the patient leaves triage with her initial evaluation done, doctors and nurses routinely record in their charts, in medical jargon, the condition, course of treatment, and prognosis of the patient.

Once the medical condition of the patient is determined and the appropriate emergency, surgical, or medical treatment begins, what is called a "treatment algorithm" takes place. For instance, if a patient arrives at an emergency room suffering from injuries resulting from a hit-and-run accident, a mugging or any other criminal assault, or a medical problem such as a contagious disease, an investigation begins to find out under what circumstances the assault, disease, or accident occurred. There are too many instances when victims of domestic violence, regardless of the symptoms, illness, or injuries that brought them into the hospital, are not subject to that same scrupulous investigation. This is another example of how domestic violence is considered in a negative context, separately from other crimes, injuries, or illnesses.

Patients whose medical problems are the result of spousal abuse, after they come out of triage, should be evaluated in another kind of triage or treatment algorithm, relevant to their specific physical and emotional problems. Once again, while domestic violence should be treated differently than other crimes, and its victims treated separately from other patients, neither "differently" nor "separately" should mean less scrupulously.

Doctors, nurses, or an advocate for battered women on staff at the hospital should question these patients as soon as possible to elicit specific details about how the trauma occurred and under what circumstances. The results of that evaluation should be included in the patient's medical chart, either in the patient's own words or in language that is clear and understandable to nonmedical readers. After that second level of diagnostic intervention is completed, it would be determined (depending on the laws in effect in that particular hospital, city, and state, and depending on the specific circumstances of the victim) when to call the police or social service workers, the priority in every situation being the safety of the victim and her children.

The most important consideration as it concerns the victim of this particular crime is that health care providers, when compiling data for a patient history, not only learn the specific events surrounding her medical condition, but also put those facts in context, so that the victim and perpetrator become two real and existing human beings—the injured party and the party who injured. Only by gathering every possible aspect of the information concerning the victim's condition—past and present—can doctors and nurses begin an effective course of preventive treatment, which is part of the basic care that it is the obligation of all physicians to offer their patients.

All symptoms, injuries, findings, and observations during examination of a victim of partner assault must be *recorded* in an official hospital chart. It is unrealistic to imagine that the specialized medical language doctors are taught can be changed in everyday practice, especially when they are describing technicalities in emergency situations. When doctors record circumstantial facts concerning injuries and traumas that are neither technical nor diagnostic, however, the language used should be nonmedical. Only then can the police effectively understand the victim's medical condition and whether it is the result of criminal activity. If the police do become involved, their record must also be accurate and something a prosecutor can understand and use to present a legal case to a court so that a judge and jury can grasp the criminal implications of the injuries that the victim sustained.

It would be even more effective if all written or oral facts concerning the victim's injuries, when presented in a courtroom, were either recited by the victim herself in her own words or read by either a lawyer or a medical expert. When a victim describes an assault by saying, "My husband hit me with a baseball bat," it has far more impact on a judge and jury than a jargon-ridden medical report that describes the injury as "trauma to patient's head by blunt object." In other words, what must be clear at every stage is that injuries, traumas, and even the death of victims of this crime are caused by criminals, people, men these women know.

The worst result of combining medical language and battered women is that a devastating injury described with these dispassionate and abstract words offers little connection to real human suffering and pain. "The language and framework of medicine," Warshaw points out, "structure interactions in ways that make it almost impossible for battered women to voice their concerns." Specifically, she contends, it is the written text of medicine, or the medical record, that obscures the injury and trauma that the victim has sustained. "Even if every doctor recorded every injury and trauma suffered by the battered woman," Warshaw continues, "there would still be glaring omissions . . . since most of the time, the woman herself is missing from the report." While the woman is missing because she is transformed into a generic victim, another glaring omission in most medical records is the perpetrator.

In a paper called "Limitations of the Medical Model in the Care of Battered Women," Warshaw talks about how the patient's perspective of an injury or illness is ignored when medical language is used in reports, instead of the patient's complaints in her own words. "What that does," Warshaw says, "is to present a scientific discourse that describes only what the clinician [health care provider] observes."

In order to understand why there are limitations in the medical model in the care of battered women, it is important to understand the difference between the terms "medical model" and "patient model." In medicine, especially in psychiatry, there are two specific models used: in the *patient model,* the patient takes the responsibility for his or her care and treatment; in the *medical model,* which is the more paternalistic approach to medicine, the physician is the only one responsible for deciding when the patient comes in and what the course of treatment will be.

Specifically, the patient model, as it works in psychiatry, is a prevention plan rather than a treatment plan, since rather than treating the illness, the patient does certain exercises, using biofeedback or meditation, to prevent the illness from reoccurring. Take stress, for example, which is a condition that can't be cured by taking a particular medication, since stress is the result of the patient's perception of his own surroundings. The psychiatric approach, when utilizing the patient model, would be to change the patient's perception of his surroundings, which would (hopefully) eliminate those feelings of stress. The limitation of the patient model is that not every patient is capable of participating or deciding on an appropriate treatment plan. As it pertains to the patient who is also a battered woman, the patient model is inevitably destined to fail. Regardless of any positive attitude, or effort to perceive her surroundings in a way that would eliminate stress and depression, or specific exercises that would help her take charge of her life to prevent illness, the victim of domestic violence is unable to avoid injury, trauma, stress, or fear, real or imagined, since each of those symptoms or illnesses is caused by the violent behavior of a specific external force, namely, her abuser.

The battered woman, therefore, can be treated more effectively by using the medical model, which means that health care providers must take charge of her course of treatment as well as initiate preventive measures that will insure her future safety. Treating the battered woman more effectively by the medical model rather than the patient model has a tremendous influence on laws covering mandated recording and reporting of domestic violence. Following through with a consistent course of treatment or method for removing the cause of the medical or psychological symptoms can mean the difference between success and failure when it comes to saving lives.

The paper that Dr. Warshaw presented, "Limitations of the Medical Model in the Care of Battered Women," specifically deals with the language used when questioning the patient who is being treated in the medical model in order to make an accurate diagnosis to effect an appropriate course of treatment. Dr. Warshaw offers an example.

A resident, who couldn't figure out his physical findings, once asked me to see a woman who had pain and redness under her right ear. I came into the room, introduced myself, looked at the patient, and asked if someone hit her. When she answered in the affirmative, I asked her who. She hesitated only a moment before telling me that her boyfriend hit her and when I asked why she hadn't told the resident, her response was that he hadn't asked.

When Warshaw confronted the resident, he claimed that he *had* asked the patient if "there had been any trauma." But asking a patient if there had been "trauma" was a poor way of asking her the more direct question "Who hit you?" or "Did someone hit you?" "The truth is," Warshaw continues, "that the resident was reluctant to ask what he thought were sensitive and intrusive questions about the woman's personal life."

By using medical jargon, the resident was able to phrase a question in a way that the patient would not understand and that would not make him uncomfortable asking. At the same time, the resident was also able to answer truthfully when he claimed that he had asked the patient if she had been hit. The only discrepancy is that he had used medical terms that confused the patient, and as a result discouraged a truthful response.

Warshaw goes on to say that there are endless accounts by battered women who claim that the questions posed by the majority of health care providers are either so impersonal or so confusing that even if they wanted to tell the truth about what happened to them, they wouldn't know how to begin. "The relationship between patient and doctor is based on trust and communication," Warshaw says, "and the problem is that society creates a false atmosphere where women think that they have told their stories to someone in a position to help them. The reality is that they haven't told anything mainly because they weren't aware that they had been asked."

It is an exercise in futility if doctors ask questions that patients don't understand. It is also useless if patients believe they have responded truthfully to their doctors and that their problems are understood. How can any physician hope to get a complete and relevant history of a patient when the dialogue between them is in two different languages? The most dangerous consequence of this kind of miscommunication is that patients don't reveal all the necessary facts, while doctors don't have all the necessary information to make an accurate diagnosis or administer appropriate treatment.

By their own admission, health care providers realize how difficult it is to convince a battered woman to be forthcoming about her injuries. Confusing the victim during that first contact, when her medical and emotional history are taken, can only create yet another chasm between doctor and patient. "Most [women] feel ashamed or frightened to report that their injuries are the result of abuse by a husband or boyfriend," Warshaw maintains. "Turning the horror into an abstraction further discourages the victim from talking openly."

In 1994, at Cook County Hospital in Chicago, Carol Warshaw conducted a review over a two-week period of fifty-two emergency room charts of women who had been deliberately injured by another person. What she found in almost every case was that physicians used disembodied language to describe a traumatic event. For example, in one report, a doctor wrote that "patient was beaten to face and head with a fist" as if there were a fist that had acted on its own rather than being attached to the arm of a human being, aka the victim's assailant. Describing injuries in that kind of language focuses on the mechanism of the injury, how the blow impacted on the body, with neither an explanation of who directed the blow nor any indication that the face and head that was its target happened to belong to the woman who was physically sitting in front of the physician.

How far can this go?

"A 42 year old woman presents with significant facial swelling and altered mental state after repeatedly being struck by a blunt object." Further down in the chart, the following was added: "Blow to head by stick with nail on it and injury on left wrist caused by jackhammer."

The reason for the assault, according to the patient, was, "My husband began beating me when I refused to give him money for drugs that I saved to buy a new washing machine."

Another report said, "A 28 year old gravida % para 4 female presents with spontaneous abortion after abdominal trauma secondary to being kicked."

The reason for the assault, according to the victim, was, "We had four kids already, and my husband wanted me to get an abortion. I wanted the baby, what was one more or less?"

By the use of medical shorthand, the victim of the attack, the patient, is reduced to an inanimate object, rather than the object or the victim of a criminal assault. Using the passive voice, as in "hit by a fist," further reduces the emotional trauma while concentrating on the mechanism of the physical injury. Removing the fist from the person attached to it obliterates the possibility of holding that person responsible. Logically, a disembodied fist cannot be arrested for assault nor can it be the object of an order of protection.

As it stands now, the language of hospitals and physicians makes it appear that victims of spousal abuse were more likely to be assaulted by a series of abstract nouns than by their partners, more likely to be victims of nebulous verbs than of another person's violent actions. As a result, not only is the trauma that the patient experienced diminished and obscured but the ongoing trauma in which the patient exists is often ignored.

What must happen is that health care providers should ask:

Who hit you?
How did this happen?
What is your relationship to that person?
Has this happened before?
Is it safe for you to return home?
Do you have another place to stay?
What do you want to do about it?

Following the medical model as it applies to battered women, if there were protocols for mandated recording under all circumstances established throughout all hospitals, that last question might be supplemented by the assurance "All photographs taken of your injuries and all statements concerning how you sustained those injuries will be sealed in your personal medical file and kept strictly confidential until you decide to use it to press charges against your assailant." And if there were protocols in place throughout all hospitals for mandated reporting under certain circumstances, that last question might be supplemented by the assurance "There are systems in place to protect you and your children from your assailant when the police arrest him for assault."

When it comes to mandated recording and reporting in hospitals, the only consideration should be victim safety. Questioning victims of assault should be followed in all cases by bringing in advocates for battered women, who must be available or on staff in the hospital twenty-four hours a day, seven days a week. These are the professionals who can recommend safety options, which must also be in place within the legal and social service systems to protect the victim and her children while the judicial system deals with her assailant. All data concerning the reasons and circumstances for the injuries sustained by the victim are essential in offering substantiating evidence and should be recorded in hospital records in nonmedical jargon that makes it clear and understandable whose fist punched the victim in the mouth or whose hand held the jackhammer that fractured her wrist. Without that, domestic violence remains an illness or epidemic whose cause is generic rather than specific, with fists, jackhammers, knives, and blunt instruments becoming euphemisms for flesh-and-blood assailants. After all, battered women do not catch a disease called domestic violence from random fists, blunt instruments, guns, or knives that produce bruises, fractures, or knife or gunshot wounds, and for which there is no known cure.

After a medical crisis has passed, however, and after

doctors and nurses leave committee meetings where each case has been discussed and dissected in medical terms, the next relevant issues to be considered are the human and emotional data, as well as what measures are needed to prevent another occurrence.

As it concerns domestic violence, practicing preventive medicine means preventing another assault, which in all probability will be more violent and life threatening than the previous one. To prevent another assault means identifying a victim of spousal abuse, intervening on her behalf, and changing medical language so that those within the legal and social service systems can understand that the medical problems she suffered were the result of a crime committed against her. Only then will there be sufficient evidence to convict the person who committed the crime.

Using simple language to record and report the victim's medical condition to systems outside the medical profession creates a response within those other systems that will be more immediate and effective. Communicating in language that obscures and confuses the issues of this crime is as dangerous a medical practice as encouraging a battered woman, during a time of crisis, to make her own choices about her safety.

The First Line
of Defense

CALL HER EMILY, NICOLE, or Tracey. Make her white or African American. Or call her by any other name and make her any other religion or nationality—Chinese, Arabic, Catholic, Moslem, Hispanic, Buddhist. Assume she has a college education, postgraduate degree, or high school diploma, or has dropped out after grammar school, or is unable to read and write. Pretend she is a professional, a doctor or a lawyer, has a high-paying job, middle-level income, or is on public assistance. Presume that she is married, single, divorced, or widowed; has children, or is childless; grew up in a loving and supportive family, or one that was dysfunctional. Imagine that she is rich, poor, or middle class; liberated, or dependent; smart, dumb, weak, or strong.

To compile a profile of the typical battered woman is as impossible as predicting who will die in the next earthquake, who will survive a terrorist attack, or who will win the lottery. The only common characteristics found in every battered woman are that she is female and that she experiences abuse at the hands of a former or current intimate partner. The only accurate method of predicting where and when domestic violence will occur is to assume that it can happen anywhere and everywhere.

Hospitals are often the first line of defense for victims of domestic violence; they are perceived as neutral, safe, accessible, and they lack the stigma of social service agencies or the police. Despite those two characteristics (female and abused) found in every victim of domestic violence, and despite the similarities in the injuries and traumas that she suffers, and despite the same excuses and reasons that she often gives for having sustained those injuries and traumas, when she enters a hospital or doctor's office as a patient, she is unique.

Every battered woman, just like every victim of stranger crime, or every patient suffering from the same disease, or every trauma victim injured by a similar piece of machinery or in an automobile or airplane accident, has her own history, psychological tendencies, emotional priorities, blood type, genetic weaknesses, and personal concerns, all of which are recorded in her medical chart.

If there is one common difference between the victim of domestic violence and victims of other crimes or accidents who seek care at a hospital emergency room, it is that the average battered woman usually has no primary care physician. Emergency room or public clinic staff are often the only non–family members from whom she seeks help. This puts them in the unique position of providing intervention and identification that go beyond administering medical treatment. If the battered woman is lucky, given her special circumstances, doctors and nurses can be the determining forces in stopping the violence inflicted on her. If she is unlucky, and doctors and nurses don't take the necessary time to get the true picture of her complaints, the only remaining option is too often to transfer her down to the morgue.

Empowering medical personnel to record the victim's injuries in all cases and to report them in certain cases is the only adequate response if that final outcome is to be avoided and women and children are to be rescued from life-threatening situations. It *is* our job to interfere. It *is* our responsibility to act, under all circumstances, and not condone violence and murder even by omission. And depending on our specific expertise, training, and skills, it *is* our responsibility to interfere, intervene, and respond in any way we can.

When there are children who either are present during episodes of domestic violence or are victims themselves, not mandating medical personnel to make decisions in the best interests of the battered woman often means that those children are taken away from their mothers and placed in foster homes. It is an eventuality that not only causes innocent children to suffer, but once again penalizes innocent women for having been victims of a crime.

There is room in this polemic for something that falls between mandated reporting in every situation, which some advocates for battered women claim disempowers them, and no reporting at all, which can cost women their lives or leave them in ongoing situations of abuse. While mandated *reporting* should be implemented under certain precise circumstances and conditions, mandated *recording* should be done in every case where a battered woman seeks care at a hospital or in the office of a private physician.

If mandated recording were made part of the law in every state throughout the country, as well as included in all medical protocols and practices, victims of this crime would be empowered in ways that would be tangible and realistic. Documenting injuries resulting from domestic abuse at the time they occur, regardless of whether they are superficial, psychological, or life threatening, would enable each victim to stand on her own, armed with the necessary proof to confront her assailant in a court of law. Mandated recording is a guarantee to the victim of this crime that she has the option to choose when, where, if, and how, without prejudice—days, weeks, months, or years later—she will proceed legally against her assailant. Freedom means choice. Choice is empowerment.

Included in the victim's confidential medical file would also be answers, in the victim's own words, to those questions compiled by Charlotte Klein and her Brigade concerning her personal relationship, violence in the home, and whether, where, and when she has reported other incidents of spousal assault to the police, hospitals, or doctors, even in other cities, states, or countries. It is important to know if the victim—like Emily, Nicole, and Tracey—has been a victim of abuse on prior occasions, even if those prior occasions were in a foreign country and are consequently not admissible in an American court. In all cases where there is a history of abuse, at least a pattern would be established that should be admissible evidence to show, if nothing else, that the victim is in an ongoing situation of danger since, by definition, abuse will always escalate in its intensity and frequency.

Once again, the only consideration should be patient confidentiality. All files and records of statements made about her abuse and her abuser, as well as all medical findings, X rays, and photographs of her injuries, would remain in her medical record, which by uniform law throughout the United States is open to public scrutiny only by court order. There should be no exceptions.

The requirement to record all incidents of domestic violence should be based on the assumption that all incidents of assault and terrorization by an intimate partner are considered potential homicides. Mandated recording should occur, therefore, regardless of the symptoms or injuries sustained by the victim of this crime, even if they are not life threatening and even if they are not physical but merely fears on the part of the victim that brought her into the safety of a hospital emergency room or the office of her private physician. Mandated recording should be an automatic part of that second level of triage, or treatment algorithm, as it pertains to victims of domestic violence.

Recording injuries means first photographing them, which calls for a Polaroid camera, film, and five minutes for someone to snap the picture—less time, manpower, or money than to receive a murder victim, call a coroner, or pay for a lengthy trial. Color photographs, which usually fall under the same state laws that cover X rays, should be taken from different angles, full-body and close-up, and where possible, a coin or other easily identifiable object should be placed near the injury to illustrate its size. The patient's face should be shown in at least one picture, and in all cases, the photographs should be marked with the patient's name, the location of the injury, and the names of the photographer and others present. Routine scannings, X rays, and image studies should also be made, and a complete medical and social history taken by the examining physician. With records now on computer disks or microfilm, there can be no excuses such as lack of space or facilities to hold these files for an indefinite period of time.

One of the most common fears that most battered women with children have is that if they report the crime that was committed against them or seek treatment for their injuries, social service workers, the police, or the courts will step in and remove their children from their care, branding them as unfit. One of the special circumstances under which mandated reporting should be put into practice is when women seeking medical help for injuries sustained by a current or former partner have minor children living in the home. Still, the choice of whether or not to press charges against their assailant is theirs, and when they are in the hospital or office of a private physician, they should be given that choice, or empowered to make their own decisions. Battered women must be made to understand that if they choose the option of pressing charges against their batterers, they will not risk losing their children. In addition, given the way this new system of mandated reporting would be set up (as discussed later on in this chapter), it would also provide another way to identify victims of this crime, specifically through their minor children. The logic is that since mandated reporting of child abuse is already written into the law, it would provide further protection of children.

Encouraging battered women to come forward before it is too late and providing and assuring them that, by doing so, they can find safety for themselves and their children would give them freedom from fear. They would no longer be penalized as crime victims, nor would the crime committed against them be judged "differently" in any negative sense. Even in those cases where battered women, living in a constant situation of tension and abuse, abuse their own children, a form of amnesty would be granted: once removed from the violent situation, they would be monitored and given psychological support to prove that they are nonabusive and loving parents.

Cathy Richardson is an example. Richardson, thirty-four years old and a former law-enforcement officer, is currently serving a sentence of twenty years to life in Bedford Hills Women's Prison in Bedford Hills, New York, for second-degree murder in the death of her abusive boyfriend. Cathy admits that when the beatings and abuse got so bad that she feared for her children, she would abuse them herself. "I started beating them to keep them quiet," Cathy admits, "because I figured that it was better for them if I abused them than if Jeff did it. At least, I could control my violence."

The most important result would be that the external situation in which battered women live would be the reason for their behavior. These mandated reporting procedures under these circumstances not only empower women to make the best choices but support them so they are not held responsible for the violence they suffer at the hands of their partners or the abuse their children suffer because of the situation. A further benefit is that it reduces the trauma suffered by children who live in an abusive home by making sure they are not only safe but in a safe situation with their mothers. And, it gives law enforcement a greater opportunity to mount cases against batterers that result in convictions.

For women without children, mandated reporting would go into effect under new guidelines that redefine misdemeanors and felonies as they specifically concern victims of domestic violence. When police are summoned in response to a crime of domestic violence, instead of using standard guidelines that define a misdemeanor and a felony in cases of stranger crime, a separate definition of misdemeanor and felony would be implemented for injuries sustained by a woman at the hands of a former or current intimate partner. For the victim of partner abuse, a felony would depend not on how hard she is hit or how severe her injuries are, but on whether she was assaulted by an intimate partner in the privacy of her own home, or was assaulted in the street or anywhere else by an assailant with whom she was currently living. A common residence should automatically signal proximity between victim and assailant, which means that the assailant has constant access to his victim. In every case, however, the place of the crime and/or the victim's relationship to the perpetrator should signal health care providers and police that the victim is in an ongoing life-threatening situation that can and will escalate.

If women who had minor children living with them refused to press charges against their abusive partners, they would risk, only under those circumstances, losing their children to foster care. This choice would, therefore, serve as an incentive for women to extricate themselves from a violent situation as well as allow police and the courts to carry out the law as it applies to minors without causing additional hardship by tearing children away from their mothers.

It has been found that the average battered woman leaves her abuser at least eight times before she leaves for good—if she is lucky, alive. The battered woman should be assured that every one of those forays in and out of that violent situation are not failed attempts to leave but rather legitimate attempts to research alternatives and options. Each time the victim leaves, she learns another piece of useful information or makes another life-saving contact that will eventually help her to build a new life. In all cases, however, where there are minor children making those forays in and out of the home as well, they should not be subjected to danger while their mothers explore their options or gather the nerve to take legal action.

From the physician's and hospital's point of view, the only obstacle to mandated reporting should be how and when court testimony is given. In order for medical records to be admissible in court, the doctor must be prepared to testify that the records were made during the regular course of business at the time of the examination or interview, that the records were made in accordance with routinely followed practices, and that the records were properly stored, with access limited to professional staff.

Testifying in court, however, can be a time-consuming and lengthy process in which busy doctors and hospital staff lose precious hours otherwise devoted to their work. Special arrangements should be made with the courts that would encourage doctors and nurses to testify by calling them only on the day and hour that their testimony is to be heard. In cases where there is no jury trial, testimony should be recorded on videotape. Where there is a jury trial, cameras should be set up in a hospital or doctor's office and linked to a courtroom; this would enable lawyers to question them without additional time lost by traveling back and forth to court.

Time and money are always the excuses given for not instituting programs, protocols, and laws; specifically, it is argued that increased budgetary allowances are required to put a system in place with adequate funds to pay for advocates for battered women on staff or on call twenty-four hours a day, seven days a week, in hospitals, as well as for installing a computer linkup between hospital emergency rooms within the same city.

There are systems already in place that, if functioning efficiently, could offer incentives that would in turn provide the necessary funding for these programs. Federal officials estimate that domestic violence costs American companies approximately $4 billion a year in lower productivity, staff turnover, absenteeism, and excessive use of medical benefits. Wouldn't it make sense for each company or corporation, therefore, to contribute to a separate fund that would supplement the cost of additional staff in all public hospitals throughout their cities? Additionally, those insurance companies which provide health care coverage for these corporations and small companies could be solicited to donate funds as well under a tax-rebate program that could finance shelters on the hospital premises. As well, insurance companies that provide malpractice coverage for doctors and other health care providers might also contribute in order to cut down on costs when legal action is taken against any health care provider if and when a victim is released and subsequently suffers additional injuries.

It's common sense that reducing the number of emergency room visits and repeat injuries would save all of us money, just as mandated recording, keeping up-to-date and complete records, could potentially save money for the courts by eliminating lengthy trials or, in the optimal situation, by acting as a deterrent to the abuser. Given the theory that a hospital, clinic, or office of a private physician is the first place where a battered woman seeks help, it is incumbent upon the health care system to establish a record of abuse that guarantees the victim the choice of utilizing the social service and legal systems already in place.

If the medical system fails the battered woman, it becomes a foregone conclusion that the social service and legal system will fail her as well, because she may never get there. Before the linkage Attorney General Reno called for in her speech can be made between the medical and criminal systems, concrete changes and protocols must be put into place, in all hospitals throughout the country, that would not only treat the medical aspect of this problem, but also provide clear documentation to enable the criminal justice system to take over and do its part. If a victim of domestic violence is given the choice of medical treatment, returning to her abuser, or pressing charges against him, she has been betrayed not only by her partner, but also by a medical system that fails to intervene as it does in all other incidents of violent crime.

Currently, most states in the United States have written into law mandated reporting of infectious diseases and animal bites as well as cases of gunshot wounds and aggravated assault. There are certain states, however, that have programs in effect in hospitals that call for varying degrees of mandated reporting and recording under specific circumstances. While these programs are not ideal, they merit mention, if only to understand the areas in which improvement and change should be made.

For the past fifteen years, Kentucky has required doctors, nurses, hospitals, and the police to report any known or suspected adult abuse to the state's Department of Social Services. Following that mandate, a letter was sent to every doctor and nurse licensed in the state, informing them of their responsibility concerning mandated reporting of domestic violence under the law. The way the law was written gave health care workers an incentive to comply, since in all reports of domestic abuse that turned out to be wrong, the doctor or nurse was protected from any lawsuit brought either by the patient (alleged victim) or her partner (alleged perpetrator). On the other hand, if any health care provider failed to report a suspected case of domestic abuse, he or she was subject to penalty for failing to comply to the state's mandate.

The principal consideration in Kentucky is victim safety. Hospital regulations require that all records of spousal abuse be sealed, guaranteeing the victim that her abuser will never know that her injuries were made a matter of hospital record or that she named him as the perpetrator of those injuries. The system in Kentucky assures the victim that official records exist that she or the district attorney can use at their discretion should they decide to press criminal charges against her abuser.

Suppose those protocols in Kentucky were slightly different. For instance, any doctor or nurse who fails to record accurately those injuries sustained in any situation of domestic abuse would be subject to censure by the American Medical Association.

If any doctor or nurse fails to probe into the cause of a patient's injuries and, instead, accepts a blatantly implausible explanation as to how they occurred, causing the victim to return to her abuser only to suffer more injuries, that health care provider would also be held either criminally or civilly liable, depending on the extent of the patient's subsequent injuries.

As well, failure to separate a female patient from her partner at the time of her admission to the hospital or emergency room or during an office visit with her private physician, which would prevent her from responding honestly to questions posed by that health care provider, would also be subject to penalties by the state's medical licensing committee for having put the patient in greater *criminal* danger.

Under American Medical Association guidelines that adhere to all state and federal law, the suggested penalties that would apply to cases of spousal assault are already in place under other medical circumstances. For instance, when a doctor ignores certain warning signs or symptoms of an illness or disease that causes the patient additional suffering, he can be found guilty of malpractice.

When a doctor prescribes the wrong drug, an incorrect dose of anesthetic, or amputates the wrong limb, he can also be found guilty of malpractice.

Putting these laws into effect in cases of domestic violence would give an incentive for insurance companies to donate money to finance additional programs and staff to care for battered women, as mentioned earlier. In fact, this donation would be justified by an anticipated decrease in malpractice suits.

On the basis of work by Anne Flitcraft and Evan Stark of Yale University, it was found that in the state of Connecticut during the 1970s, doctors were identifying only 4 percent of domestic violence cases. As a result, mandatory reporting in Connecticut was passed in the legislature as a five-year experiment. There was a negative and extremely dangerous side to this policy, however. If a private doctor or hospital failed to report a domestic violence case that came to their attention, an attorney representing a batterer could then use the noncompliance of the health care provider to his client's advantage. A typical cross-examination of a battered woman who had pressed charges against her abusive partner during a court trial went something like this:

> DEFENDANT'S ATTORNEY: You told us you were treated by Doctor X or at X hospital for injuries.
> PLAINTIFF: Yes.

DEFENDANT'S ATTORNEY: You testified that you told your doctor (or hospital workers) that your husband (partner) inflicted those injuries.

PLAINTIFF: I did.

DEFENDANT'S ATTORNEY: Did your doctor inform you that he was making a report of those injuries as provided under the law of mandated medical reporting?

PLAINTIFF: No.

DEFENDANT'S ATTORNEY: Did you ever learn that he had made such a report?

PLAINTIFF: No.

DEFENDANT'S ATTORNEY (turning to the judge): Your Honor, I would like the court to take note that there is no indication in the doctor's or hospital's records of any assault by the plaintiff's spouse that was ever introduced as evidence.

DEFENDANT'S ATTORNEY (summation): The plaintiff told her own doctor that her husband had caused her injuries. Her doctor, required by law to report any injuries that he believes are the result of domestic violence, never reported them. It is evident that her own doctor, who examined her and saw those injuries, did not believe her story and as a consequence never reported it.

By not adhering to the mandated reporting laws in Connecticut, doctors created a legal situation as harmful to the victim as that in cases when prosecuting attorneys use years of spousal abuse to prove premeditation when a battered woman finally kills her batterer. As a result of the negative repercussions caused by noncompliance with the law by health care providers, mandated reporting in Connecticut was not reinstated at the end of that five-year experimental period. It wasn't until Tracey Thurman's case provoked public outrage and cost the Torrington police over $2 million that the law was reevaluated.

What resulted was another effort in Connecticut to institute a coordinated community response to domestic violence, which included adequate budget increases to make that coordinated system work. While the state of Connecticut adopted a comprehensive domestic violence law calling for the arrest of abusive spouses, there was nothing written into the law to engage the support of the American Medical Association and social service and judicial systems to cooperate or comply. Still, in the year that followed, 1986, the number of arrests for domestic assault increased 93 percent, from 12,400 to 23,830. In the years after that, however, when still nothing had been written into the law to make that compliance official, reported cases of domestic violence decreased drastically.

For the past three years Massachusetts has considered domestic violence as a crime. While the system is still not complete, there are two specific hospitals that should serve as examples for the entire country.

One of the best programs for battered women is found at Massachusetts General Hospital in Boston. And one of the most unique and successful programs for identifying battered women through their minor children is found at Children's Hospital, also in Boston.

Although in Massachusetts it is not required under the law to report incidents of domestic violence, these two programs have protocols in place either to record all injuries and traumas or to utilize existing laws that require health care providers to report and record all injuries and traumas sustained by minor children.

Trisha Mian works at the Massachusetts General Hospital as a psychiatric clinical nurse, dealing directly with victims of domestic violence. She is one of four people on staff whose job it is to identify and intervene when battered women come to the hospital seeking medical treatment for their injuries and traumas. Working with Trisha are two social workers, who cover shifts Monday through Friday from eight-thirty in the morning until eleven-thirty at night, and occasionally on Saturday evenings, times when incidents of domestic violence are most likely to occur. In addition, they all carry beepers that keep them in touch with and available to the hospital twenty-four hours a day, seven days a week, in case of emergency.

Trisha's job takes her anywhere in the hospital from the emergency room to waiting rooms (both in the medical unit and near the operating room) to the gynecological clinic to parts of the ambulatory care center. She describes her job: "I'm involved in a couple of different ways, establishing guidelines or protocols for patients who come into the emergency room, training the nursing staff on how to identify battered women when they are in crisis and following up after they leave."

When a patient enters the emergency room with suspicious injuries or traumas, Trisha is immediately notified. Her job begins as soon as the patient is stabilized medically. According to Trisha, the majority of battered women who seek medical assistance initially claim that they were assaulted by a stranger or involved in an accident. "Despite our best efforts," Trisha admits, "not every victim arrives with one story and leaves with the truth." Still, any woman with suspicious injuries who insists that she is not the victim of domestic abuse will be told by Trisha that her condition presents another scenario. "The problem is that many times the woman is brought in by her batterer, who hovers around and refuses to leave her alone, which makes it difficult for the victim to tell the truth, even if she wanted to."

In those cases when the patient is not alone, Trisha explains to the husband or boyfriend that hospital procedure calls for him to wait outside while his wife or girlfriend is being assessed. "Sometimes it's the woman who resists more than the man," Trisha explains, "because she's terrified of alienating him. After all, she's got to go home with this man, and we're only seeing a slice of their relationship." Regardless of the circumstances of each individual case, whenever a victim of suspected domestic abuse arrives at the hospital, with or without her partner, the security police are notified that there is a potentially dangerous situation in progress.

"As soon as I'm able to talk to the woman alone," Trisha continues, "the first thing I do is assure her that I understand how frightened she is and while I really want to help, I won't do anything that might jeopardize her safety."

If the patient still resists and refuses to discuss her injuries, Trisha will leave the woman alone for ten minutes to think things over before she tries to intervene again. During her next contact with the woman, Trisha explains that the goal of the domestic violence program at Massachusetts General Hospital is to empower her to make the best choices by taking into account her particular situation. "There are many occasions," Trisha explains, "where the best choice for a battered woman is to return home with her batterer and not risk a more severe beating. On the other hand, if a woman is really looking for help, we can get her into a shelter or we can call the police to get her a temporary restraining order, and in those cases where she's willing to press charges, the police *will* arrest him. Our policy is to support the victim and do whatever she wants."

Despite a policy that calls for empowering the victim to make her own choices, in cases where family violence is suspected, all patients are questioned—in private and with the guarantee of confidentiality. Any patient suspected of having been battered is asked direct questions such as "Are you in a relationship where you have been physically hurt or threatened by your partner?" After the patient is assured that everyone believes her story, she is told that under no circumstances does she deserve to be treated violently. In all cases, after the abuse has been admitted and discussed, the doctor or nurse calls the advocate—Trisha or one of her colleagues—who proceeds to list all the various options available, such as going to a shelter or staying with friends or family. In extreme cases, when there is no available shelter space and no friend or family member nearby and the victim is too frightened to return home, she is kept in the emergency room until other arrangements are made.

Mandated reporting automatically goes into effect at MGH if a woman arrives at the emergency room with life-

threatening injuries or presents a scenario where there is
even a remote possibility of more deadly injury. In those
cases, police are notified under the same guidelines that are
used for reporting gunshot wounds or infectious diseases as
well as any felony committed during a stranger crime. To aid
the victim further, doctors and nurses record the name and
badge numbers of the investigating officers, along with any
action that was taken. Despite the best efforts by police and
hospital staff, however, there can still be resistance by the
victim to cooperate as well as a failure of cooperative effort
between different systems.

What is missing as of now in Massachusetts is a computerized system between hospitals and offices of private physicians that can determine immediately if the patient has
sought care for similar symptoms or injuries elsewhere within
the state. If there were a computerized system, and if the
answer to that query were affirmative, then regardless of the
extent of her injuries on that particular occasion, mandated
reporting could go into effect automatically, taking into consideration those guidelines that define misdemeanor and
felony in crimes of spousal assault. (This would require a
new law.) Remember, the injury or crime that brings the
victim to the police, hospital, or office of the private physician is not necessarily the first or the most severe she has
suffered at the hands of her abuser. The point is to act when
she is available, reachable, in need, and above all, alive.

In all cases, women seeking medical care in hospital
emergency rooms who resist revealing the true facts concerning their injuries or who refuse services made available to
them should be told by all health care providers, including
advocates and social workers, that what has happened to
them is a crime. The difference between telling a battered
woman that she is the victim of a crime because it is a hospital rule and having programs in place that deal effectively
with the crime as well as protecting the victim is the difference between crash dieting and permanently changing
eating and exercise habits. One is guaranteed to fail, while
the other, over time, will succeed.

In the four years since Trisha has been with the domestic violence program at the Massachusetts General Hospital, she has seen a variety of women from a wide range of social, economic, and ethnic backgrounds. "I've seen women come in who are married to doctors on staff," Trisha reports, "and I've even dealt with women doctors who are married to doctors. In fact, we had one case of a couple, both doctors, where the wife came in badly beaten. But before I could even finish listing the services available to her under our domestic violence program, her husband came down and got her and they left together."

Trisha has learned to recognize the different excuses that battered women give for their injuries. "We did a chart review here last year of seven hundred women who came into the emergency room," she says. "Quite a number of professional women who came in with head injuries claimed they were walking down the street, got dizzy, and tripped on the sidewalk." According to Trisha, professional women who remain in abusive relationships are usually the ones who claim that their partners are going to change because they have access to therapists. "They're the ones who make the mistake of entering into couple therapy," Trisha says, before adding, "what we tell them is that the beatings will never end; nothing will change except to get worse."

Conversely, the battered woman who is less financially independent is more apt to tell the truth and more likely to refuse intervention and instead remain in the abusive relationship. "For them, living with occasional abuse is better than leaving their home and moving into a shelter," Trisha explains, "better than pressing charges and having their partner carted off to jail, where he can't support the family."

Trisha offers several examples of how the police, private doctors, or the hospital have failed women who first sought help in the emergency room.

A successful investment banker arrived at an emergency room seeking treatment for cigarette burns on her hands and arms. "She told the nurse that her partner had a burn fetish," Trisha says, "as if that were an acceptable explanation for her injuries." During the next six months, the woman appeared at the same emergency room on fifteen separate occasions with more severe burns to her face and body. Each time that the woman sought medical care, the nurse tried to convince her to get a restraining order to remove her partner from the condominium that they shared and that the woman owned and for which she alone paid all monthly maintenance fees. And each time the woman claimed that she and her partner were engaged in couple therapy to cure *him* of his burn fetish. The last time the nurse saw the woman, she was in the intensive care burn unit, suffering third-degree burns over 40 percent of her body. Her partner with the burn fetish eventually scalded her with boiling water, leaving her permanently disfigured.

"The tragedy," Trisha contends, "is that this woman, by entering into couple therapy, gave her partner the message that she considered his burn fetish to be *their* problem."

Unfortunately, that is not the only example where a woman was wrongly advised by a therapist or medical doctor that couple therapy was a productive course of treatment. Not only is couple therapy *not* a productive course of treatment; it is a policy that has disastrous and dangerous consequences for the battered woman. Advocates for battered women cite the risks involved in offering couples' counseling to women involved in abusive relationships. The greatest danger is that frequently any disclosure of violence made by an abused woman during a counseling session is used against her by her batterer once they get home. In all cases, couples must be properly assessed for violent behavior before attempting to work from a family-systems perspective.

Another case that Trisha cites is that of a thirty-four-year-old woman who was brought into the emergency room along with her husband. The story the couple gave was that they had both been victims of assault by a gang of thugs while at a baseball game. What made doctors and nurses suspicious, however, was that only the woman had been injured. Trisha was summoned.

"Maria was literally beaten to a pulp with a baseball bat," Trisha begins, "and when I questioned her about whether she had reported the assault to the police, she claimed that she had." But when Trisha tried to verify her story with the police, she found that there had been no record filed of any assault concerning a couple who had been at a baseball game that happened still to be in progress. After several days of talking with Maria, on the day that she was scheduled to be released from the hospital, Trisha finally convinced her to tell the truth.

It was exactly four-fifteen on a Friday afternoon when Robert Pastor, as he was leaving the main entrance of the hospital, was arrested and charged with grievous assault on his wife, Maria Pastor. After Robert Pastor was taken downtown to the police station, Trisha accompanied Maria to the criminal court, where she swore out a complaint and secured a restraining order. Feeling safe and relieved after years of abuse, Maria was about to go home when, on a hunch, Trisha suggested that Maria come back to the hospital with her. While she didn't want to alarm the woman, she also wanted to make sure that Robert was still in custody. When they returned to the hospital, only three hours after Robert had been arrested on hospital grounds, Trisha called the police and confirmed her suspicions that Robert had already been released on bail.

Trisha asks the question, "How did pressing charges help this woman? He was already out of jail, and if I hadn't called to check, Maria would have gone home and been beaten worse than before, or killed."

In all cases of spousal assault, after a victim finally presses charges against her assailant, the police should be instructed to contact the hospital or the victim to advise them that her husband or boyfriend is being released on bail. The most ready excuse that the police give is that they do not have an adequate budget to designate an officer who would do nothing else except track those cases where a batterer was arrested to determine when and if he had been released.

The solution is that police officers should be required to do duty on that particular service on a rotating basis, even if that means having one less police officer in the station to answer the phones or putting one more person on duty during every shift. In terms of cost and time efficiency, it might prevent men who are released from jail from heading directly back to their victim and assaulting her again. In addition to providing for victim safety, it would reduce the incidents of rearrest, which involves another court hearing and eventually a trial. As a backup, in every case the hospital or doctor who treated the victim, along with the advocate on staff at the hospital who helped the victim press charges against her assailant, should be held responsible to verify the whereabouts of her assailant as well. Until that information is confirmed, the victim should not be released from the hospital or should be transferred to a safe place other than her home. Trisha Mian's response, "The hospital doesn't always have funds available to put a special person on staff just to contact the police," is accurate in most cases. However, the hospital still remains responsible, which means until funds can be raised or allocated, a volunteer who is already working in the hospital gift shop or distributing magazines and books to patients should be transferred to the advocate's office, where it would be his or her job to find out if the perpetrator has been released on bail before the victim is allowed to return home. Victim safety must have priority in all cases, regardless of any excuses, however valid, concerning inadequate budget or lack of staff.

Medicine has made a startling transition from the beginning of the twentieth century, when people succumbed to infectious diseases or benign problems, to the end of the twentieth century, where revolutionary procedures can predict and identify diseases before they manifest. The vast majority of deaths statistically noted involve risk factors pertaining to cancer, heart disease, substance abuse, and genetics. There is no reluctance on the part of any doctor to insist that a patient get a genetic test for cancer, be screened for cholesterol, cut back on alcohol, or eliminate cigarettes.

In general, the trend is to alter lifestyles to prolong healthy lives. Yet when the medical profession deals with an epidemic such as domestic violence, which has a readily identifiable cause, and can automatically interrupt the "illness" and prevent physical damage by removing the patient from a specific environment that places her at risk, the same principles that are applied to primary care prevention are ignored.

SEVEN

Out of the Mouths of Babes

CHILDREN ARE FREQUENTLY the indirect victims of domestic violence, victims who are often ignored and eventually forgotten. While there are laws across the country for mandated reporting of child abuse, these laws often work in direct conflict with what is best for both mother and child, considered as a unit.

Kentucky takes measures to assure the battered woman that any abuse she has suffered in the presence of her children will not automatically cast her as an unfit mother.

Colorado requires doctors to report to the state's Department of Public Health all criminal activity, from gunshot wounds to stolen bicycles. With regard to domestic violence, doctors are required to report all incidents to the Department of Public Health. This automatically involves the Colorado Domestic Violence Coalition, which keeps all records confidential. The state of Colorado also keeps incidents of child abuse confidential; the negative aspect of this practice is that records are not subject to discovery in cases of child custody.

While confidentiality is a positive aspect of both mandated reporting and mandated recording of injuries inflicted on minor children, the downside of that confidentiality is that it often prevents judges, when hearing custody and visitation cases, from knowing certain facts concerning the father's involvement in spousal abuse. There have been and continue to be many cases not only in Colorado but throughout the United States, in which, despite orders of protection, courts have required women to turn over their address and telephone numbers so that abusive male partners can come to the victim's home to visit the children. What has become evident is that children are frequently the secondary reason for the father's visit. The primary reason is that the visit provides a means for further abusing the woman.

The Pikul case is one of the most extreme examples of a father/abuser who got custody of his minor children after he was proven to be many things, including a wife beater and, in the end, a wife murderer.

On November 5, 1987, the day that the Steinberg/Nussbaum case broke in the newspapers, Diane Pikul was buried at Riverview Cemetery in South Bend, Indiana. In another coincidence, the Pikul family also happened to live around the corner from Joel Steinberg and Hedda Nussbaum, in New York's Greenwich Village.

Joseph Pikul, Diane's husband, was an admitted transvestite and alcoholic. Accused of murdering his wife, Pikul, in a bizarre twist of justice, was released on bail and permitted to retain custody of their two minor children.

The question of whether to allow minor children to remain in the care of the accused murderer of their mother was eventually put into the hands of Robert Wayburn, the associate general counsel for New York City's Human Resources Administration. Despite pressure brought to bear by District Attorney Robert Morgenthau, who insisted that the children be removed from Pikul's care, as well as pleas from Diane Pikul's relatives, Wayburn said he was constrained by the current law, which provided that only two people have protected parental rights to a child: the mother and father. According to Wayburn, those rights could not be taken away unless a parent were found to be unfit, or unless a judge concluded that there were extraordinary circumstances, in which case a hearing would be held to determine what would be in the best interests of the children—staying with the parent or being sent to live with other caretakers. In other words, under New York State law, for the children to be removed under the unfit-parent category, the children had to be in "imminent danger." A parent could not be charged with abuse or neglect solely based on the fact that he or she had been accused of murder, even if the victim of that murder happened to be the children's mother. Further, there wasn't even any legal precedent to fall back on, since in most cases of spousal murder, the defendant stays in jail until trial.

Represented by a battery of high-priced lawyers, Joseph Pikul managed to get himself released on $350,000 bail and was prepared to wage a high-priced custody battle as well. As Robert Wayburn viewed it, the question was whether it was permissible for Pikul to have gained parental monopoly by eliminating the competition. But, judging from social workers' reports about the children's emotional and psychological conditions, it was clear to Wayburn that they appeared to be bonded to their father without any apparent fear or any desire to live with anyone else. They were aware that their father had been accused of killing their mother. According to the little girl, her father had also assured her that he was innocent. Having lost one parent already, the children were getting much-needed security from Joseph Pikul. On that basis, Wayburn concluded that the courts would not judge Joseph Pikul an unfit parent, even while awaiting trial for the murder of his wife, the mother of their two children.

A custody suit brought by Diane's family was therefore the only option. The city would participate in the proceedings. The lengthy custody hearings began on December 18, 1987, before Judge Kristin Booth Glen, in New York State Supreme Court. Though the city had found no legal basis to initiate proceedings against Pikul, Wayburn ultimately told the judge that the Human Resources Administration opposed Pikul's continuing custody. At the request of Joseph Pikul and his lawyers, Judge Glen interviewed both children in her chambers. When she returned, the message was clear. The children loved their father and wanted to stay with him.

The children would probably have remained in Pikul's care until he was eventually found guilty of second-degree murder of his estranged wife, Diane, which he was on March 16. But, while awaiting the outcome of his trial, Joseph Pikul remarried, and it was when he attacked his second wife with a knife that he finally lost custody of his two children.

Yet in an even stranger twist of justice, after a jury convicted him of the murder of his wife on June 2, 1989, while he was awaiting sentencing, the issue of custody or conviction became moot when Joseph Pikul died in prison of AIDS.

In response to what was considered the unsolved problem of domestic violence against minor children, Massachusetts adopted Project Protect. This was an administrative policy that required the Department of Social Services to investigate every allegation of child abuse and neglect as well as every incident where children were present in the home when the mother was suffering abuse at the hands of her male partner, whether or not he was the biological father of the children.

The result of Project Protect was that every woman who sought medical care with a therapist or a physician or in a hospital emergency room was immediately reported to the Department of Social Services, which was charged with investigating each case to determine if minor children living in the household were also at risk. In a major study of more than nine hundred children living with their mothers at battered women's shelters across Massachusetts during 1992, it was found that nearly 70 percent of the children were themselves victims of physical abuse and neglect; nearly half had been physically or sexually abused; and 5 percent had been hospitalized because of abuse. The conclusion was that family abuse was the largest single cause of death for children under the age of five.

On the basis of that study, Project Protect assumed that every child living in a home where abuse was present was also a victim. But instead of treating those facts in a way that would not further traumatize women and their children, the police were instructed to strip-search children for signs of physical abuse every time they responded to a domestic violence call. As a result, social service agencies were routinely called in to evaluate custody, which in most cases held the mother responsible for the safety of the children when they were living under the same roof as the abusive father or male partner. In fact, social service agencies across the country frequently open cases of abused or neglected children in the name of the mother, even if she has been dead for five years.

Most of the investigations under the aegis of Project Protect led to children being taken away from their mothers and placed in foster homes, which caused many women to move away or never return to court for any final order concerning their abusive partners. While Project Protect was a well-intentioned plan to reach battered women through laws that mandated reporting of child abuse, the result was that women and children were penalized, while the criminal actions of the father/partner were rarely addressed.

The same problem exists in New York State, where a Task Force on Family Violence, formed in December 1992 and cochaired by Ruth Messinger, Manhattan borough president, and Ronnie Eldridge, chairman of the City Council Subcommittee on Women, attempted to revamp a system that was responding less than adequately to all aspects of domestic violence. It was an ambitious undertaking by women who have been involved for years in the issue of domestic violence and continue in their struggle and commitment to protect the rights of battered women and their children. One of the first orders of business was to investigate the protocols already in place.

The Child Protective Services' Domestic Violence Protocol is a document prepared for the Child Welfare Agency (CWA) by the New York City Interagency Task Force on Domestic Violence (ITFDV). It is intended for use when domestic violence is found to exist in any home under investigation for child abuse or neglect. Although the document was accepted by the Child Welfare Agency in 1990, it became clear to the task force that it was an invisible document, unknown to the judges and attorneys involved in the Family Court. Even more surprising was that many CWA workers were not even aware of its existence. More alarming was that many battered women as well as their lawyers were unaware that in New York State, through the Family Court Act 842, a provision exists that provides for the "resolution of visitation and custody issues as part of an Order of Protection."

The protocol and method of implementation of this document were obviously rife with problems. First of all, it took effect only when the state hot line received a report of suspected child abuse and/or maltreatment that specifically mentioned domestic violence. Second, there was no legal reinforcement. The document was not declared a CWA policy or procedure, and it has never been issued as a CWA bulletin. In its present form it does nothing to protect battered women from having their children removed by the very governmental agency to which battered women turn as a last resort for protecting themselves and their children.

The task force heard frequent complaints that the protocol often established an adversarial relationship between the battered woman and CWA workers. Since it is the caseworker, referred most times by the health care worker, who is charged with acting in the best interests of any child, he or she can, therefore, remove the child from its mother. What that does from the moment a woman seeks care for herself or her child in any hospital emergency room is to discourage her from being open and honest about the violent situation in her home.

The recommendation by the task force was to amend and eliminate judgmental questions to make the battered woman comfortable about turning information over to the CWA caseworker. The amended protocol also suggested that not only when a caller to the Central Registry happened to mention a battered woman in the household, but whenever the child protective worker had reason to believe that the mother was also a victim of domestic violence, an investigation should be launched. The protocol would never be put into effect, however, until it was considered a CWA policy, in cooperation with health care workers, judges, and attorneys working within the context of the Family Court.

In the matter of child custody and abuse, the task force

also determined that all adult male members of families should be included in any risk assessment done by the Child Welfare Agency and, when appropriate, should be held accountable for abuse inflicted upon children. In New York City alone during the year 1992, the task force recorded 161,000 emergency calls placed to 911 to report domestic violence; 52,000 reports of child abuse and neglect involving nearly 84,000 children also came in to the State Central Registry Hotline. Further studies conducted throughout New York State projected that one in every seven to eight boys and one in every four to five girls will be sexually abused. On a national basis, it was also documented that 69 percent of all sexual abuse in the country involved children aged seventeen and younger. And in those cases, 83 percent of victims knew their abusers. These statistics, while they do much to reveal the magnitude of the problem of family violence, do little to explain its bitter depths and broad reach or to inspire solutions.

The problem is further complicated by the fact that in most homes where children are abused or neglected, the mother is blamed for the harm that comes to them—either directly or in citations for "failure to protect" her children from harm at the hands of the children's (and usually her) abuser. In a further example of what is a deadly catch-22, the task force determined, a battered woman will in too many cases avoid taking her children to a doctor for fear of having the violence in her home exposed. Such actions often lead to charges of neglect and the loss of her children, precisely the situation she feared would happen in the first place. Consequently, victims of domestic violence, already terrified of their abusers, are also terrified of the Child Welfare Agency and its power to take their children away, as well as the power that health care workers have to report child abuse to the social service system or the police. What has evolved is a situation where a battered woman is put in a position that forces her to lie.

In Section III, "Assessment of Parent/Caretaker's Ability to Protect Children," for example, the task force determined that the evaluation of whether or not to remove custody from the mother was replete with value judgments about how a battered woman should behave *if* her children were to remain in her care. Not outlined in the report were ways to remove both the woman and her children to a safe place, far from their abuser. Once again, a situation exists where the batterer goes unpunished while the victim, seen as the sole protector of the children, risks losing them as a result of violence that targeted her as well. The obvious question arises, how can a woman protect her children against violence in the home if she can't even protect herself?

Historically, violence in the family has been viewed as two distinct issues, child abuse and domestic violence. A recent study conducted at Yale/New Haven Hospital in July 1994 found that spouse abuse is the single most significant context for child abuse. Additionally, the New York City Child Welfare Agency also found that in a sample of 71 percent of the child homicides it was called to investigate, the mother was also the victim of domestic violence. Further, both studies indicate that the man who physically assaults his partner is the most common child abuser. Yet existing services and theories of intervention are unjust and basically ineffective when it comes to combating this twofold problem, since all too often the result is removing the children from their mother.

In 1985, two disturbing incidents spurred the staff of the Family Development Program at Children's Hospital in Boston to address those same issues which were perplexing the task force in New York. The first incident occurred during an evaluation ordered by the Boston Juvenile Court to explore allegations of child abuse. During the initial interview with the child's parents, the father started to pace around the room before he suddenly lunged for his wife's throat. Pulling him away, the staff had little idea of what to do next.

The second incident was disturbing in a different way. Asked to evaluate a family whose children were in foster care in order to make a final custody recommendation to the court, the Family Development Program team interviewed the mother and the children. They found that the children were deeply attached to their mother, who had never mistreated them. The problem, it turned out, was that the mother returned repeatedly to a man (the father of her children) who beat her and who, on occasion, also assaulted the children. Because of the potential danger to the children, the hospital staff felt it impossible to recommend that the children be returned to their mother. With the unsettling feeling that they were punishing a nonabusive mother for a violent father's behavior, the staff prepared its findings for the court. Their report proved to be unnecessary, since on the day of the custody review, the mother failed to appear. What was subsequently learned was that on the night before the hearing, she was so severely beaten by her husband that she had been rushed to the hospital. Months later, despite the reasons for her failure to appear, her parental rights were terminated.

Both cases created an upsetting dilemma for the Children's Hospital staff handling these situations. The questions that plagued them were "Shouldn't we have done something more?" "Was it in the best interest of these children to offer so little to their mother?" "Would the case have had a better outcome if the mother had adequate help?" And thinking beyond those two specific incidents, the staff also wondered, "Can we really help or protect children if we ignore the abuse of their mothers?"

The response was that the Family Development Program began researching to find out how extensive the problem of spousal battering was and found that in approximately 40 to 50 percent of child abuse cases, the women were also battered. The question that followed was, how could they, in all good conscience, urge battered women to leave dangerous situations if there was little in the way of concrete assistance available to them? Or, worse, how could they encourage women to report abuse if they knew that, by doing so, they risked losing their children?

In response, the staff began looking for new ways to

assist these women, models for intervention within existing pediatric health care facilities as well as child protective agencies. They found none. They then set about inquiring within the professional community for ways in which others handled cases involving battered women and abused children. There again, they heard only frustration in response. What was obviously needed was new interventions, protocols, and programs. Borrowing from the ideas of the battered-women's-shelter movement, the staff decided to create a program that offered advocacy and support to abused mothers at the same time that the hospital provided protection for the children. Protecting women, they argued, fit perfectly with the hospital's ongoing commitment toward children.

In the five years since the AWAKE program has been in effect at Boston Children's Hospital, it has handled more than six hundred cases of abused women. In a small evaluation study of forty-six of these women, who were followed for sixteen months, approximately 80 percent of the mothers reported that they and their children were no longer living with their assailants and were no longer abused. Only two children were in foster care.

What is essential in any hospital program is the ability to identify battered women. The AWAKE project tackles the problem through the children, assuming correctly, in most instances, that if a mother is experiencing physical or mental abuse, any child who is living in the home and witness to that abuse is also suffering. The objective, therefore, is to protect mother and children while, at the same time, giving the mother back her independence, dignity, and ability to protect her children, which will eventually empower her to take control of her life by making her own decisions.

While the AWAKE program treats children as the primary patients, its counselors routinely interview mothers to determine whether their children's injuries are the direct result of family violence. According to Jennifer Robertson, who runs the program, AWAKE is the first project of its kind in the United States, a model program that intervenes and advocates for battered women by offering a range of support systems to keep mother and children together. Since there are already existing laws that mandate health care providers to report all cases of child abuse to social service agencies and to the police, reaching beyond the child to the mother is another way to satisfy those who oppose mandated reporting of adult victims of domestic violence. Robertson describes the AWAKE philosophy: "We try to make people get away from the question of why the victim didn't take her children and leave the abusive situation and look instead at the tactics used by her abuser that make it impossible for her to leave."

AWAKE puts into practice a system in which battered women not only are identified through their children but are kept with their children and far from their batterer in almost every case. AWAKE recommends that in order to establish a lifesaving link between child abuse and spousal violence, physicians and hospital employees, when confronted with a case of child abuse, should be required to ask, "Is there any reason to believe that other forms of violence such as wife battering are occurring in the same household?" It is a logical transition that would trigger law enforcement agencies to step in and investigate any criminal assault against the mother. Unlike Project Protect, however, police, social workers, and the courts will not separate the victims. In those cases, the same laws covering mandated reporting of child abuse would be in effect to cover mandated reporting of domestic violence. After identification of the abused child along with the battered woman, a choice would be offered. Either the woman cooperates with the system to bring charges against her abuser, or if she refuses, she risks losing her children.

Robertson claims that while men who abuse their wives and girlfriends also restrict their visits to hospitals and private physicians for fear of discovery, they are less apt to restrict their children from seeking routine medical care. "These men don't want to get in trouble with school authorities over vaccinations or other contagious diseases, and so allow their children access to routine pediatric visits," Robertson maintains. "As a result, any child in every service at Children's Hospital—whether for injuries suspected to be the result of abuse; psychosomatic symptoms resulting from stress, anxiety, or fear; or on medical floors for treatment completely unrelated to domestic violence—opens the way for health care workers to question their mothers regarding the situation at home. From that moment, if there is any suspicion of abuse, all records are kept confidential, while mother and child are given access to a system whose goal is to support, protect, and eventually provide shelter and other options for the mother and child to live safely." Not only are all records kept confidential, but any reference on the child's medical chart, found attached to the metal rim of the bed, indicates only the letter *A*, for AWAKE, indicating that the program is involved with the mother and the child. In that way, if the batterer/father visits the child in the hospital and reads the medical chart, he has no way of knowing that measures are being taken to prosecute him and to find an alternative safe home for his family.

AWAKE is also the only program in practice that recommends not removing abused children from their mothers even in those cases where the mother has either by omission or commission inflicted violence on the child. Rather, the male abuser is held responsible, since it is assumed that he has put the woman in the untenable position of not being able to protect herself, or he has made her psychologically incapable of functioning as a good parent. The AWAKE program not only considers characteristics attributed to hostages and prisoners of war to be similar to those of battered women, but considers rescuing those women hostages as a positive action rather than as disempowering them. In all cases, removing both mother and child to a safe environment is the recommended policy.

While AWAKE has proven effective in identifying battered mothers of child abuse victims and providing them with services that unite the two problems against a common abuser, rather than separating mother and child, the program also works for the benefit of the entire family. Robertson explains, "If there is any hope of rehabilitating or uniting the abuser with his partner and children, we are there to offer support and help in order to stabilize the situation."

Despite the growing body of evidence that batterers of women are also often child abusers, most city and state agencies have so far failed to develop procedures and protocols that recognize and address that linkage. According to Robertson, AWAKE is very aware of that connection throughout all the services available at Children's Hospital. "The program is in place which acts and advises before the violence escalates to where routine checkups in the pediatric clinic become admissions into emergency rooms," she explains. "It's another way of getting around mandated reporting for adult victims of domestic violence by including the mother's abuse along with accepted rules of mandated reporting of child abuse."

As the system is currently set up in most hospitals throughout the United States, there is little incentive for any woman to act according to the law to protect her children from abuse in the home or to report honestly how she herself was injured when she has sought medical treatment at a hospital emergency room. While the ideal would be to establish programs modeled on AWAKE in all pediatric hospitals or in pediatric services, laws concerning child abuse should also be implemented for all battered women with children, even in cases when the children are unharmed.

Those who are opposed to mandated reporting for adult victims of domestic violence are supportive of keeping abused children with their mothers, even if the mother is also inflicting abuse on them. At some point, there must be a reckoning; it must be established that in order to have the privilege of keeping children, certain responsibilities toward those children must be fulfilled. Battered women must cooperate with the system to insure the appropriate punishment of those men—husbands, partners, and fathers—who are either inflicting that abuse or causing it to happen.

Currently, the only mention of the link between domestic violence and child abuse in protocols used throughout the medical system is written in the following way: "battering is a major factor in a range of psychosocial problems including suicide attempts, alcoholism, and child abuse." What that suggests is that battered women might be excused if they beat their children, given the physical and emotional stress and abuse they are enduring themselves. Battered women should not be excused from abusing their children, but learn how to be good parents by being empowered to escape the violence.

Protocols should be put into effect whereby women with minor children living in the home are offered a choice without stigma or prejudice. Rather than summarily removing children from their mothers in cases where there is abuse in the home, these protocols should leave the choice to the mother: either leave the abuser and cooperate with the court to remove the abuser from the home, or risk losing your children to foster care until the home situation is deemed safe. If, however, those women refuse to report the violence or fail to cooperate in convicting the abuser, only then should they face the possibility of losing their children.

While a democracy must consider the rights of all people, under certain crisis situations and emergencies the state must have the right to protect its citizens until they are once again in a position to make their own decisions. Assault with or without a deadly weapon, rape with or without a history of prior consent, and abuse or neglect of a minor child are all criminal acts covered under the existing criminal justice system. If there is a lag time for social condemnation of spousal assault to filter into the criminal court system, women should not have to pay a deadly price under the guise of empowerment. Nor should children, however, have to pay a deadly price so that society can satisfy its own concept of rights and empowerment.

Physicians have always kept detailed records and compiled statistics of patients suffering from various diseases or viruses without necessarily asking or receiving their permission. This documentation is done under the heading of research and for the purpose of finding cures and better drugs to treat various medical conditions. Doctors are rarely accused of disempowering patients suffering from more recognized, mainstream, and noncontroversial diseases when they report medical findings and specific cases to national health organizations or government-sponsored research programs. Protecting a woman from continued domestic abuse or, in extreme cases, death should present no dilemma.

Something is wrong with our priorities if domestic abusers are not treated the same as perpetrators of stranger crime and are ultimately given only minimal sentences under existing laws. Something is even more seriously wrong with our moral judgment if women are given the luxury of choice in emergency situations that put innocent children at risk of physical harm or emotional trauma.

EIGHT

The Veil of Privacy

IF FOR THE BATTERED WOMAN the first line of defense against her abuser is a hospital emergency room or the office of a private physician, the first line of defense against the batterer is the police. It is the police who are first on the crime scene to evaluate the condition of the victim, the physical evidence in the house, and the potential culpability of the batterer. It is the police who must also determine the next appropriate course of action, which may include medical attention for the victim, and if so, arrange for the care of any minor children. In the case of domestic violence, the responsibility of the police goes beyond arresting a criminal; it also influences the final disposition of the case in very different ways than in stranger crime. When it comes to police response, those differences are yet another example of how domestic violence is set apart from other crimes.

Incidents of violence within the private domain, or in the home, that occur between intimate partners have always been considered by the police as less serious than violence that has the potential of affecting a mass number of people. Once again, it is a matter of a quantitative approach to crime as opposed to any qualitative consideration. Violence in the home has always been accorded a low priority because it has limited visibility, occurs within a sphere that is traditionally considered private in any democracy, and is perpetrated against victims by assailants who are known to them, often intimately. In the past, the police, who have seen just about every possible variation of human misery imaginable, have treated domestic violence the same as they have treated rape or violent crimes against prostitutes. Police tended to assume that the victims (women) of those crimes were where they should not have been, or that they should have known better, or that they should have been able to prevent the crime from happening in the first place. Just as everybody has his or her own set of ethics and standards when confronting any situation or job, the police also react according to their own stereotype of what they consider appropriate female behavior from either victims or offenders in any crime.

The problem with police allowing their personal opinions to interfere with an objective appraisal of a crime is that good police work calls for objectivity. Although not all police officers harbor negative prejudgments about women, the rules and formal structure of internal policy and procedure within most police departments are inherently gender biased.

The first patrolwoman was appointed in Los Angeles in 1903. Her job consisted of assisting detectives in cases involving women and children. In 1910, Los Angeles appointed its first regularly paid policewoman, but it wasn't until 1916 that twenty-five other cities in twenty different states also hired women police officers. Any opposition from male police officers toward women in the force has always been justified by the excuse that women lack the physical force to do the job. As recently as 1975, in a study of male police officers conducted by the Crime Prevention Survey in California, it was found that 91.2 percent of male police officers believed that women lacked the physical strength required to do the job. In addition, 57 percent of male officers stated that women would be totally unable to cope with family disturbances. Since 1972, while the Equal Employment Opportunity Commission has been able to stop police efforts aimed at edging women out and to eliminate separate tasks for women, promotion prospects for women officers remain inferior to men's.

Feminist groups and advocates for battered women have always made great efforts to protect the rights of all women crime victims regardless of their social or economic position, of whether they are Mary Magdalene or Mother Teresa, of whether they know or have known their aggressors. While police and society in general have come a long way when it comes to considering rape victims as the usual crime victims, prostitutes who are murdered as the usual murder victims, and perpetrators of those crimes no less guilty because of the profession or attire of their victims, when it comes to violence in the home, police attitudes still have a long way to go.

When police are confronted with a crime of domestic violence, the immediate decisions that they are required to make have far-reaching legal, medical, and social consequences for everyone concerned. Any personal judgments they may have about guilt or innocence, blame or responsibility, can make the difference between life and death for the victim.

The division between crimes committed in the public domain and crimes committed in the sanctity of the home still exists within the law. It is the basis for two different sets of regulations concerning police involvement and reporting of each type of crime. Since police are usually the first on the scene of any crime, their initial judgments and reports influence prosecutors and judges when it comes to taking any subsequent legal action against criminals.

Historically, the law has always distinguished between public and private matters, which left the family under the control of the husband and father. English common law made the husband and wife legally one entity, that of the husband. When a woman married, she ceased to exist before the law and instead was "protected and covered" by her husband. If she ran up debts, physically aggressed a neighbor, or stole property, her husband was summoned to the bar of justice. Since a man was regarded as head of the household and responsible for his wife, the law considered it his duty to use whatever means necessary to control not only her behavior but that of his children and servants as well. As a consequence, society drew a veil of privacy around any measures taken within the walls of the man's "castle," thereby shielding him from public scrutiny and legal repercussions. There is that terrible scene in *Crime and Punishment* where a horse is bludgeoned to death by its owner, who whips him with a crowbar. "It's my goods," the owner exclaims as the horse bleeds to death. In the same context, wife beating has its roots in history, given the basic premise that women are the property of their husbands. It was only when morality got in the way of human nature that society reacted. Laws began to change when men began committing crimes against their wives and children that, had they committed them against strangers, would have resulted in their being convicted of assault and remanded to jail.

By the middle of the nineteenth century, many states within the United States, although influenced by English common law, began to restrict the rights of men to abuse or inflict physical punishment against their wives and children. Few states, however, provided any legal repercussions for men who disobeyed those restrictions. Until 1984, the law continued to uphold a different set of laws for the criminal assault of a legal wife and for the same assault inflicted on a female partner, cohabitant, or stranger. One of those differences was that any legal wife could not be compelled to testify against her husband in court. This marital exemption was justified by a concern to preserve the sanctity of marriage and had little bearing on whether the victim of the assault happened to be the assailant's wife. It was not until 1984 that spousal violence against a legal wife was no longer treated as a minor criminal infraction or as a common assault.

Feminists and advocates for battered women fought long and hard to change legal and social judgments so that women who were not legally married would be included in the definition of a legal spouse. Not only did their efforts result in changing historical perceptions but they also succeeded in having women who were not legally married to their abusers, such as cohabitants or girlfriends, included in the category of crimes committed between intimate partners.

It is a category that, by definition, considers those crimes less serious than stranger crime. As a matter of fact, former wives are thrown into that category as well. The only irony when it comes to police response to victims of spousal assault is that there are now more women in the category listed above, who are more vulnerable under a law that separates stranger crime from domestic violence.

Janine Ferris Pirro is the district attorney for Westchester County and an eminent advocate for battered women. On November 1, 1977, new legislation was passed in New York State that on record gave battered women the right to be heard either in Criminal or Family Court, providing they made what would be an irrevocable choice within seventy-two hours. "Nobody really understood the law," District Attorney Pirro says, "not the battered women or even the court, clerks, or police, or maybe no one wanted to understand. On the surface, the law changed in New York, which meant that prosecutors had the right to bring these cases into Criminal Court and the victims had the right to be considered legitimate crime victims."

In November 1978, the federal government sent out what is called a request for proposals, or RFP, advising certain counties, cities, and states that there was federal money available for domestic violence programs if anyone wanted to get involved. At the time, Janine Ferris Pirro was a young prosecutor with an active interest in the issue of domestic violence. "I found in our criminal justice system," she explains, "that women were not recognized as equals; women didn't have a voice; they were forgotten, considered inconsequential and unimportant. I remember doing an appeal on a sixteen-year-old kid who was hired by a man to kill his wife, the mother of his three little children. It affected me like nothing else and probably tailored my whole career."

Pirro requested federal funds from the Department of Justice Law Enforcement Assistance Administration to start a special program for victims of spousal assault. In response to the proposals sent out, four sites were selected around the country—White Plains, Miami, Philadelphia, and San Diego.

"The government was interested in tackling the problem of domestic violence on a national scale, but even before tackling it," Pirro says, "they didn't know what the problem was or how pervasive it had become. The attitude was that if a woman was abused enough she would eventually leave and save the system the time and money to prosecute her abuser. There was this sense that women were either masochists or that they accepted the notion that sex was better after a beating."

According to Pirro, Westchester was selected because it was an affluent suburban, greater-metropolitan community, which the federal government doubted would have a problem with domestic violence. "As it turned out, Westchester was one of the only programs that outlived the cutting of funds by President Carter in the early eighties, because we made a political issue out of it," Pirro continues. "Carl Vegari, the district attorney at the time, while supportive of the program, warned when there were no more federal funds, the program would be dismantled."

The attitude within the criminal justice system is no different from the attitude within the medical community that maintains that a victim of domestic violence will eventually seek care and treatment when her injuries are serious enough. "I remember testifying at a hearing," Pirro continues, "where the main speaker was laughing and ignoring me. After a few minutes, I just stopped trying to compete with him and said, 'If you laugh at me, you're laughing at battered women everywhere.' "

What Pirro realized was that the reaction of that speaker was the rule rather than the exception. What she also realized was that the only way she could make an impact on anyone in a position to help was by sheer determination, which is exactly what she did and is still doing today.

After Pirro got the funding, she called a meeting of the forty-three chiefs of police from each autonomous section of Westchester. "The first thing these men said to me was, 'Where's the coffee, Janine?' "

The next thing they said to the young prosecutor was,

"Janine, there isn't a man in this room who doesn't think it's all right to beat his wife."

When District Attorney Carl Vegari's warning became a reality and funds were cut for the program, Pirro became a one-woman fund-raising effort, approaching Democrats, Republicans, wealthy women, actresses, corporations, anyone and everyone, asking, begging, pleading with them all to support her domestic violence unit, which consisted of several paralegals and a Spanish interpreter. Successful enough to keep the program running under two separate New York State governors, Carey and Cuomo, Pirro drafted legislation to make the Criminal Court System easier for victims of domestic violence to negotiate. It is an effort that continues today, given the difficulties victims of this crime still face in any criminal arena.

While there have been substantial changes in the law in the past decade concerning spousal abuse, those changes have primarily concentrated on providing more remedies (usually of a civil nature) to the battered wife or female partner. The result has been double edged in that the wife/partner's right to protection under criminal law has been weakened. In most cases, she is simply edged out of the criminal justice system in all but the most serious of crimes. This is one of the reasons that in New York State (one of the last states to change) as of January 1995, the law was changed that had previously forced a woman to make that irrevocable decision within seventy-two hours whether to be heard in Criminal Court or Family Court. But even with the new law, which is almost uniform across the country, serious contradictions still exist.

A two-tier justice system has always presented serious problems when it comes to protecting women from male violence in the home, since historically the primary concern of the family court has always been to protect the "sanctity of the family at all costs." Consequently, the Family Court in New York State, the Probate Court in Massachusetts, or its comparable civil and circuit courts in other states, were the courts that heard most domestic violence cases. Although most crimes of spousal assault were as serious as crimes brought before judges and juries in a criminal setting, prosecutors generally refused to prosecute domestic violence cases in the criminal court. Once again, it was advocates for battered women who succeeded in getting criminal jurisdictions over some of these cases, where at least there was a chance for them to be heard in a criminal setting.

Judge Laura Drager, who sits in Criminal Court in New York City, is another important advocate for battered women. "The focus in Family Court," Judge Drager explains, "was always to keep the relationship together. Advocates who argued that these cases should be heard in Criminal Court claimed that the issue wasn't to save a relationship but rather prosecute criminal behavior."

Judge Virginia Knaplund is the chief justice of the County Court in Scarsdale and another important advocate for battered women. She explains, "New York was the only state in the whole country which said that a victim of a particular crime could choose between bringing the case before the Criminal Court or the Civil Court, and usually that meant Family Court. The reason was because the system claimed women were so undecided that they'd tie up all the courts if we let them go into both courts."

It should make no difference whether the victim knows her assailant, is married to him, living with him, or separated from him. The only fact that should be considered in order for a case to be heard in criminal court is whether the crime committed is covered under the criminal statutes.

While in favor of the new domestic violence law, whereby the victim is not forced to choose between Family and Criminal Court and is no longer limited to seventy-two hours to make up her mind, Judge Drager also believes that the problem is amorphous and therefore cannot ever be an either/or situation. "In some instances I agree that these cases should be heard in Criminal Court, but that depends on the case and the people involved. There is a tendency to lump all domestic violence cases together based on the crime, which, I believe, is a mistake. People are at different stages in their relationships. Some women are ready to leave; some aren't; some don't want to go that far to press charges in Criminal Court, and maybe that particular situation may not call for criminal action because each case varies. We've been finding how difficult it is to generalize in domestic violence cases as opposed to stranger crime."

While the goal now in Family Court is not necessarily to keep the family together, the problem is that a woman who decides to prosecute her partner in Criminal Court may decide three months later that she wants to return to Family Court and continue the case there. While it is now legal for her to change courts, there are potentially serious problems that can happen. Judge Drager explains, "If the victim started in Criminal Court and got an order of protection, for instance, and then returned to Family Court because her partner reoffended or violated that order, or if the reverse happens, there are no cross-reference numbers available so that police and judges are aware of any previous violation. The police can arrest only if there has been a felony, murder, or violation of a restraining order. If the charge is only a misdemeanor, without knowing if the assailant is already in contempt for violating an order, he can't be held."

The change in the law, which gave battered women the right to be heard in either court, or change courts in the middle of a case, or have the same case pending in both courts, however, only created an illusion of choice, equality, and justice. In reality, the legal response remains the same, since that divide under the law still exists between violence against wives or intimate partners, which is considered *private*, and violence against random victims, which is considered *public*. What also remains unchanged and counterproductive is that police are still put in the position of upholding and reinforcing that public/private gap, since it continues to exist within the justice system. The result is that there is still a distinct separation in which crimes of violence are based on relationships rather than laws.

The police response to any call of spousal assault, therefore, is hampered from the inception, even if the individual police officer has no particular negative perception about women in general or a woman in particular as crime victims. What is even more dangerous for battered women is that the police, in all cases of violent crime, have specific duties and responsibilities that influence any subsequent action taken by prosecutors and the courts. Once again, depending on where the crime occurred and the relationship between victim and assailant, those police duties and responsibilities differ from duties concerning stranger crime.

When it comes to assault, or violent, threatening, and suspicious behavior on the streets, prosecutors rely almost exclusively on police evidence. In fact, in many cases of street crime, when the victim has been murdered or refuses to testify, the police are the chief and often the only witnesses for the prosecution.

When a crime occurs in a private home, the responsibility of the police is to evaluate the case on the spot for the prosecution, determining whether it has sufficient merit to be presented for further legal action. From the moment the police arrive on the scene of any crime of domestic violence, they must anticipate the views of the prosecutor on the strength of the evidence they discover, the likelihood of a conviction, the credibility of all witnesses, and whether such a prosecution would be in the public's best interests. What this means is that the police have it within their power to decide on the merits of any case of domestic assault by evaluating what they believe would be the prosecution's interpretation of the facts. The result in many such cases is that the police evaluate on the basis of whether there can be a successful outcome, rather than concentrating on the severity of the crime that was committed. And in those cases when the police judge that a prosecutor would decline to take a case to court for lack of evidence or on the basis of other considerations—such as that the perpetrator was a first offender or that the chances were high that the victim would refuse to testify—they often don't even bother making a report at all. As a further example of the enormity of police responsibility and power, when the police consider that a case should be brought to the attention of the prosecutor, they are the ones who also decide the appropriate level of assault with which to charge the batterer.

In all violent crimes, each assault category has specific elements that must be present to constitute that a crime has been committed. For example, to charge a person with assault and battery with intent to kill, the police must determine that the means or force used was capable of causing death. The implications of those criteria for domestic violence, however, can be catastrophic.

If any differentiation should be made between public and private crime, the level of assault in a crime of domestic violence should not be based on the same criteria used in stranger crime. As has been discussed, there must be different rules for defining a felony and a misdemeanor in crimes of domestic violence and stranger crime. To expand on those differences: In order to remove the batterer from the house or prevent him from coming near his victim, the initial charge should in all cases be assault with intent to kill, regardless of the extent of injuries sustained by the victim. That charge should be based on the proximity of victim to assailant. Any argument that arresting the batterer for attempted murder without probable cause is in direct conflict with his civil rights is false. Prosecutors can always determine if the charge should be maintained or reduced before the case gets to court. Remember, anyone who is stopped for speeding by the police is technically arrested, which does not necessarily mean that the arrest goes on any permanent record. On the other hand, not arresting the batterer for attempted murder when there is probable cause is in direct conflict with the victim's civil rights, specifically, her right to protection under the law, which in these cases can mean the difference between life and death. From there, charging the batterer with a specific level of assault should be based on the following new criteria.

The new basis to define what is a misdemeanor or a felony in crimes between intimate partners would entail *mandatory* change, cooperation, and communication between all systems in place in society. For instance, the degree and severity of the abuse suffered by the victim involves medical input; risk involving any minor children living in the house involves social service input; risk concerning the possibility of future and more deadly attacks involves medical, judicial, and social service input; decisions about incarcerating the batterer or releasing him on parole on the condition that he participate in a batterers' intervention program (discussed later) for a period of no less than six months involve input by the courts; whether he is a first-time offender *on record* or has a history of drug or alcohol abuse involves input by those who run the batterers' intervention programs in conjunction with the courts and the police.

The justification for this new division in the law should be that all cases of spousal assault are different from stranger crime. From the beginning, the assailant in all cases of domestic violence not only knows where to find the victim, but often has keys to her house, which more than often is also his house.

A further difference should be made when it comes to granting bail. In regular assault cases, the accused is granted bail on the grounds of the likelihood that he will show up for trial. The conditions for bail in cases of domestic abuse should be based solely on the potential danger the accused presents to his victim. It should make no difference whether he is an unemployed drug addict with no fixed address, a well-loved actor with a weekly television series, or a philanthropist, a pillar of the community. The issue of color should make no difference—that doesn't mean black, white, yellow, or brown, but rather green, for money. Once again, victim safety should be the only issue under consideration.

In addition to a guarantee of victim safety in the short term, arresting the batterer on the spot and taking him to jail, where he would be incarcerated without bail until his hearing, gives prosecutors an advantage that they currently do not have in the long term.

Amy Sharf is a prosecuting attorney in Essex County, Massachusetts. According to Sharf, in most instances the assailant's attorney is able to get to the victim before the court and convince her to drop the charges. "So many cases have fallen apart," Sharf contends, "because the assailant is free and the victim is terrified, so when her partner's attorney contacts her, she has every incentive not to go forward with the case."

Maintaining the current division under the law between private and public crimes may give the victim of domestic violence more choices, but the result is less protection. As well, it influences police response, which in turn presents the victim with the impossible option of coming forward and pressing charges alone, without the automatic support of the police or the protection of the prosecution and the courts.

While domestic violence has never been viewed as a central theme in any debate on crime prevention, progress has been made, given a national awareness of the problem when isolated cases of spousal assault and murder become front-page news. Still, police tend to justify their nonintervention or limited intervention by claiming that the victim, in so many cases, is reluctant to prosecute, even and especially after she has made the initial complaint.

It would seem far more logical for police and prosecutors to accord this crime a higher priority than stranger crime and make every effort to prosecute without victim involvement, precisely because victims of domestic violence are reluctant in so many cases to go forward.

NINE

Cry Abuse

AN AMERICAN POLICE FOUNDATION study in 1976 revealed that men who seriously assaulted or murdered their wives or girlfriends were often men who had already committed violence against the same or previous partners in the past. It was also discovered, as a result of this study, that early intervention could interrupt the escalating chain of violence that usually results in more serious cases of spousal assault and often homicide. On the basis of these major findings, police departments throughout the United States called for a more rigorous on-the-spot intervention policy when it came to cases of domestic assault. The problem was that the American Police Foundation study was unable to determine which measures taken by the police on the scene were the most effective against the batterer.

Lawrence Sherman, a criminologist who studied urban police departments in the United States from the late 1970s to the late 1980s, was one of the principal designers, along with Richard Berk, of the Minneapolis Domestic Violence Experiment. The research that Sherman and Berk did and that influenced their Minneapolis Experiment in 1981 tested three specific police responses to simple domestic assault: arresting suspects, ordering suspects to leave the house for a period of no less than eight hours to cool off, and providing information and advice to the victim and assailant that was tantamount to suggesting that both parties seek counseling.

The police who took part in this experiment were randomly assigned a particular response, and the results of each response were subsequently evaluated six months later, on the basis of interviews conducted with victims about any reoccurrence of violence.

The broader or more general questions to which Sherman and Berk sought answers were: Does calling the police deter further violence? Or does police presence only aggravate the situation? And if calling the police does deter repeated violence, which is the most effective police response?

The study was based on a sample of 252 men. It was determined that the men who had been arrested were the least likely to abuse again, as compared to those men who were simply ordered out of the house for eight hours to cool off. In only 10 percent of the cases in which an arrest was made did the perpetrator assault his partner again, while violence reoccurred in 19 percent of cases in which the police had only issued a warning, and in 24 percent of the cases in which police ordered the assailant to leave the house for eight hours to cool off.

The problem with this study and with all similar studies is that the results must be treated with caution. Giving random assignments to the police meant their judgments were based on the same criteria used for stranger crime. Further, police officers also continued to use the same criteria for determining which cases of domestic violence would result in any successful prosecution in the courts. If they judged a case to be a waste of time, they simply did not bother reporting it at all. Also, as Sherman and Berk noted themselves, of all the police officers involved in the experiment, three had turned in almost 28 percent of all the cases, which again substantiates the thesis that police bring with them their own set of moral values on this subject.

The other important variable in the study had to do with the degree of intervention made by each police officer. For example, of the 136 men who were arrested during the

Minneapolis Experiment, only three were ever formally charged. While it is a small number, even the authors of the study point out that "booking has a bite": arrest, even without follow-through to prosecution, is an important deterrent to further violence. Another point worth noting is that most of the suspects arrested were kept in jail overnight, rather than being released several hours later. In fact, in cases when a suspect was not kept overnight but released several hours after his arrest, the deterrent factor was reduced. The conclusion could be drawn, therefore, that being handcuffed and put into the back of a police car, driven downtown to the police station, fingerprinted, booked, and put into a cell for the night does make an impression on these men. Despite those results concerning incarceration and length of time a suspect was held, however, Lawrence Sherman drew a second conclusion concerning the influence that incarceration had on the reoccurrence of violence.

Sherman concluded that arrest made little impact on those men who already had criminal records, while those who didn't were sufficiently affected by the experience not to reoffend. Arrest an employed, married, white high school graduate for spousal abuse, Sherman contended, and he was less likely to reoffend. Arrest a marginal man (unemployed, unmarried, high school dropout) who was African American or a member of another racial minority, someone who had "nothing to lose," and his arrest would only result in increased violence toward his partner.

What Sherman did not take into consideration when he made that determination was the countless exceptions, the most recent of which, of course, is O. J. Simpson, who had everything to lose when he battered his wife and yet was a repeat offender. Nor did he take into consideration someone like Salvatore Mangiano, for example, an out-of-work construction worker with a long criminal record ranging from disorderly conduct to assault, who had "nothing to lose" when he battered his wife. Yet after Mangiano was arrested eight years ago for spousal assault, he never committed another act of violence against his wife and, in fact, went on to become a respected counselor at a batterers' intervention program in Quincy, Massachusetts.

And then there is Burt Pugach, another example of a man who had everything to lose by hurting the woman he supposedly loved.

Once a well-respected and successful lawyer, Burt Pugach fell madly in love with Linda Riss. So in love that it didn't matter to Burt that he happened to be married when he met Linda, or that he risked everything that was supposed to be sacred to spend furtive hours and days with her. According to many reports, Burt couldn't bear the thought of ever losing her to another man. He couldn't imagine Linda's beautiful face on a pillow next to anyone else's but his.

They dated for years until Linda finally realized that Burt was never going to leave his wife and marry her. According to people close to Linda, she was not only fed up but vulnerable when she met a single guy who told her that all he wanted was to spend the rest of his life making her happy. When he proposed marriage, Linda accepted. She broke up with Burt.

Burt Pugach's reported reaction was not unlike that of Charles Thurman and other abusers who have been rebuffed. They all alluded to a kind of white light flashing before their eyes or filling their heads, causing them to lose their memory and apparently disabling their sense of right and wrong. At the time, those close to Pugach said that he couldn't think clearly.

As a successful attorney, Burt Pugach was able to hire three men to throw lye in Linda's face, ensuring that no other man would wake up every morning and see Linda's beautiful face lying on a pillow.

Disfigured and blind, Linda Riss testified against Burt Pugach. She was a very powerful witness who made a devastating impression on the jury, who returned a guilty verdict against Burt. Burt Pugach was sentenced to fourteen years in the Attica State Penitentiary in upstate New York.

Every year while he was in prison, Burt went before the parole board to make a plea for his release based on good behavior, and every year Linda appeared at the district attorney's office to insist that Burt serve out his entire sentence for ruining her life. Finally, fourteen years later, Burt was released. He headed for the old neighborhood in Queens. When he saw Linda, he gently took her arm to help her negotiate the curb. Without a word of protest, Linda allowed Burt to guide her safely down the street. Within months, they were married.

There are some who might consider the Burt Pugach/ Linda Riss story an example where a happy ending is possible after one tragic incident occurred in what was otherwise a nonviolent love affair. There are others, however, who might find it difficult to believe that there had never been a history of violence before Burt arranged for lye to be thrown in Linda's face.

Linda Riss explained her change of heart by telling people that the past should remain the past, that she forgave Burt, and that she did not want to be alone. Burt Pugach was quoted saying, "The guy who dumped her when she got sick never really loved her the way I do."

Another study, conducted at the same time as Sherman's Minneapolis Domestic Violence Experiment and also concerned with the arrest and incarceration of batterers, produced extremely interesting results—so interesting, in fact, that they should serve as a basis for police policy throughout the United States.

In May 1981, the London Police Force in Ontario, Canada, instituted a policy that directed the police to charge, on every occasion, men who assaulted their partners. The study in Ontario revealed that in 1983 alone, the third year that the policy was in effect, a 2500 percent increase in men who were actually arrested and charged. Out of those 443 cases, 298 had been charged directly by the police, while in 22 cases, it was the victims who brought charges against their abusers. The comparative figures for 1979, the year before this policy was implemented, show that police charged in only 12 cases, while victims charged in 92, for a total of 104 prosecutions out of 444 reported cases. Although the total amount of cases that were *reported* did not increase, the important figure has to do with the percentage of cases that were successfully *prosecuted*. And that rose from 23 percent in 1979 to 72 percent in 1983. Further, the study revealed that in every case in which the police were the ones who brought charges, the victims were nonetheless consulted as to what they perceived were the appropriate charges and subsequent fines or punishment to be imposed on their abusers.

The most positive and productive way to empower a victim of domestic violence is to include her in all decisions concerning specific punitive measures taken against her batterer. One does not empower a victim of domestic violence by giving her the choice of *whether or not* punitive measures should be taken against her batterer; that is negative and dangerous. In the Ontario study, battered women were made a part of the judicial system and therefore automatically protected under the law when their batterers faced prosecution for their crimes. It is a policy that directly responds to Judge Laura Drager's concerns about where a victim might be in her relationship with her abuser, which can ultimately affect the response of prosecutors and judges. Where the victim might be in her relationship should affect the response of prosecutors and judges only after they have discussed with her what she wants to do.

Elizabeth Loewy is a district attorney in New York City who spent several years heading up the Domestic Violence Unit. According to Loewy, "If men know from the beginning that, regardless of what threats they make to the victim, it makes no difference because it's out of the victim's hands, it's him against the state, the problem of intimidation or lying to drop the charges wouldn't be an issue. The reason a woman is in danger is because suddenly she has power and control over her batterer."

Again, the most effective and just way to empower victims of domestic crime is to consult them in every case when their abuser is arrested as to what they view is the appropriate charge and subsequent fine or punishment.

The logic behind this policy is that each victim knows

best her and her children's needs and priorities, as well as what it takes to change the behavior of her abuser. In cases when the victim does not care about changing her abuser's behavior since she has no intention of ever living with him or seeing him again, she is still in the best position to know how much time she needs to find a safe place to live, a new job, a first job, job training, or simply how much time it will take her to gather her strength, contact those who can support her, and ultimately begin a new life without fear of violence.

Empowering the victim to share in the decision concerning the extent of punishment also insures the safety of other women who, had the batterer gone unpunished, might subsequently have become his victims.

Further, in the Ontario experiment, in 9 percent of those cases in which the police wanted to charge the batterer but the victim was reluctant to cooperate, the police went ahead and charged without the victim. The result was that, in cases in which the victim was reluctant to press charges and the police took over, victims reported a reduction in or termination of the violence.

Although the Ontario sample is small, the experiment's findings reveal that independent police intervention is not only effective when it comes to protecting the victim, but also encouraging to officers, whose responsibility it is to make judgments for the prosecution concerning the potential success of any case. If the study in any way neglected to cover all eventualities, it was that it did not establish definitively whether women who did *not* call the police fared better or worse than those who did. Put simply, is it more effective a deterrent if the victim calls the police, regardless of the outcome, or if she tries to deal with the violence without any outside intervention?

The National Crime Survey conducted a victim study that addressed that issue. The results showed that calling the police, however good or bad their response, did, in fact, deter repeated violence. According to that survey, from 1978 until 1982, a total of 2.1 million women were estimated to be victims of spousal violence. Of those, 1.1 million, or about 52 percent, called the police themselves, or neighbors or bystanders did. During a six-month period after an incident of violence in which the police were summoned, those victims reported no further incidents. Of those victims who did not call the police, 180,000, or 16 percent, reported further victimization. The findings indicate that calling the police in itself acts as a deterrent to repeated abuse. Following that logic, if the police, when called, actually arrested the batterer, it would not only protect the victim immediately, but stop what has been proven to be an escalating pattern of violence in this type of crime.

The most highly charged debate concerning arresting the batterer goes back to the 1970s and has to do with discretionary and nondiscretionary arrest laws. Again, Lawrence Sherman addressed that issue in the Minneapolis Domestic Violence Experiment. The conclusion that Sherman drew then was that, while the police should be empowered in any domestic violence call to make arrests without warrants if there was *just cause*, there should be no mandatory arrest laws.

Sherman suggested that mandated arrest would force the police to arrest all batterers regardless of special circumstances. What this would do, he warned police, was to eliminate police discretion as well as create a precedent that would allow women to use battering as a negotiation point in any divorce action. In fact, the most frequently used excuse by police is that, even if there is no divorce action pending, must-arrest laws can put innocent men at risk if wives and girlfriends are simply vindictive.

The same argument used by those who oppose the death penalty can be used here. While there are many criminals who are guilty of heinous crimes, who exhibit little hope of ever being rehabilitated, and whose death seems the most logical solution to remove them permanently from society, the moral dilemma arises when and if one innocent person is put to death.

The incidence of women lying about having been

abused, beaten, or raped by their partners is statistically so
low that removing one innocent man from a house where a
woman falsely accuses him of violence is worth all the incidents in which men who are guilty of abuse will be automatically arrested and the lives of their partners saved. And since
an arrest does not necessarily go on anyone's permanent
record, there is sufficient opportunity to determine if the
accused was, indeed, the victim of a vindictive spouse or
girlfriend.

Charlotte Watson is another vocal and important advocate for battered women and the director of a women's shelter in Yonkers, New York. She says, "Everyone thinks women
are demons, that they use the court and legal system to
harass their husbands. These are the same people who can't
imagine how humiliating it is for a woman to go through the
court system; it's like women crying rape. Who's going to cry
rape and go through that whole humiliating process if it's
not true?"

According to Judge Laura Drager, women do lie in
court. But when and why they lie is surprising. "Most of
the time, when women lie," Judge Drager explains, "they're
trying to convince us to drop the charges after their partners
have used coercion and threats that make these women so
terrified that they'll do or say anything, even try to convince
the court that they lied when they claimed they had been
abused. If I believed for a minute that victims made things
up, I would be in favor of not prosecuting. But victims don't
make things up, because they're so frightened down the line
to carry through and prosecute their partners for battering."

Judge Knaplund is one of the few judges who will open
up her courtroom at any hour of the night or on weekends
to hear cases of domestic assault. On the basis of her years
of experience, Judge Knaplund agrees that most women
would go to any length to avoid appearing in court against
their partners. She recalls an extraordinary story of one battered woman who actually paid her abuser protection money
to leave her alone. "The horrible part of this story," Judge
Knaplund continues, "is that when the woman was finally

shot and killed by her boyfriend in a grocery store, the police found an order of protection in her pocketbook."

Douglas Gaudette has been working with batterers for more than fourteen years. Currently, he is the director of the Lawrence Mental Health Center in Lawrence, Massachusetts, an alternative program for batterers that is connected to the Essex County Criminal Court. One of the unique aspects of this program is that the court makes participation a condition of parole for all batterers.

Douglas Gaudette believes that while some women have hidden agendas and will fabricate information and charges, it is something that happens rarely. "I can't say that has never happened," Gaudette admits; "maybe somewhere in the world, but we don't normally see that, since it's a very painful process for women to have to go to court and stand there giving this information, while the batterer is also standing there. It's just so overwhelming that the majority of women wouldn't make up something and put themselves through that."

While the debate continues throughout the country concerning nondiscretionary arrest laws, what has become clear is that it is not only the *best* way to protect the victim, but also the best way to protect the police from any potential lawsuits brought against individual officers for false arrest. But even when there are must-arrest laws in effect, police are still reluctant to arrest in cases of domestic assault.

In New York, for instance, there is a must-arrest, or mandated arrest, policy for batterers, which goes into effect if any one of an estimated seventy-five thousand orders of protection granted by the criminal or family courts is violated; if the victim has bruises or other injuries and wants to press charges; if the officer has witnessed harassment of the victim or a similar violation and the victim is willing to comply; or if the assault is serious enough to be considered a felony. Usually, it is too little too late. One has only to remember that California also has a must-arrest policy, which was in effect when Nicole Brown Simpson ran out of her house wearing only sweat pants and bra, with bruises all over her face and handprints on her neck. "You never do anything," she cried to the police. "You always come here and you never arrest him."

Officer Don Edwards responded to a domestic violence call from a woman in Queens who called 911 to report that her husband trashed her apartment and tried to slash her with a nine-inch hunting knife. "Do you want him arrested?" Officer Edwards asked the woman and got no response. According to Officer Edwards, "All I heard was a heavy silence on the other end of the telephone."

"Do you want him arrested?" Officer Edwards asked again.

Finally, after another long pause, according to Edwards, the woman uttered a "halfhearted" yes.

By his own admission, Officer Edwards and his partner did not make a tremendous effort to pick up the man who tried to slash his wife—a clearly cynical approach to an all too familiar problem. "The woman was hesitant," Officer Edwards explains, "and we've had too much experience handling domestic violence cases when the woman starts out as hesitant and attacks the police when they come to arrest her abuser. It just isn't worth it, because there're enough criminals out there doing harm to the general population. In most cases when it ends badly, the police officer either needs a lawyer or a doctor."

Most police officers throughout the country will admit that intervening in wife or partner assault is one of the most formidable tasks they confront. What they won't always admit is that just like health care providers, they bring their own perceptions of how women should behave and what the acceptable boundaries of violence are within a relationship. And those judgments influence whether or not they will arrest. If there were nondiscretionary arrest policies, however, neither would their job be as formidable nor would their opinions be as relevant to any eventual legal response.

In 1982, Linda Knopf started a domestic violence program at the YWCA in Greenwich, Connecticut, which she still runs. The program in Greenwich is one of eighteen domestic violence programs in Connecticut. According to Knopf, victims of domestic violence are provided with information on the legal system, the rights of women, and an advocate who will accompany them to court, help them fill out the complicated legal forms to get a restraining order, make a petition for support or custody, or anything else they need. An advocate from the Y will also stay with the victim throughout any hearing or trial to offer her moral support. Lastly, the Y, under Linda Knopf's supervision, runs a weekly support group for victims of domestic violence, whether they have or have not attempted to go through the legal system. "Part of this support group," Knopf explains, "is to build self-esteem, to make these women feel capable of getting out of the situation without feeling pushed by advocates or intimidated by the police."

Asked about the police who arrive on the scene of any domestic violence call, Knopf says, "We have so many cases when the police arrive at a house and they see a woman who is out of control and hysterical, which is natural since she has just been beaten or raped or threatened, or her kids have been harmed or her pet has been killed. At the same time, the police see her batterer, who appears cool and calm, so the police are naturally going to view the situation as they see it at the time. If the police aren't properly educated and trained, they'll believe in every case that the woman is crazy or violent or, in the worst case, that she's only harassing her partner to win a custody battle or to get a larger financial settlement in a divorce case. Don't forget, police are made up of the same psychological and emotional mix as any group of civilians."

Lydia Martinez is a police officer and a specialist in domestic violence who works out of the Chief of Patrol's Office in New York City. According to Martinez, any hesitancy on the part of the police results not only from concern for their personal safety or from any personal agenda, but also from a consideration of the victim's rights. "The police officer is not only exposed to the threat of personal injury every time he or she responds to a call of spousal assault,"

Martinez contends, "but is also a witness to a personal tragedy that frequently involves not only a man and woman but
their children as well. Not allowing the victim to be heard
often makes the situation worse."

Not arresting the batterer, however, is often a guarantee
that the victim will never be heard.

TEN

Rights Versus Wrongs

IN AN EARLIER CHAPTER, different criteria were suggested for mandated recording and mandated reporting of a victim's injuries in a medical setting. Also discussed earlier were different criteria, based partly on the London Police Force experiment, concerning legal measures to be taken against the batterer. While each situation must be evaluated according to the circumstances, needs, and wishes of the victim, any debate on nondiscretionary, or must-arrest, laws must also make victim safety and the safety of minor children the first priority. The only questions that should be considered concerning the police, before the prosecution and courts are even involved, are: Is the response of the police good enough? Do the police, as the first line of defense against the batterer, make the victim feel safe?

According to the Uniform Crime Reports from the Federal Bureau of Investigation in Washington, the police response to a call of spousal abuse leaves the impression that many ambiguities and contradictions still exist. For example, following is the wording, taken directly from one of those reports, that covers regulations for police to follow when they arrive on the scene of a crime of domestic violence:

> A prevalent factor which surrounds wife beating
> is alcoholic intoxication. In the majority of cases, the

abusive husband is drunk when he assaults his wife. What this means to the officer is that the victim is in real danger and the suspect is not in a condition to accept a reasonable resolution to the situation.

Regarding police perception that the batterer is usually drunk, the report once again reveals the difference between domestic violence and stranger crime. If that same victim were being beaten, assaulted, threatened, raped, or psychologically traumatized by an unknown assailant, drunk or sober, the police wouldn't hesitate to make an arrest, rather than trying to find a "reasonable resolution," like social workers, family therapists, or sponsors from Alcoholics Anonymous. As for the batterer frequently being drunk, intoxication is never the cause for a man battering his partner; rather, any batterer who is intoxicated may have fewer inhibitions, which is why he attacks his victim more viciously than if he were sober.

The report, therefore, denotes a profound misunderstanding and lack of education on the part of the police when it comes to the reasons men batter women.

Why should the police even attempt to offer a "reasonable" solution to someone, drunk or sober, who has committed a criminal act? The full impact of the report's statement leads one to believe that police continue to consider that wife beating or spousal assault is an isolated incident, caused by alcohol or drugs, or, under certain other circumstances, brought on by stress, financial problems, or something that the victim has done to provoke the abuse—all worst-case scenarios that amount to the dangerous perception that domestic violence is not a crime but rather a reaction on the part of the perpetrator to his victim.

As for "reasonable" solutions or "reasonable" reactions, feminists and advocates for battered women succeeded in changing those perceptions, but only in those cases where the victim reacted in the extreme.

During the late 1970s and early 1980s, it was the women's movement that not only exposed the plight of the battered woman and the lack of adequate police protection, but also presented in a new light the "battered woman turned homicide defendant." An increasing number of women who had killed their abusive husbands or boyfriends were claiming provocation or self-defense. The women's movement successfully challenged some of the traditional legal assumptions and precedents that had been established regarding homicide and self-defense. Their greatest achievement was that they were able to get a new definition of what was "reasonable" when it came to using deadly force as self-defense. The points that were addressed and that formed the basis for that new definition were these: what causes provocation; the psychological effects of battering on a woman over time; a battered woman's perception of what is imminent danger; how long is "imminent"; and under what circumstances.

The most famous example of a woman who murdered her abusive husband and was acquitted is Francine Hughes, whose story was the subject of a book, *The Burning Bed,* written by Faith McNulty. Unfortunately, the outcome of Francine Hughes's case, just like that of Tracey Thurman's— while both were landmark decisions—remains the exception to what usually happens.

In 1977, after years of rape, battery, and terror, which continued even after she was divorced, Francine Hughes poured kerosene on her sleeping ex-husband and struck a match. What made the case so sensational was that Francine Hughes's legal defense was that she was temporarily insane as a result of the severity of her ex-husband's abuse. While the courts, in most cases, might have been prepared to acknowledge a plea of self-defense if a woman killed a violent husband or boyfriend in the middle of an attack to save her own life, in the case of Francine Hughes, because she killed her ex-husband while he was sleeping, the court was introduced to a new concept.

The defense presented on behalf of Francine Hughes stated that while she was suffering from "learned helplessness," she had also been driven to violence, which culminated at the moment when she struck the match. In what appeared to be a total contradiction, the jury decided that, at the same time that Hughes had been rendered helpless as a result of continued abuse, she had also been driven crazy enough to take violent action.

While the women's movement and advocates for battered women made a significant impact on the legal definition of what is regarded as "reasonable" concerning battered women who react in the extreme by killing their abusers, they did not change either the definition or nuance of "reasonable" as they pertain to any response by the perpetrator. It would appear that from a legal and personal standpoint, the battered woman stands a better chance of protecting herself if she kills her batterer than if she calls the police.

In the Minneapolis Experiment, Lawrence Sherman focused on the battered woman as the murder victim rather than on her murderer to argue against nondiscretionary arrest laws. Sherman took the position that not only should the police have *discretion* to arrest but if they chose *not* to, and as a result the victim is subsequently maimed or murdered, they should also not be held responsible for failure to protect the victim if the assault was a first-time misdemeanor. It wasn't surprising that Sherman's position was supported not only by the police but also by the judicial system, which concluded that in the majority of cases, victims refused to press charges anyway after the heat of the moment, which results in a loss of time and manpower that could have been directed to more serious crimes and more cooperative victims.

In 1976, in response to what was becoming standard police practice, legal aid attorneys filed suit against the chief of police in Oakland, California, for "breach of statutory duty to arrest" under California Penal Code section 836, on behalf of women in general and black women in particular who were victims of domestic violence *(Scott* v. *Hart)*. In his defense, the chief of police responded by denying any attempt to discriminate against women. The plaintiffs argued, however, that discriminatory intent existed, since there was a disproportionate impact on one particular class—women —because women are disproportionately the greater number of domestic violence victims and in domestic violence cases there was a departure from normal procedure, since arrest was to be used as a last resort.

By November 1978, a comprehensive settlement was approved by the court, providing that "no arrest-avoidance policy" was to be used. The court retained jurisdiction for three years in order to monitor the implementation of the new policy. In response, police promised to make arrests when they had probable cause to believe a felonious assault had occurred in the context of domestic violence or when a misdemeanor occurred in their presence.

In 1980, a group of battered women in New York sued the police commissioner of the city of New York for failing to enforce laws against men who committed spousal assault (*Bruno* v. *Codd*). The trial judge who heard the case ruled that the police, regardless of the severity of the charge, could not automatically decline to make an arrest simply because the assailant was either married or living with the victim.

By 1980, in response to the efforts of feminists and advocates for battered women, a national organization of police chiefs formed the Police Executive Research Forum, which conducted a study on domestic violence. The decision they reached was that police should be trained to arrest perpetrators of domestic assault under the same laws as perpetrators of stranger assault were arrested. As a result of the above-mentioned lawsuits, heated debate within the social service and judicial systems, and vocal public opinion, Attorney General William French Smith, in 1983, became the first public official to acknowledge the "insidious criminal problem of domestic violence and the fact that it never received the national attention it deserved."

What followed for a while was a widespread adoption of this new, proarrest policy until gradually, police, prosecutors, and the courts reverted to their old habits—until 1985, when the situation exploded once again into the public's consciousness after the Tracey Thurman case.

Once again, the judicial system responded by reevaluat-
ing "reasonable" response as it concerned the police who
arrived on the scene and tried to elicit a reasonable response
from the perpetrator. Another evaluation followed concerning the merits of nondiscretionary arrest laws as they concerned crimes of domestic violence or crimes occurring in
private between intimate partners.

Massachusetts is one of the few states that has a nondiscretionary arrest policy. According to Sara Buehl, a survivor
of domestic violence who is now a district attorney and vocal
advocate for battered women in Massachusetts, the police
themselves prefer it. "They are less afraid of getting shot
during a domestic violence call," Buehl claims, "than they
are of getting sued by either the victim or her assailant."

Nondiscretionary arrest laws would not only guarantee
protection from lawsuits against individual police officers,
but would also make those familiar questions "Why doesn't
she just leave?" and "Why was the batterer allowed to stay?"
superfluous.

When it comes to any issue of domestic violence, Douglas Gaudette concentrates on short-term solutions. Of nondiscretionary arrest laws, he says, "In every case, the batterer
shouldn't be anywhere near the victim, but instead, he
should be locked up. The reason the victim is forced to flee
is because the police have discretion, which means they're
afraid of getting sued for false arrest. Here in Massachusetts,
if the police have reason to believe that a woman has been
assaulted, they can lock the guy up and ask questions later,
and they don't have to worry about being sued because
they're only following orders."

According to Judge Kevin Herlihy, who sits on the Criminal Court in Essex County and works closely with Gaudette
and the Lawrence Mental Health Center's program for batterers, "The police prefer nondiscretionary arrest laws because, in all cases, it makes them immune from prosecution
by removing the gray, which means, in terms of short-term
protection for the victim, the issue becomes black or white."

Douglas Gaudette began his career by teaching about

domestic violence at the Police Academy in Boston, Massachusetts. "My focus was not so much on getting the police to respond to the mandates of the law," Gaudette explains, "but to be more sensitive toward victims of this kind of crime in general. The main theme I wanted to get across to the police was that they couldn't look at a victim of domestic violence the same way they looked at a victim whose car radio was stolen, because in almost every case, there are undercurrents that need to be addressed if they're going to intervene appropriately."

In every case of domestic violence, without exception, those undercurrents are the result of a current or past relationship between victim and assailant. According to Jonathan Cohen, who is a counselor at a batterers' intervention program in Rockland County, New York, the police have never understood that in order to respond adequately, they must take into account the relationship between victim and assailant.

The Rockland County program is based on a philosophy that places domestic violence in a category of other discriminating behavior perpetrated by white males against minorities and women. "This goes beyond the actual confrontation between the police, victim, and abuser," Cohen maintains. "For me, there needs to be a complete transformation in the judicial system. Appealing to certain components of the legal system is fraught with immense problems, dangers, and built-in failure. Appealing to the police to protect battered women is almost a redundancy since, institutionally speaking, the police have been one of the primary instruments in protecting men's violence against women. For those of us doing this work and working within the system, we've learned to live with some painful contradictions. We do our best to train and educate the police, we push for legal reforms, and yet, we do this without great illusions. It was a great victory to get orders of protection, but they're only as good as the paper they're written on. Mandated arrest laws, harsher penalties for batterers are all wonderful ideas on the books, but they have to be enforced."

To give an abuser a warning without imposing any penalty should that warning be ignored is tantamount to giving no warning at all. The assumption is that removing the abuser from the home is sufficient to protect the victim. That assumption is wrong. The only way to protect the victim is by incarcerating the batterer until his hearing, after which he is either released on bail, depending on those conditions stated in a prior chapter, or is kept in jail until his trial. In either case, whether he is convicted and sentenced to jail or is convicted and sentenced to probation, he should automatically be required to participate in a court-supervised batterers' intervention program. These programs must be in place both in prisons and outside.

If the batterer is not convicted—and there are so many reasons and technicalities for a judge or jury to find a defendant not guilty—he should still be required to attend a program that teaches men about equality, dignity, and respect, as well as how to have a difference of opinion without having a brawl. Men who were arrested for battering and released or subsequently acquitted should consider the program educational rather than punitive. In all cases, however, regardless of the legal outcome, the name of every individual who participates in a batterers' intervention or education program should be filed away in a central computer for future reference. For the innocent man, it should be considered a precaution; for the guilty, a further protection for his victim.

According to statistics compiled by the FBI, one-third of all spousal homicides are committed against women by men when the parties are no longer living together. According to those same statistics, one-fourth of all aggravated assaults or murders are committed against women by men who have already been arrested for battery. A nonmolestation injunction, therefore, without an accompanying arrest is not a deterrent. Jonathan Cohen is right. Injunctions or orders of protection without a coinciding arrest order are not worth the paper they are printed on. Arrest must be mandatory under all circumstances. If not, women are not sufficiently protected.

The Family Court Act of 1962, which was amended in

1977, in New York City and Washington, D.C., provides for "dealing with such instances of disorderly conduct and assaults." When a victim or her lawyer files a petition, the court can issue a summons or arrest warrant in cases where the "safety of the petitioner is endangered," or the court can "dismiss the petition, suspend judgment for six months, or grant a civil protection order." There are seven conditions for which an order of protection can be granted and that implicate the batterer:

To stay away from the home, the other spouse, and the child

To permit a parent to visit the child at stated periods

To abstain from offensive conduct against the child or against the other parent or against any person to whom custody of the child is awarded

To give proper attention to the care of the home

To refrain from acts of commission or omission that tend to make the home not a proper place for the child

To notify the court or probation service immediately of any change of residence or employment

To cooperate in seeking and accepting medical and/ or psychiatric diagnosis and treatment, including family casework or child guidance for himself, his family, or child

In 1979, the Protection from Abuse Act was passed in Kansas, allowing family members to seek injunctive relief from abuse. This move came about as a result of local and statewide reform efforts, including input by the Governor's Committee on Domestic Violence. The act is closely in line with civil remedies available in virtually all other states, beginning in Pennsylvania.

To obtain protection, the victim must first file a petition. Within ten days the victim is required to prove the allegation. In the meantime, an ex parte* order may be granted, order-

* Ex parte: On one side only; by or for one party or done on behalf of one party only.

ing the offender to "refrain from abuse," granting exclusive possession of the house to the victim, or evicting one of the parties. Since 1979, other states have implemented similar legislation (for example, the Family Violence Protection Act in 1982 in Wyoming and the Spouse Abuse Act in 1981 in Utah). The problem is that the degree of evidence required in these civil cases is as high as in criminal cases, where a witness's statement, a police officer's statement, and medical evidence are required. Many women who are aware of the amount of evidence needed to satisfy a court before an order is granted may not bother making the application at all. If, however, the victim knew that at least medical evidence of her injuries existed in her confidential hospital record, she would perhaps be more confident about using the system to achieve a positive result. This is one more example showing that any specific system in place breaks down if other systems are not working properly.

From a judge's point of view, treating every case of domestic violence as a potential homicide can be an overwhelming task. Judge Kevin Herlihy explains: "There must be a court to dispose of domestic violence summarily, which means prosecutors must have an eye like in the medical business to do what is called triage so they can focus on the more serious stuff. We don't have the luxury of treating every case like a life-and-death matter, since we average eighty-two cases a day, and that doesn't include civil or juvenile. Out of those eighty-two cases, twenty percent are domestic violence cases where the assailant is up on a misdemeanor charge, which means the sentence is maximum two and a half years. If you talk about a success rate, either we never see the guy again for the same charge or we see him up for murder."

Under the law, provisions exist that when a victim of domestic assault seeks police assistance, the police *must arrest* the abuser when they have reasonable cause to believe a felony or misdemeanor has been committed or when the abuser has violated the "stay away" provision of a temporary or permanent order of protection. The problem is that most of the time the police have no way of knowing if an order of protection has been violated, since most abusers simply destroy them. While women are told to make photocopies and keep them hidden around the house, it is not always possible, nor is it guaranteed that the abuser will not discover the copies and destroy them as well. As it stands now, in order for any victim to get a copy of an incident report that her batterer has destroyed, to prove that there was a violation of an order of protection, she has to write to the precinct that filed the report, and eventually that precinct will send her a copy, but that can take days or weeks. The danger is that she could be more severely injured in the interim, or dead.

To insure victim safety by guaranteeing an appropriate police response as well as to make it futile for batterers to destroy protection orders, the police must have access to a computer, either in their patrol cars or at least back at the station. Every time police respond to a domestic violence call, they must be able to access information on a computer that would give a brief history of the assailant as well as updated information concerning orders of protection or bench warrants that are outstanding or that he has violated. It is difficult to believe that parking tickets or moving violations are more important than human lives. If police have immediate access to information from the motor vehicle bureau to identify scofflaws, they should also have immediate access to information that would identify batterers who are potential killers. Only then could police enforce must-arrest laws, knowing an order of protection was violated, which would provide them with *probable cause.*

According to Judge Herlihy, chances are that batterers will eventually run a red light or drive while intoxicated or commit other minor traffic infractions. "If those domestic violence orders can't be put under a separate system, they should be tied into the motor vehicle computer and even go on the guy's driver's license. In that way, when the police pull someone over, they can not only check into his driving history but also learn if he's in violation of an outstanding order of protection," Judge Herlihy explains. "What that does is save the victim from having to go down to court every few days to swear out a temporary order of protection in case her abuser shows up, so she can call the police in time to serve him."

The most extreme problem when it comes to computerizing orders of protection are the cases where a batterer calls his partner from Puerto Rico, for example, and threatens her. "Obviously," Judge Herlihy contends, "the police can't seal off all the airports, but what can be done, at least, is to institute a computer hookup between the criminal court and family court throughout every state with the goal of having a national computerized system that can track outstanding violations in other states as well. Only then will one hand know what the other is doing."

Amy Sharf in her capacity as district attorney in Essex County Criminal Court works closely with Douglas Gaudette and his batterers' intervention program. Sharf wants to go even further: "Not only would I like to see a hookup between Probate [family court] and District Court," Sharf says, "but I'd like to have probation records hooked up interstate. Batterers move their families around because the situation is embarrassing to them. They move across the state or to different states, so by the time they come here, it seems like they have no record. Sometimes after I talk to the victim, I learn they just moved from North Carolina, but to call up the records there takes time, because it's not automatic or hooked up. Or maybe I find out from a victim that, by the way, her partner was given probation for beating her in Georgia, which means instead of looking at a guy who's a first offender, I'm now looking at a guy who's been convicted in other states, except—guess what—lots of times I can't tell the jury that the defendant has been convicted before because the judge won't allow it."

Another difficult problem that the police face is gaining entry to a private house, which is precisely why police need to be protected from possible false-arrest lawsuits. Without that computerized system which would furnish sufficient evidence that a crime has been committed, the police are rendered powerless. While the police are taught to try and gain entry by requesting permission from whoever answers the door, if permission is refused and the police have reason to believe that the victim is in a life-threatening danger, they also know that getting a warrant is time consuming under emergency conditions.

There are certain circumstances when police are permitted to make what is called a "forced entry"; they fall under the heading of "probable cause"—for instance, if police claim they heard cries for help, saw weapons brandished or obvious signs of a struggle, or were able to get an eyewitness account that a felony occurred and the victim is still inside the house. If, however, the police are unable to claim any of the above but still believe the victim is in danger, Douglas Gaudette offers an alternative solution: "When I lecture at the police academy, I tell police that if you go to a house and have every reason to believe that the victim is in danger or she's afraid to open the door because there could be a gun to her head, you get into the house any way you can. For example, 'I smell gas, I'm coming in.' "

Once the police have gained access to the house, their job becomes even more formidable. Not only must the officer be the eyes and ears for any potential case brought by a prosecutor but the police must also remember to separate the parties as well as keep any children and other residents or visitors away from the victim and the abuser so as not to compromise their potential status as witnesses. In addition, they must also attempt to keep the parties out of the kitchen area, since there is the likelihood of getting access to weapons such as knives.

The next problem that the police face is how to gather evidence that will hold up in court. Under the law, there is something called "excited utterances," which means that anything the victim or her assailant says in a moment of hysteria or crisis can be used as evidence in court. The police, however, must record those excited utterances on the spot or be able to testify exactly what was said by whom under what circumstances.

Manhattan district attorney Elizabeth Loewy elaborates:

"In domestic violence cases, these guys talk; they're so angry when the police get there because of the misconception that the problem is a family matter. They're so outraged that often they make incriminating statements, admitting the entire crime and then adding that it's a family matter. We encourage the police and we do a lot of training in police stations to bring those statements to us." Loewy offers examples of excited utterances that were recorded by the police and presented as evidence in court:

> "I punched her once because she never has dinner ready when I come home. She's always out shopping."
> "The bitch lied about money so I ripped up the checkbook, cut the credit cards in half, and shoved her away from the stove."

In the first case, the punch resulted in the woman losing consciousness, which resulted in her having brain surgery, which left her partially paralyzed; in the second case, shoving her away from the stove caused third-degree burns on the woman's legs when her assailant threw a pot of steaming spaghetti at her.

"Given the mindset of these abusers," Loewy continues, "who don't consider that a crime has been committed, if we can get the police to remember those statements [excited utterances] we can use them as evidence in the event the victim refuses to testify."

"Essex County draws a fine line between forcing a victim to testify," Judge Herlihy explains. "You need to respect the victim's wishes although you can still proceed without the victim's testimony. After all, we can't put a victim on the stand who was murdered, which means that we shouldn't need to put a victim on the stand to testify who beat her, as long as we have medical evidence of her injuries. Police need to be trained to write better police reports, to notice what's going on in the house, and to write down any excited utterances they hear, such as victims who are in an excited state saying, 'He hit me again; he's always hitting me.' That's admissible evidence, and we need the courts to accept police reports in lieu of first-person testimony.''

The question of what is admissible evidence is also open to debate. The law says that what the police see at every crime scene is admissible evidence unless the alleged assailant is already on probation, and then hearsay evidence is permissible. "A police report is hearsay testimony," Judge Herlihy explains, "if in their report they refer to what the victim said, unless it falls under the heading of excited utterances." Once again, the problem is how to differentiate.

"If the victim is screaming when the police arrive," Judge Herlihy continues, "as to what was done to her, as opposed to what she calmly recites back at the station when the police take a formal statement, that's the difference. Frankly, I am all in favor in proceeding without a victim's testimony; it's much safer for the victim."

In what seems to be yet another contradiction, police are under instructions to stop any suspect from making what are called "res gestae" statements, or statements made without police questioning that could incriminate the suspect before he has been read his rights. Yet prosecutors, judges, and those who work with batterers in alternative-to-violence programs depend on the police recording excited utterances so they can prosecute without the victim's testimony in the event she changes her mind, refuses, or is physically incapacitated. The guidelines to distinguish between res gestae statements and excited utterances must be defined precisely when it comes to crimes between intimate partners.

Most states hold that general on-the-scene questioning is not considered interrogation within the meaning of the Supreme Court decision in the *Miranda* or *Escobedo* cases. Police are instructed, therefore, to "interview as soon as possible" the alleged perpetrator, the victim, and neighbors who either heard screams or who can detail other violent incidents in the past. At the same time, those same states also require that police must determine if the incident of wife beating is accidental, a matter of self-defense, or criminally committed; that falls under the heading of a "fact-finding" process. Another contradiction arises when police are not only required to determine the nature of the assault, but are also expected to elicit information from the suspect, which could incriminate him, by asking questions that would be considered as an "interrogation." As a result, police officers on the scene often find themselves in what is called a situation of "threshold confessions." It is not an uncommon situation in family-related offenses for a suspected abuser to make a confession at the beginning of police involvement that is usually in response to an innocuous question such as, "What's going on here?"

In order to protect the victim from any potential claims by a defense attorney who might later say that his client was not read his rights before being questioned, the following must be addressed as they pertain only to domestic violence: Can excited utterances be used in a court of law as evidence against a batterer? Are there conflicting legalities that prevent them from being used?

The difference is crucial when it comes to cases of spousal assault, since any incriminating statements made by the perpetrator on the scene are often the only evidence the prosecution has to go forward with its case, especially if the victim is unwilling or unable to testify. The law should be amended, therefore, so that excited utterances take precedence over res gestae statements in all cases of spousal assault.

There will be many arguments against this policy, beginning and ending with the issue of depriving the suspect of his rights. In response, the reality is that victims of domestic violence are deprived of their rights all the time. They are not sufficiently protected under the law as broadly or effectively as, or equally with, victims of stranger crime; nor are their rights as well protected as those of their assailants. Setting different rules for stranger crime and incidents of domestic violence that are caused, for example, in the victim's house by a current or former intimate partner might make battered women *as* well protected as, although certainly not *more* protected than, any other crime victim or criminal suspect. It is another example of going to the extreme in order to achieve the norm.

There are other contradictions when it comes to police protocols, rules, and regulations concerning domestic violence. For instance, if the victim refuses medical aid and if the police on the scene judge her injuries to be serious enough, they have the right to transport the victim to the hospital, even against her will.

According to police regulations, "physical evidence typically takes three forms in cases of spousal abuse; injuries of the victims, evidentiary articles such as a blood-stained blouse or weapon that substantiates the attack, and the crime scene itself." The regulations go on to say that "the victim's account of the injuries sustained must be corroborated by a doctor. Information about the injuries should be obtained from him, including descriptions of the location, size, shape, and direction of all cuts and bruises. Whenever feasible, photographs of the injuries should be made."

If one of the three forms of physical evidence set by the police are the victim's injuries, and if those rules of evidence stipulate that any account of the victim's injuries should be substantiated by a doctor, mandated reporting and mandated recording within the medical system is once again at issue.

According to police policy, the victim, for her own protection, can be temporarily robbed of her rights when she has consciously declared that she does not want treatment for her injuries, and police can transport her anyway to the hospital. Why are doctors, nurses, and other hospital staff prevented from taking over temporarily as well to protect the victim from further violence—a step that can ultimately save her life? Why have mandated reporting and mandated recording in a medical setting become controversial issues?

In the case where the police are already involved, mandated reporting is not relevant. Given police involvement, then if, as a matter of regulation, hospitals record the victim's injuries, that record might influence those recommendations made by police to prosecutors concerning the merits of going forward.

Additionally, police regulations also maintain that the police themselves should take photographs of the crime scene and of the victim. There is no mention, however, of making photographic equipment part of the regulation uniform, which includes gun, handcuffs, badge, and so forth. Police officers, just like hospital personnel and private physicians, must have a Polaroid camera with film at all times in their police car. Every successful and effective response to this crime means *mandated* change, cooperation, and communication between all systems.

Concerning Douglas Gaudette's suggestion of getting access to the house under any pretext, as in, "I smell gas," he adds that police should also be aware of and make notes of physical evidence strewn around the house, such as a phone cord that has been pulled out from the wall, pictures smashed, or furniture overturned. Ideally, police should seek information from a neighbor who either heard the fight or saw something.

"We've been working a lot with the police, and since we also are allowed access to the police report as it pertains to the charges and arrest of the perpetrator who enters our program," Gaudette explains, "we are in a position to ask our police to write good reports, investigate these cases as if they were already murder cases, take pictures of injuries, record statements of witnesses or children, and subpoena medical records." Which goes back to the beginning of the story, will there *be* medical records to subpoena? "If there's an officer who's not up to what's happening with domestic violence," Gaudette continues, "I try to educate and explain to him how important it is to understand."

According to standard police policy, when the police arrive on the scene of a crime of spousal assault, it is important to make contact with the victim to make her feel safe, confident, and willing to tell her story. "Crucial to the success of an interview is the manner in which the officer shows an interest in the victim's account of her predic-

ament..." the report reads: "this requires effective listening, and effective listening demands concentration, and
understanding of what is being said, and an awareness of the
importance of non-verbal communication."

More crucial than knowing how to listen and making
the victim feel comfortable is getting the victim alone so that
she is able to tell her story without her assailant in the same
room. It is a policy to which Trisha Mian adheres all the time
at Massachusetts General Hospital, separating the victim
from her abuser when questioning a battered woman as to
how she was injured. So many batterers are able to terrorize
and control their partners by merely a gesture or a look. If
police are not trained to do more than listen attentively,
make eye contact, encourage the victim to continue her story
by using neutral words and phrases, it is almost a given that
the victim will be unable to overcome the embarrassment
and emotional stress of recounting the incident, especially if
her abuser is still in the house, even if he is being guarded
or contained in another room.

The optimal situation would be, if there are signs of
a struggle or evidence that the victim has been physically
assaulted, to remove her abuser immediately from the house
after he has made any statements or excited utterances concerning the attack. Ideally, in all cases, a female police officer
should be the one to question the victim; this might eliminate any embarrassment.

Recounting an incident in which a husband, ex-
husband, boyfriend, or ex-boyfriend entered the house and
used current intimacy or a previous relationship to inflict
harm is almost as painful as the physical symptoms incurred
from that beating. According to Judge Virginia Knaplund,
"When a woman gets a beating from her partner, it can be
more intimate an act than sex."

The relationship between a police officer and any victim
of domestic violence is also intimate. They meet at a time
when in her own best interests, the victim is forced to share
some of the most painful details of her personal life, to reveal
to a total stranger secrets that she has never confided in close

friends or family members. For those brief minutes or hours when the police officer arrives in the middle of that crisis, he or she becomes the most important person in the victim's life.

If male police officers insist upon differentiating between crime victims, or if they insist upon bringing their personal perceptions of women along on the job, it might work in favor of battered women if those officers made the following effort: Whenever a policeman arrives on the scene of a domestic violence call and finds himself automatically categorizing the crime or judging the victim's role in the assault, he should stop and imagine that the victim is his mother, sister, or daughter and that she was just beaten, raped, or murdered by someone she knew or once knew and loved.

ELEVEN

Behind Closed Doors

"ONCE A REPORT of domestic violence is filed within the system," Judge Virginia Knaplund asks, "what exactly is the system prepared to do?"

Often, the people who are in place to deal with the victims of this crime are overworked and poorly trained. Frequently, the programs geared to protect the victim and punish the perpetrator are understaffed and underfinanced, and lack basic equipment and resources for communicating and cooperating successfully between themselves or throughout other systems. These are all reasons that account for Judge Knaplund's question. When the response to this crime is inadequate, if victims have learned anything, it is not "learned helplessness" but rather "learned system distrust," which becomes evident only after the damage is done.

Alisa Deltufo is another advocate for battered women and the director of the Family Violence Project in New York, which is connected to the Legal Action Center for the Homeless.

"What the battered woman has really learned," Deltufo claims, "is exactly what she didn't want to know in the first place. Why bother calling the police to get an order of protection when it's not going to keep away her assailant? Why try to get into a shelter program when there is either no space, or there are so many rules with which she can't possibly comply because of her particular situation? Why bother bringing charges against her assailant in two different courts, Family and Criminal, if the courts work at cross-purposes because there's no computer linkup? Why even bother going to court at all if she has no one to help her negotiate the complicated court system, or watch her kids while she fills out forms or has to testify against their father? Call it 'system helplessness' or call it anything else, as long as society stops blaming the victim.''

Domestic violence is a learned process of reactive behavior that becomes obvious only after the victim is abused, after the system fails her, after she has already been established and defined as a battered woman, which automatically works against her when she is blamed for not using the system to stop the abuse from happening in the first place. Domestic violence is learned abuse, or learned expectation of the metaphoric fist, that reproduces itself through generations. It is the cancer of family relations that targets grandmother, mother, and daughter, destroying lives and bodies in its wake.

"There is false advertising out there that is doing a great disservice to battered women," Deltufo continues, "because they believe help is available when it isn't. A battered woman has this false idea that the violence will stop if she does X, Y, and Z. When the violence doesn't stop, she feels more helpless and more trapped than before, when she had a whole series of as yet untried options.''

More than false advertising, there is a lack of funds, facilities, and properly trained staff to implement long-term programs and short-term solutions. The result is that society is neither properly educated about domestic violence in the abstract nor sufficiently outraged when confronted with its reality.

We must say again that the public must begin by viewing domestic violence as a crime, the degree of which depends only on the level, intent, or reoccurrence of the assault. Society must stop blaming the victim for having any involvement or responsibility in a crime that was committed against her. If the victim is at all responsible, it is only because she once picked, for a variety of reasons that are ultimately irrelevant, the wrong partner in her life and is currently unable or fearful to leave him.

The horrifying truth is that the only time victims of this crime are treated the same as victims of stranger crime is when a murder has been committed. Only then is a united voice heard, in which opprobrium is heaped on the entire legal, social service, and judicial system for not having done more to prevent the murder, either by protecting the victim or by punishing the criminal more severely for his past crimes. Not instituting preventive policies is not only devastating to human life, but also costly.

Money that could be used precisely for implementing long-term programs and short-term solutions is spent instead on trials, after which batterers are either incarcerated or sentenced to death.

Jimmy Breslin, the author and newspaper columnist, has his own opinion on what would be a successful preventive measure. When police or health care providers doubt a batterer's guilt because his terrified victim tries to cover up the facts, Breslin suggests: "Every time a woman goes to a hospital emergency room or every time the cops come to the house and she's black and blue and beaten up and she tells them that a kitchen cabinet fell on her, the doctors or the cops should ask to see the wall where that kitchen cabinet fell."

Breslin's proposed response to domestic violence may sound simplistic, but it isn't. If implemented in all its forms, or taken broadly, that response might produce a decrease in repeat assaults or an increase in convictions.

If every person who came in contact with the victim, her batterer, and the crime scene, or every person working within the medical, legal, social service, and judicial systems, took whatever measures necessary to prove that a crime was committed and that the reason the victim is lying to protect her assailant is that she fears for her life, the results might be startling. Not only would more kitchen cabinets be found securely attached to undamaged walls, but every other excuse given could be eliminated as spurious as well. More time and care could be taken as well to make the victim feel safe by offering her viable options and by proving to her that there are concrete programs and laws within the system that will come to her aid. Police, prosecutors, and judges could also concentrate on using the system already in place to punish her assailant.

"Inspecting kitchen walls" should be used only as a euphemism for confronting the batterer and making him understand that it is no longer up to his victim to decide whether or not to press charges. It is solely a question of him against the justice system.

Ronnie Eldridge is a New York City councilwoman who, along with her husband, Jimmy Breslin, has been dealing with the problem of domestic violence for more than twenty years. Eldridge's assessment of the situation is as follows: "The thing that's wrong with the whole system is that it's backwards." Beginning with the shelter system, it's the batterer who should be put out of his home and made to live in some kind of a dormitory-type arrangement while he's forced to participate in a treatment program. The fact that women and children are the ones who are forced to flee, escaping to family, friends, or into a shelter, forces them to undergo the additional trauma of leaving their familiar surroundings."

Lucy Friedman, who runs the Victim Services Agency in New York, receives approximately 242 calls a day on their hot line. According to Friedman, thirty-five of these calls are requests for beds for families (battered women and their children), whose average size is 2.5 people. "Unfortunately, there are usually only ten family spaces available," Friedman explains, "which means families are often placed out of state or are told to call the next day. If the abuser was remanded to a shelter, the need for bed space would be greatly reduced. For a woman and her children to pick up and leave is also more complicated, since her needs and the needs of her children are greater."

Forcing the batterer to leave and enter into a shelter is not only cost and space effective but penalizes the criminal instead of the victim. In opposition to this practice, it might be argued once again that it would be in violation of the batterer's rights. Officer Lydia Martinez comments: "When the victim leaves to go to a shelter, it is a voluntary act. How can anyone force the batterer to leave unless he has been arrested?"

The response to Martinez is that forcing the batterer into a shelter would happen *after* he was arrested and re-leased, either on bail or on probation. Douglas Gaudette puts it simply: "The batterer can go anywhere he likes, except anywhere near the victim."

Eldridge has been working toward a solution whereby the batterer would be removed from circulation, either in-carcerated or released on parole and remanded into a batter-ers' treatment program; he would live in a shelter designated especially for batterers. "One bed, one abuser," Eldridge says; "a lot less space than is now needed for a woman and her children."

Space is not the only problem that exists within the shelter system. Another is the uniform rule that excludes male children over the age of fourteen from entering into a shelter with their mothers, as they are considered in a femi-nist context to be young men. Witnessing physical or sexual abuse of their mothers or younger siblings is the main reason why these teenage boys run away from home and end up on the streets. In some cases, excluding women with teenage sons or not providing alternative shelter arrangements can cause situations that are even more devastating.

Cheryl Cummings is forty-seven years old and has al-ready spent five of her twenty-five-years-to-life sentence in Bedford Hills prison for killing her boyfriend. What makes Cheryl's case so frustrating is that it shows that the system not only failed Cheryl from the beginning but is now making an example out of her to teach women what happens to them if they take action against their abusive partners on their own.

Cheryl Cummings was fourteen years old when she married her first and only husband, who was sixteen. After she had three children, it became obvious that her husband was an alcoholic; this disease eventually killed him when Cheryl was only twenty-six. A year later, in 1971, Cheryl's mother also died from alcoholism, leaving her as the sole custodian of not only her own three children but also of her two younger sisters and a retarded brother. "I was the sole support of the entire family," Cheryl relates, "and without a husband, I worked two, sometimes three jobs to make ends meet. I was a cashier, waitress, home attendant. I worked in a factory. I did anything to earn money."

After all the children grew up and moved out, Cheryl was left only with her severely retarded brother to care for in a city-subsidized apartment in Far Rockaway, Queens. "My brother was like a baby, but I was making good money, so I could hire someone to look after him during the day when I was at work and even at night when I went to school to learn how to be a really good cashier."

When Cheryl met John, he told her that he had a child by another woman but had separated from her, had little contact, and was anxious to make a new life. It was Cheryl who was hesitant to make any commitment, since John was several years younger. But John convinced her that age made no difference and he was in love with her and anxious to move into her apartment so they could make a life together. "In the beginning, he was working as an electrician," Cheryl says, "and I had my own car, so I was driving myself back and forth to work. After a while, John lost his job, which was when he began to stop me from driving. He became very jealous and insisted that he should drive me and pick me up."

After about eight months, people around the housing project where Cheryl lived began telling her that John was using and dealing cocaine and crack, which, in retrospect, Cheryl believes was the reason he lost his job and became so paranoid. "He used to come home and run into the bathroom, pull the shower curtain back, and ask me where I was

hiding the man; that's how bad things got." Before long,
John would sit in the car in front of the supermarket where
Cheryl worked. Her register happened to be in front of a big
window that ran the length of the store. John would spend
the whole day or evening, depending on Cheryl's shift, just
staring at her. "He would accuse me of holding a customer's
hand too long when I gave him change," Cheryl recalls,
"and that's when he began hitting me." According to
Cheryl, the beatings got so bad that she would sometimes
have to wear dark glasses to work to hide her black eyes
and swollen face, and when she couldn't hide a split lip or
fractured hand, she would call in sick. "By then," Cheryl
says, "I wanted him out of my life, and I even got an order
of protection once, but John just ripped it up."

Another concern Cheryl had was that she had already
broken one of the housing rules by allowing John to live with
her. The rules stated that only someone related by blood or
a legal husband was allowed to reside with her in the apartment. "I lived there for fourteen years," Cheryl explains,
"and if I got thrown out, where was I going to go? That was
my only home, and I couldn't afford to move."

While the apartment was officially in Cheryl's name, she
couldn't change the locks to get John out because of the
rules in city-subsidized housing projects. While Cheryl was
able to get an order of protection without involving the housing authority police, she was unable to call the police to
come to her apartment to enforce the order because automatically they were obliged to bring along the housing authority police, which would have jeopardized her status
there. "My son had been in trouble," Cheryl explains, "because he went to jail, and in the end he was shot in the street
and killed by gang members, so I was already on the list as a
problem tenant."

John kept a loaded gun in his toolbox. As his abuse of
Cheryl escalated, he began taking the gun out and shooting
randomly out the window. "After a couple of days of doing
that," Cheryl says, "he would take the gun out and put it to
my head and pull the trigger, like Russian roulette. I would

hear the gun click and I didn't know, sometimes I thought I was dead." In fact, once Cheryl actually called the police, according to her, they came and did nothing, even after Cheryl told them that John had a gun. During the trial, when Cheryl's lawyer offered that fact as evidence, the police denied they had ever come and claimed there was no record of having ever answered a call at Cheryl's apartment.

The events leading up to the murder are still painful for Cheryl to remember. The abuse not only continued but escalated. "Once he tied me up in the car and sodomized me," Cheryl says. "Another time, he dragged me by my hair to the roof of the building [fourteen floors] and pushed me over the ledge, holding me by my ankles, until I promised not to make him leave."

The night that Cheryl shot John, she claims, it was because of a small detail that terrified her so much that she was absolutely convinced that John intended to kill her. "Every time he shot the gun out the window," she begins, "he would put it to my head afterward and play Russian roulette before he would lock it back up in his toolbox. Every time he did the same exact thing, and I can't count the times he did it that way, but on that particular night, he did something different."

On that final night, John took the gun out of his toolbox and shot it out the window, but instead of grabbing Cheryl as he usually did and putting the gun to her temple, he took her hand. "He rubbed my hand gently," Cheryl says quietly, "and he never did that before, and told me really calmly that he was going to kill me and go back to Puerto Rico to live with his child and his child's mother where the police would never find him." After that, according to Cheryl, John went to bed, but instead of locking the gun up in the toolbox, he left it lying on the table. "I was sure he was going to kill me," Cheryl repeats.

As Cheryl tells it, she just "did it." She says simply, "I picked up the gun from the table, went into the bedroom, and shot him."

So John is dead and Cheryl is facing life in prison without any chance of parole until she is sixty-seven years old.

What is so astounding about Cheryl's story is that almost every regulation, rule, program, or law within the legal, social service, medical, and judicial systems worked against her —beginning with the rules and regulations concerning a tenant who lives in public housing, which made Cheryl fearful of calling the police as well as seeking care at a city hospital; continuing with Cheryl getting an order of protection, which John ripped up; and then hearing during her trial that, on the only occasion when Cheryl did call the police, they never made a report, obviously because they decided that the case did not have enough merit for the prosecution to prosecute.

And finally, Cheryl paid dearly for the prosecution's position that any attempt to portray John as a batterer was only "putting the victim on trial."

On the other side of the defense table, how many cases are there when the woman is murdered by her partner and is subsequently put on trial by her partner's lawyer in an attempt to prove that she was a bad wife or mother and simply deserved to die? In an especially shocking example of this double standard, only last year, in Maryland, a trucker returned home unexpectedly because of bad weather. He found his wife in bed with another man. Curiously, he shot and killed only his wife, allowing her lover to leave unharmed. When it came time for sentencing, the judge gave the man only eighteen months in prison along with an apology. "I'm sorry I have to give you any time at all," the judge said, "because obviously, no man under the same circumstances would have done less."

The case of Cheryl Cummings is a perfect example of how the victory won by Francine Hughes when she was acquitted of murdering her husband was an exception that did not create a legal precedent for other battered women who kill their batterers in self-defense. In the future, at least, what happened to Linda should provide a justification for changing and amending laws, policies, and regulations within the legal and judicial systems so that battered women have equal rights under the law.

Judith Kahan is the executive director of the Center for

the Elimination of Violence in the Family and also the director of a battered women's shelter in Brooklyn, New York.
Kahan cites other groups of women who do not benefit from
the shelter programs for domestic violence victims. They are
the handicapped, elderly, and rich. According to Kahan,
there is a general and erroneous belief that if a woman has
money she can just move out of her home and stop the
abuse. On any financial level, it is often difficult for a woman
to change her family's economic lifestyle by leaving an abusive relationship. For the rich woman, it means removing her
children from private schools, taking them away from their
friends, and knowing that her husband will cut off such mate-
rial luxuries as toys, trips, clothes, and camp. In most cases,
there is even less sympathy for these women, since they are
assumed to be privileged and therefore able either to control
the violence in their homes or use that privileged position to
find alternative solutions. In either case, those assumptions
are wrong, prejudicial, and dangerous.

Caroline Schneider is a psychologist, married to a lawyer, and the mother of two small children. Caroline believed
that she could handle the situation with her violent husband,
although the violence finally became too frequent and too
life threatening. After years of physical and mental abuse,
she finally sought professional counseling after an especially
violent episode. In front of the children, her lawyer husband
beat Caroline on the legs before dragging her to the kitchen
stove, where he set her hair on fire. Despite the escalation
of violence and the advice she received from her therapist,
Caroline felt that she couldn't take the children and leave
her husband since all of her assets were in both their names.
Her fear was not unfounded, since several lawyers advised
Caroline that leaving would constitute abandonment and
leaving with the children could possibly result in charges of
kidnapping being brought against her by her husband. (FBI
figures for 1995 indicate that any *woman* who has absconded
with her children is usually found within six months.) The
financial implications were that Caroline would risk losing
the family home and living without sufficient support during

what would undoubtedly be a long and drawn-out divorce proceeding, financed by her husband. In fact, her husband threatened to use his money and connections to have Caroline declared an unfit mother so that he would gain sole custody of his children, all this in an effort to dissuade her from leaving or, if that was unsuccessful, from suing for divorce to gain her share of their property. Caroline decided, like many women in her financial and emotional situation, that staying in a constantly violent situation was better than the risk of losing her children forever.

Not only are women judged harshly by the judicial system for vacillating when it comes to pressing charges against their abusers, but they are also criticized for returning to their abusers, even if they were able to get into a shelter. The more often a battered woman leaves and returns, the more frustrated and impatient everyone becomes with her—lawyers, judges, the courts, even battered women advocates.

According to Judith Kahan, a survey taken of women running shelter programs throughout the United States in 1995 showed that, the more often a battered woman leaves her abuser, the more likely she will eventually leave permanently.

"Women may leave and return dozens of times," Kahan claims, "but each time she stays away five more minutes or she learns one more technique, one more telephone number, one more option, has more money put aside; it's like doing research. What she does is to gather resources for herself, tuck away a few more dollars. The problem is that at the same time she's doing this and getting stronger, it's also the most dangerous time for her, when she's attempting to leave or after she's left, because there's a seventy-five percent greater chance of her being killed by her batterer."

Again, if the battered woman is going through this process of gathering strength alone and not bringing along minor children, what she needs most is support, trust, and patience from everyone within every system in place to help her. As long as she is not the victim of a felony (under new definitions of misdemeanors and felonies as they apply to crimes of domestic violence), what she does not need is to be blamed or called crazy or masochistic for going back.

In February 1995, a new commission on domestic violence was formed and met at Safespace in Miami, Florida, a model shelter for battered women. American Bar Association leaders and their counterparts from other national organizations, including the American Medical Association, the National Education Association, and the National Resource Center on Domestic Violence, had a dialogue with survivors of domestic violence and victim advocates to discuss what should be done on a national basis to help victims of spousal abuse. There, finally, the following issues were discussed and considered important enough to be recommended: mandatory arrest policies, personal injury and civil rights lawsuits, and improving the efficacy of civil orders of protection as opposed to criminal sanctions as a way to prevent further battering. Dr. Robert McAffee, head of the AMA, made the following statement: "America is at war with itself and terrorism in the home is a major part of that war. Doctors, lawyers, judges, social workers, police officers, and victim advocates can make a difference with a commitment to work together on this issue, in every state, in every community."

Until that happens, we should consider the battered woman a prisoner, a hostage, a victim of someone with whom she believed she was sharing a dream, not a nightmare.

TWELVE

Intimate Enemies

SHARON SMOLICK runs the domestic violence program at Bedford Hills Women's Prison in Bedford Hills, New York, one of the best programs for battered women in the country, offering a chance for women to understand how to identify violence in their lives and how not to blame themselves for having been victims. "Our goal," Smolick explains, "is to create a safe, supportive environment for women to begin to identify, share, and address the experiences of victimization in their lives. Within that framework, we attempt to develop an understanding of the impact that victimization has had on each woman, and the implications that it has in terms of addressing change in her life."

Most of the women who participate in Smolick's program murdered their abusive partners and will spend years of their lives in prison. For the women at Bedford Hills, Smolick's program offers an opportunity to share their experiences and receive support and comfort.

The Bedford Hills prison is a community of approximately seven hundred women, the majority of whom are in their late twenties to early thirties, primarily African American, and from New York City. Forty-nine percent of the women are imprisoned for what is categorized as a violent felony (34 percent for murder, manslaughter, or attempted murder). While the average minimum sentence these women serve is eight and a third years, the reality is that close to two hundred women are serving sentences in excess of ten-year minimums, while one hundred women will be imprisoned for at least twenty years or more. Without exception, all of these women have suffered abuse at the hands of a family member for their entire lives.

Peggy Green, an inmate serving twenty-five to life for the murder of her common law husband, explains: "I was not a silent victim, I was not passive, and I learned my strength and anger very young. But striking out did me no good; but then nothing else did either. I went for help and no one listened. When I was being beaten, I went to the police and they sent me back home and I was beaten more. When I told the foster care workers about the foster fathers who were molesting me and their wives who were beating me, they defended them. And when I tried to tell the psychiatrists, they analyzed and asked lots of questions, but did nothing about the situation."

For Peggy, as for many of the inmates here, this is the first real peace and support they've had in years. But what about battered women on the outside, who also need access to programs? And what about their children and the men who abuse them? Where are the programs for them?

A domestic violence program like the one at Bedford Hills should be put into effect in every church, synagogue, school, university, government agency, and private corporation across the country. Programs must be in place to help women know if they are living with a batterer, as well as to help them develop a safety plan to escape without resorting to methods that will only put them in another prison for the rest of their lives.

There must also be programs for men before they face the criminal justice system, to enable them to learn about how to have a relationship without physical or emotional violence. And there must be classes given in schools so that boys and girls can learn while they are still young how to have a healthy, violence-free relationship.

Phyllis Frank of the Rockland County Batterers' Intervention Program maintains that domestic violence is a gender crime that will never be eradicated unless there is education about and a change in the role of men and women throughout society. "From a purely judicial viewpoint, in the long term," Frank says, "social attitudes must change, education and therapy groups must be implemented, all in an effort to make men aware and to protect women and children from violence."

When children enter school, programs must be in place to reinforce a sense of equality and dignity that parents should be—but too often are not—teaching at home. Schools must include in every curriculum not only reading, writing, arithmetic, and sex education, but also management control, so that a difference of opinion or disagreement will not automatically erupt into violent behavior. Children must also be given lessons in gender roles, which include division of household chores, inclusion of girls in sports events, and lessons for both sexes that deal with displaying emotions. The message that must be sent to boys and girls is that there is no place for violent behavior in any intimate relationship. They should also be taught that violence committed by one partner against another is a crime that automatically becomes police business.

From the beginning, mothers must teach their sons to respect women regardless of their financial contribution to any family unit, or whether their primary job is in an office or running the home. Mothers must teach daughters that it is unacceptable for little boys to pull their hair or pinch, punch, push, or slap them as a show of affection. Mothers must teach sons and daughters that it is not the unilateral responsibility of the woman to make any relationship or marriage work, but rather, that any successful relationship takes a dual effort.

From the beginning, fathers must set an example for their sons, treating female members of the family as well as all women with respect and dignity. Fathers must also set an example for their daughters by not treating their wives and mothers as servants or objects. Equality and dignity may be unalienable rights for every citizen under the Constitution, but individual equality and dignity in any ongoing relationship must be a reciprocal and conscious effort.

Education can make a difference in changing male behavior toward women in general, especially if it is done when boys are still young enough to learn, before ingrained habits or moral judgments are formed.

Judge Kevin Herlihy contends that even after men are identified as batterers, jail is a waste of time and money if they are not obliged to enter a program that teaches them about gender roles, respect, and equality. "After all, usually the batterer isn't in jail forever unless he's on death row," Judge Herlihy says; "it isn't the end of the road. These education programs have to be in jails as well as in schools or in lieu of jail for these guys, because if not, you send a guy to jail, keep him on probation, and then, at the ripe old age of twenty-eight, release him and turn him loose on women at large and have him start battering someone else. If we can't deal with that, all the laws in the world won't help."

Men who are known domestic abusers should never be placed in a category of "domestic abusers"; rather, they should be considered as dangerous threats to society at large. There are too many cases where these men have gone on to injure or kill family members of their partners, including stepchildren or even their own biological children.

Judge Virginia Knaplund agrees and adds, "We must get a message to kids that it's not the victim who gets blamed when she gets battered; it's the batterer who has to take the responsibility squarely on his shoulders."

"We should be doing much more to educate men long before these guys ever get to a courtroom," Judge Herlihy continues. "We've got to start in the schools and families where there's an absence of a role model and twelve- and thirteen-year-old boys and girls think that hitting women or girls is standard procedure or a show of affection."

Long-term programs that educate men, women, and children, while important to change attitudes within society, are beneficial only if there are systems in place that deal effectively with this crime by confronting the problem and sending the right message to batterers.

"Combatting domestic violence," Douglas Gaudette warns, "will only be successful if success is measured on a cooperation between all agencies, courts, and schools. Let's face it, one process has to be immediate, given the danger these women live with on a daily basis, while the other might take hundreds of years before the definition of gender roles is changed. As it stands now, the system is not making it any easier to protect the victim and her family by providing her with the help and support that is promised, simply because police are reluctant to arrest, prosecutors are reluctant to prosecute, and judges are reluctant to sentence the batterer because they all believe they should concentrate their efforts on crimes where the victim is willing to cooperate. The reality is that society must make these men feel like criminals, not heroes."

District Attorney Amy Sharf is also pragmatic when it comes to providing women with immediate protection. "The real problem," Sharf says, "is to protect women and save lives. Sometimes, if it's impossible to convict the batterer or if there are resources lacking for batterers' programs, the most important thing is helping these women get out of a bad relationship and get on with their lives. I'm not saying these men shouldn't be punished, but when you talk about the typical case, where the victim isn't strong enough to provide us with evidence, it becomes more important to get her out of there and give her support. Instead of just changing this sexist society, we have to change the system."

The dilemma remains how to create a separate system across the board that deals exclusively with crimes of domestic violence in ways that will protect victims as well as punish their assailants. The ideal would be to combine a tough legal response with extensive social programs. But before any system, however perfect, can be put in place, from the moment that a crime is committed, there must be specific guidelines in place to recognize that it is a crime of domestic violence, whether those differences are blatant or subtle.

"Define abuse," District Attorney Elizabeth Loewy challenges, "because some of these guys never lay a hand on their partners and yet terrorize them just as effectively in other ways."

"A woman may be married for ten years," Sharf continues, "and claim she's never had an incident of violence, and then the more you talk to her, the more you realize that it's a question of degree. Some women don't consider being pushed or slapped as violent behavior, or maybe she draws the limits when he smashed her windshield when she was sitting in the car. Another woman I remember who was seven months pregnant asked me if calling her a fat pig was considered abuse. What can I say? You can't take the guy to court for that or so many other subtle or not so subtle verbal abuses. What we do is just sit around and wait until he breaks the law."

Opinions are diverse as to the best method of combatting this problem, whether by short-term or long-term solutions or a combination of both. There is no argument, however, when it comes to defining domestic violence as a crime that causes harm not only to the victim but to her children, a crime that, in essence, amounts to an attack on what society holds to be the core of our civilization—the family. In order to create an effective response, it is crucial to understand what makes this crime different as it pertains to the victim, her needs and reactions.

One of the most apparent differences between this crime and others occurs when a criminal is incarcerated for a violent stranger crime. In those cases, the system need not worry about the fate or well-being of the victim. And if there is doubt, the victim often has the opportunity to enter a witness protection program.

Judge Laura Drager offers this viewpoint: "What we mean about domestic violence being different is the disposition at the end of it. How can you put a victim of this crime in a witness protection program when that means she has to cut all contacts with family and friends? What do you do about the children in a case like that? It's as unrealistic and insufficient a solution as simply putting the perpetrator in jail. There are numerous cases where he telephones the victim from jail and threatens her when he gets out, or harasses her, or threatens to have his 'buddies' knock her off while he's in. The way the system is set up, the victim just doesn't get away."

Another difference between victims of this crime and victims of stranger crime has to do with a particular kind of trauma battered women experience while they are in court. What is needed in all courts is advocates to walk these women through a complicated legal process and stay with them to offer moral support. Often, as is *never* the case in stranger crime, the most familiar and reassuring face in the courtroom to the victim is her assailant—which only conjures up all the guilt, fear, doubt, and conflict about following through with the charges and testifying. Women find it difficult, even women who have been brutally battered for years, to watch as their abusers—the fathers of their children, the family's sole support—are being led away in handcuffs.

Judge Laura Drager believes that the best example of the difference between domestic violence and stranger crime is that, as horrible as a crime can be between strangers, at least the victim knows he or she will never see the assailant again. "In a domestic violence case," Drager explains, "especially if there are children involved, there is always going to be a connection between victim and assailant. And the closer and the more intimate the relationship is, the more difficult those issues of prosecuting or even just pressing charges are going to be."

Charlotte Watson, who runs a shelter and is an eminent advocate for battered women, elaborates: "The problem with this crime and what makes it more complicated is the access that the perpetrator has to the victim, which is why you can't treat this crime in exactly the same way. If I break into your house at three o'clock in the morning and you wake up and I'm standing over you with a gun, you'll do whatever you have to do to stay alive. If the perpetrator in a stranger crime happens to be arrested, the D.A. or the police will ask you to testify, and if you're afraid, you can always, in the extreme, move to another house and know that the court won't give out your new address. But imagine the same set of circumstances, only the perpetrator is your husband or boyfriend, and the next day the police arrest him and the D.A. asks you to testify because that's the only way they can get a conviction, even though they understand that you're afraid. But wait, the law in these cases is different, so for the next ten or twenty years, you have to tell the perpetrator where you live because of the children, and you can't go on vacation without telling him where you're going. In other words, you're going to have to see this man every week on a regular basis because of the children, and by the way, the perpetrator will be giving you support payments, so your very existence is tied into this person who held a gun over you at three o'clock in the morning. Now, given those circumstances, would you testify? And knowing that you probably won't testify, the court and the prosecutor aren't going to make a big effort to press charges, regardless of how many times this guy has been charged with assault.''

In most cases of domestic violence when children are involved, yet another judgmental question is often asked: ''What's wrong with these women? Why do they drop charges?'' If people who ask that question only understood the repercussions involved when there are children, or the conflicting laws concerning the batterer's rights to visit and stay in contact with his children, or the financial, psychological, and emotional ramifications that women and children suffer by going forward in court, that question would never be asked.

There are many cases when the law allows men who beat or murder their wives to have access to or custody of their children. Judges may require women to give their addresses and phone numbers to the court so that the father/abuser has access to his children despite any order of protection that she might have. And if the woman refuses, she can be held in contempt. What most women don't know, however, and what most lawyers and judges either forget or don't bother to remember, is that there is a provision in domestic relations law stating that when there is "risk either to the child or the custodian [mother], the judge shall not make her give her address to her abuser."

There are also many cases when judges refuse to incarcerate a batterer because they either don't want to break up the family, deprive the children of a father, or deprive the family of financial support. In stranger crimes, those same men would be put in jail without thought to their civil or social status or rights. The way the system treats the batterer who has children is also responsible for that old familiar question "Why doesn't the woman just leave?" Yet again, there are women, especially those who have children with their abusers, who leave all the time, and it doesn't necessarily get them away from their partners or prevent their partners from pursuing them.

There are many examples of men who use their time with their children as a means of inflicting abuse on their partners. In fact, not only is there a provision in domestic relations law that protects women; there is also a case that has acquired cult status by battered women, feminists, and advocates for battered women and that should have set a definite precedent.

Jeanne Farkas left her husband. She also got a restraining order against him. Neither seemed to work, since Howard Farkas still had visitation rights to their son, Jonathan, which he used to continue his abuse of his estranged wife, slapping and cursing her when she dropped Jonathan off and picked him up. One particularly brutal attack occurred when Howard Farkas pulled up in his car in front of Jeanne's house. Jonathan was dozing in the front seat. Getting out of the car, Howard ordered Jeanne to get her son. When she leaned in, he slammed the car door on her back, breaking the window and sending Jeanne to the hospital.

After years of what Jeanne Farkas described as a relentlessly violent marriage and subsequent separation, she filed for divorce and won sole custody of Jonathan. In 1992, Judge Elliot Wilk cited the car door incident as an egregious exam-

ple of the way Howard Farkas had taken advantage of his
visitation rights to his son to harass and injure his former
wife. The judge cut off almost all contact between father
and son, allowing only prescreened letters and taped and
videotaped messages. With the court's permission, Jeanne
and Jonathan moved out of state so Howard could never find
them again. In his opinion, Judge Wilk wrote, "To permit
Mr. Farkas to learn the whereabouts [of his former wife and
son] would be a betrayal to them both."

Judge Wilk's decision in *Farkas* v. *Farkas* broke new
ground in case law for battered women in New York by ruling
that courts *must* consider violence in the marriage as a factor
when deciding custody arrangements. Unlike thirty-eight
other states, which have explicit laws requiring judges to
hear evidence on marital violence in custody cases, New
York's judiciary can and frequently does ignore such history.
What makes this case so bizarre, however, is that it is as
difficult to find as Jeanne Farkas. It has never been published
in law books or cited as precedent in another judge's reported decision, which is why it has become a cult case for
the battered women's advocacy network. What was hoped,
logically, by advocates for battered women after the Farkas
case was decided, was that it would enable women with extensive proof of abuse at the hands of their husbands to gain
sole custody of their children. That it didn't do so is further
proof of the fact that the abuse of these women will not
necessarily stop after their day in court.

A solution is possible. Charlotte Watson has been working on creating supervised visitation centers where those
abusers who are not incarcerated would be able to visit their
children in an area that is controlled and monitored by the
court. Trained staff along with security guards would be on
duty at all times. There would be a separate entrance for
batterers and one where victims can drop off the children
without any possibility of confrontation, either accidentally
or on purpose. "The government should pay for these centers," Watson maintains, "because you're talking about protecting someone within the Constitution for safety, which is

a reasonable government expense. I would rather have a center where the funding comes out of the county budget than have our county executive have two or three cars with telephones and a six-digit salary. It's a question of priorities."

Practically, those visitation centers would cost less than incarcerating a man for assault or, in the extreme, paying for a murder trial. "But unfortunately, that's a long way off," Watson admits, "since we can't even get supervision for a battered woman when she's in court to get an order of protection or to press charges against her abuser. If judges, district attorneys, and the police understood how difficult it is for a woman all alone, they wouldn't complain that women constantly vacillate, that they don't know what they want."

Children's experiences in court while they wait for their mothers to fill out papers for a restraining order, or to file a petition for support, or to testify against their abusive partners can be traumatic. As well as centers for batterers to visit their children, there should be centers where children can be safely deposited while their mothers go through the lengthy process of waiting, filling out forms, talking to prosecutors, and trying to devise alternate safety plans concerning where they will sleep that night.

The Yonkers court, thanks to the efforts of Charlotte Watson and others, provides drop-off child care centers where battered women can leave their children to be supervised and entertained while they handle their legal affairs in court. The center in Yonkers should serve as an example, since it is also open twenty-four hours a day, seven days a week, and prepared to receive minor children whose mothers are seriously enough injured to be hospitalized. Furthermore, in the event there is no shelter space available, such child care centers should take minor children in situations where the mother must spend the night in a hospital emergency room.

The problem of children of battered women exists throughout the country, from California to Massachusetts, and courts are just beginning to recognize the need to temper justice with child care. In many states, such as New Jersey, there are specifically designated children's waiting rooms in some county courthouses, furnished with donated toys and staffed with volunteer baby-sitters. More than just providing a baby-sitting service, these centers—given an increase of homelessness, AIDS, drug abuse, and poverty—are also the first place where women can learn more about permanent policies, including health care and social service programs, that affect them and their children. While there are many members of the judiciary who believe that they have been appointed or elected to dispense justice from on high and therefore should not be forced to get involved with the human service aspect of the problem, it is time to change those attitudes within the law. If not, and if courts don't make an effort to become user friendly, not only will women continue to drop charges, but they would have to be masochistic or crazy not to. It is another example of a catch-22. Let us not forget that if any woman does not use the judicial system against her batterer and as a result her children are harmed, the judgment is often, "Any woman who doesn't protect her children from a batterer has to be crazy, masochistic, and therefore an unfit mother."

Yet given the failure within the system—putting the rights of the batterer before the rights of the victim and her children—it is no wonder that in so many cases women end up losing everything, often tragically.

"The best thinking now," according to Linda Knopf, "is to have legislation that creates policies that require procedure that, within the letter of the law, hold men totally accountable for the crimes they commit against their partners. There must be a coalition of service providers within every community from every institution, agency, and organization that deals only with domestic violence, which includes both victims and offenders. A system must be coordinated where there are no holes for people to get by, and that means starting with the criminal justice system and including the mental and health care systems, education, bringing in corporations for training and sensitivity programs, as they have on other issues, everything to offer support and leadership for this effort. Without it, there will be more and more women" abused and killed.

Linda Knopf's goal is an ambitious one, to which Jonathan Cohen and Phyllis Frank, both from Rockland County Batterers' Intervention Program, subscribe.

"Regarding sexism and battery," Phyllis Frank elaborates, "no piece of paper, treaty, or law is going to protect any woman from being battered, or stop any man from battering, unless there's mandatory education in all public, private, and parochial schools on a long-term basis concerning the recognition of unacceptable controlling or violent behavior."

District Attorney Elizabeth Loewy, however, insists that it is the criminal justice system that must be changed or amended to provide for these kinds of cases. "To me, if you take the approach that you've got to change society," Loewy argues, "it's never going to happen; it's too esoteric. It's got to be much more of a hands-on approach which will protect the woman."

The criminal justice system as it exists today does not comprise courts of justice but rather courts of law. Prosecutors are never certain that they will get a conviction, even if the evidence seems to be indisputably in their favor, which is the reason for so many negotiated plea bargains. If they can be assured of a conviction, even for a less severe crime, they will take it rather than risk losing the case entirely.

According to District Attorney Sharf, "If the victim is cooperative, it's sometimes better to negotiate a plea to assure a conviction, because these guys know how to manipulate the system or terrorize their partners so they won't testify. Or, the women just don't show up, or they assert marital privilege, which means it takes a lot of work for the prosecution to build a case. We go forward on a case-by-case basis, even where victims cite marital privilege, or we'll go forward even if a victim doesn't want to testify. We'll evaluate each case and see how strong it is, which is why it's so important to be able to get the defendant's prior record. If we can get it, and if he's got a long history of abuse, even if the victim comes in and refuses to testify, we'll prosecute."

According to District Attorney Sharf, one of the main reasons for the victim's hesitation is that she knows from experience that the judicial system is not always sympathetic. "Whether there are men or women on the jury," Sharf says, "they always ask the same questions: 'Why did she stay and take the abuse? Why did she go back after all the restraining orders? Why did she change her mind and vacate those orders?' "

One of the reasons the city of Lawrence, Massachusetts, does such an effective job when it comes to prosecuting batterers and protecting victims is that there is extensive cooperation between all systems in place.

"There are a lot of agencies working together," Douglas Gaudette explains. "For example, there's a team within the district attorney's office that deals only with domestic violence, and a court with two judges, Kevin Herlihy and Michael Stella, who take an active approach, as well as women's programs that are involved, and a batterers' program that is connected with the court."

Douglas Gaudette claims that the reason the batterers' intervention program that he runs is so effective is the daily input and cooperation of others within the social service and judicial systems. "By ourself, we are useless," he says. "What makes us successful is that we work with the courts, and we probably intervene more with the courts than any other program, and by courts, I mean judges, probation clerks, prosecuting attorneys, defense attorneys, and battered women. Part of our success depends especially on victims who write to us and tell us if their partners are still violent, what kind of violence, what progress they are making if they're still living together. This is all information that we use when we intervene, since we adjust and readjust our response to these guys all the time to assess what the chances are of them reoffending."

No one can predict whether a violent man will reoffend. While it has been proven that men with previous records are more likely to reoffend and men with no previous records are less likely to reoffend, the reality is that every reoffender, at one time or another in his life, was a first-time abuser. It is not enough to rely on the court's judgments unless the court works closely with the people who are actually seeing the batterer in sessions where he talks about his violent behavior and expresses his opinions concerning women in general and his partner in particular. To insure the protection of the victim, it should make no difference if her abuser is a first-time offender or a repeat felon, at least until any trial or conviction. In the interim, it should be a matter of routine in all cases to assume that the batterer will reoffend. The issue to be considered is to safeguard—legally—against an assault reoccurring. How?

Battered women need protection. Protection means separation. Separation means exclusion from the home or a court order that forces the batterer to keep a certain distance away from the victim, or prevents him from stalking her.

Currently, there are only twenty states that have stalking laws or laws pending that call for imprisonment or fines for "intentionally, maliciously and repeatedly following or harassing another person and threatening that other person with death or great bodily harm." California happens to be one of them—which nevertheless did not help Nicole Brown Simpson when she was stalked, followed, and spied on by her ex-husband.

Stalking as a sole act is not considered criminal, even though in most cases it causes the victim to lose her freedom of movement, speech, housing, job, health, or peace of mind and therefore is a direct violation of her civil rights. In cases of domestic violence, laws should be changed throughout the country so that imprisonment for stalking is used as preventive detention for a dangerous act that in almost all cases precedes assault or murder. In all cases, men who are known domestic abusers should not be placed in a category of "domestic abusers," but rather viewed as dangerous threats to society at large.

The key word for effecting a legal, medical, judicial, or

social service system that works is *communication*. The most important factor in linking up all of these systems so that they function at top efficiency is *cooperation*. The most important overall goal throughout society when it comes to stopping this crime is *change*.

Without communication, cooperation, and change, there will continue to be a myriad of confused definitions, unrealistic responses, and archaic reactions in the matter of domestic violence.

While society is used to dealing with conventional crimes and conventional criminals, it is unprepared to deal with a crime such as domestic violence that involves such a wide range of human emotions. In all cases, domestic violence is a unique area of criminal behavior. "Ask a criminal why he committed a crime and he'll give you a reason," Judge Herlihy explains. "Ask a wife beater and he'll say an argument got out of hand or it's a personal matter."

Or as Jimmy Breslin explains it, "These guys give reasons like the house was cold, the food was cold, the wife was cold. My sense is a wife beater is like a hunchback, you either are or you aren't. The point is that decent people walk away when they get annoyed or angry."

Unfortunately, the law was not written for decent people.

THIRTEEN

Trunk
of the Elephant

CHANGES WITHIN the medical, legal, and social service systems are all vital to protecting the victim and prosecuting her assailant. The place where the accused and his victim confront what will be an absolute and realistic ending to their case occurs within the judicial system, or in the courts. Here also changes must be made not only to insure an appropriate response to a crime that has been committed, but also to insure that judges who sit in these courts understand the law and all its nuances.

Many states have changed or amended their laws to enable law enforcement to function more effectively, as well as to offer better services to the victims of this particular crime. Unfortunately, even when efforts have been made concretely and in writing, in many cases ambiguities and confusion still exist. For example, under laws that are in effect in most states, victims of domestic violence need no longer wait until the family court or any comparable courts are in session to get help. Women in crisis may go before a local, city, village, or town judge at any hour of the night or on weekends to ask for a temporary order of protection or ask that an arrest be made when an order has been violated.

Judge Virginia Knaplund is one of those judges who will get up in the middle of the night to hear a case of spousal

assault. She is also someone who can explain the problems
with the way the law was written.

"It's the case of the blind man holding the elephant's
trunk and proclaiming it a snake," Judge Knaplund begins.
"It's just not clear. For example, when I open up my courtroom, I unlock the door, turn on the lights, and usher in the
police, victim, and assailant, and we do our business. In most
courtrooms across this state and in large cities throughout
the country, there are unions, which means that the judge
can't always turn on the lights or unlock the door. He or
she has to call in the union people to make the courtroom
operational. So, while the law states that the victim has the
right to a hearing immediately, and even if the judge is
willing, there is nothing written concerning appropriation of
funds to pay the union people to come in and do their job."

The Court Administration, which sets the guidelines,
rules, and regulations for all judges throughout the country,
has created a situation where there is an inherent confusion
as to what is required and what is left to the discretion of any
individual magistrate. "The Court Administration claims,"
Judge Knaplund continues, "that the legislature didn't say
that the judge was forced to get out of bed in the middle of
the night, but that the judge could if he or she felt it was
appropriate. Now, that's playing a childish game with people's lives if the system is willing to risk women being killed
because they're not willing to force judges [on a rotating]
basis to get up, either by paying the union people to come
in or allowing the judge to work without the union." Unfortunately, Judge Knaplund's commonsense approach is an
exceedingly rare one.

Another contradiction within the judicial system occurs
when it comes to using the family, probate, or civil courts to
hear cases of domestic violence. Judges who sit in these
courts are not required to have a background in family law
but, rather, must only have practiced law in general in the
state for at least ten years. What that means, in the extreme
case, is that a judge who spent a career practicing real estate
or tax law can sit in the family court and adjudicate cases of

domestic relations or, more precisely, judge cases of domestic violence. According to one New York State Supreme Court judge, "Some of these judges haven't even opened a Family Court Act law book since law school, and suddenly they're deciding where people's kids should go, based on their own agendas and experiences."

This is a dangerous practice that is not present in other professions. For example, it would make no sense for someone to consult a cardiologist for a toothache or a psychiatrist to take out an appendix, even if they are both doctors. Nor would it make sense for someone to go to a bakery to buy meat. Why then, are people with no experience in the area of family law allowed to preside over cases in any type of family court setting?

The answer is that judges in the United States are either elected or appointed. In most other countries, judges are required to have special training, and that does not necessarily mean that they have to be lawyers. According to Paul Lombard, a domestic relations lawyer in France, "Judges here have to go to a special school because it is a separate profession than studying the law to become a lawyer."

One prerequisite in the appointing of judges to the family court should be that they have spent their legal careers specializing in domestic law. According to Judge Kevin Herlihy, at a training facility for judges on domestic violence that he attended, he was surprised to see that the majority of judges in his section sat either in land court or in superior court. "There were no district court judges there," Judge Herlihy adds, "and these are the people who should learn why a batterer needs to go to jail."

Judges have the power to decide property cases, which can take everything away from one person in favor of another. They preside over murder trials, custody battles, divorce, and all other aspects of life, which means that judges in the United States have more power on a daily basis than the president of the United States. Yet there are no specific regulations set down for judges to be given routine psychological and medical tests to determine that they are in good health, or random or routine alcohol and drug tests. Ironically, most people who deal with other people's lives, such as pilots or subway drivers, are subject to random drug and alcohol tests, as are professional athletes, who are tested before and after a game.

District Attorney Elizabeth Loewy is concerned about other problems within both the family and criminal courts when it comes to dealing with these kinds of cases. From her perspective as a district attorney within the Criminal Court system, Loewy has a problem concerning the separation of these courts when it comes to hearing any specific case that could be pending in both. "Maybe the answer is to join the courts [Family and Criminal], since the idea of separating Family and Criminal court may not be the best way of handling these cases. The information I usually have at the arraignment of a batterer is his criminal record, which may or may not have anything to do with a charge of spousal battering. The problem is that the information I get about him comes from an interview he's had with the Criminal Justice Agency (CJA) or with the police, since I haven't even had time to speak directly to the victim yet. Any information about the family situation comes from the accused's defense attorney because he's the one who's had the opportunity to speak to the accused, where I haven't."

According to Loewy, the defense attorney has first access not only to the accused, but also to the victim. "This presents a problem in many different areas of the case," Loewy continues, "because the defense attorney, for example, might tell me that the accused is willing to stay away from the victim but he's a good father and he wants to see his kids. Now, we all know the issue of what happens to children who don't see their parents, and at that point, I have no history of these people."

What would make it easier for any prosecutor to handle these cases and to know how to respond to requests from the perpetrator's attorney would be for the victim to be brought to speak to the prosecutor before the hearing. District Attorney Loewy is in favor of having an escort bring the victim directly to the district attorney's office so she can be interviewed before her abuser has his hearing; if she lives too far away, arrangements should be made for someone to watch her children and for some kind of video hookup in her precinct, or at least a telephone hookup, so the victim can speak electronically to the prosecutor. "If we could talk to the woman, we could at least find out if there was a past history of violence, prior cases, anything pending in another court, and what she wants to do," Loewy explains.

In October 1992, the District Attorney's Office in Essex County, Massachusetts, started a domestic violence unit that worked closely with victims of this crime from the beginning, before the case came to court. One of the philosophies of the program was that if the victim felt she had someone within the court system with whom she could connect, she would be more likely not only to follow through, but also to turn over information that would be essential in bringing down a conviction against her batterer. District Attorney Amy Sharf explains: "When a case first comes to our attention from the police, we would immediately get in touch with the victim and arrange to meet with her, just to let her know that we're here and concerned and available to help her. If she needed, we could also give her referrals for different services in the area, counseling agencies, shelters, every resource, so that she didn't feel all alone."

The program in Essex County also works closely with the Lawrence Mental Health Center, which sponsors Douglas Gaudette's intervention program for batterers. There is full cooperation so that the batterer and his violence can be monitored through the victim. Once an abuser is referred to the batterers' treatment program, the District Attorney's Office also turns over any special information about him that could be helpful for them to know—such as whether the incident that resulted in his participation in the program or his prosecution was the first incident of abuse or there had been a long history of prior abuse.

Ellen Ferland is a counselor with the Essex County batterers' program who believes that relying on the batterer to tell the truth about his history of violence is useless. "If we relied on the batterer to tell us," Ferland explains, "he'll usually claim that it was the first incident. Since we have access and a relationship with the victim, she is the one who can tell us that it's been going on for years, for example, and specifically, this is what he does, these are the ways he's controlling me, et cetera, and these are the things that we can address once he gets into the program."

Making the batterer's police file available to the batterers' intervention program, as is done at the Lawrence Mental Health Center, makes it impossible for him to lie or deny his behavior. "What that does," Gaudette explains, "is to create more proof of the batterer's crimes, abuses, and ongoing emotional intimidation, which gives the victim enough proof either immediately or at a later date to proceed in court with the full protection of the system."

Not only should there be mandatory batterers' programs connected to every court that hears cases of domestic violence but there must be ongoing contact with the victim in all cases, or the program will not be as effective. District Attorney Loewy believes also that the batterer must be monitored even after he gets out of jail, even if he participated in a program while incarcerated.

"There's a value if the batterer was monitored and there was regular contact with the victim, because then he would understand that he was responsible to the system for any abuse that was not covered under the law. It would no longer be a matter of his intimidating his partner so she wouldn't press charges. At that point, it would be out of her hands."

Which gets back to Loewy's concern about defining abuse. For instance, the fear that many have who work with batterers is that while they might no longer engage in physical abuse because they realize that means they will be sent back to jail, they will continue to abuse their partners psychologically or verbally. The law must be amended so that it covers nonphysical abuse as well. There must be regular contact with the victim, even if she is no longer living with her abuser, so she can report any incidents of stalking, threatening, or violent or abusive behavior. Batterers, even after they finish a jail sentence or a batterers' program, will automatically have a record in a computer that they were convicted of spousal assault. Any incidents of violent abuse by those men will automatically, under the current law, put them back in court and undoubtedly in jail, while any incidents of non-violent abuse will find them automatically back in a batterers' program for an additional six months.

One of the most confusing problems with the law that allows battered women to use both courts—family and criminal—at the same time is that often the courts contradict each other in their judgments. For instance, a victim may ask the family court for an order of protection, an order for child support, or an order for temporary custody of the children. At the same time, because the case is also in the criminal court, that court can proceed and prosecute her assailant, even sentencing him to jail for the same crime that a family court judge deemed warranted an order of protection. Under the law, these two different actions can be maintained without double jeopardy concern. What is needed is communication between the courts, and the best way to effect that is to have a computerized system that keeps each court up to date on the disposition of every case.

Judge Virginia Knaplund agrees that when it comes to assuring victim safety by prosecuting batterers, there must be open lines of communication between the courts, batterers' intervention programs, social workers, and the police. "We need courts to talk to each other more openly, to have courts communicate with batterers' programs. For example, there are some courts that still won't give out information about criminal records or details of abuse to other batterers' programs because they claim it's privileged. Well, it isn't privileged if we're going to be able to talk to these men who consistently lie to us."

"If I had three wishes," Douglas Gaudette says, "one of the things I would wish is that the court always does what we tell them and that we could all communicate effectively on a moment's notice. Often there are last-minute needs for very important information that needs to be tracked down, so my needs are very basic. How can we make the program work better? The nuts and bolts need to be better. We need to communicate more effectively."

Ellen Ferland adds, "We also need more people. We're covering a lot of courts; we need to be in more than one place at one time. If we say we're going to be in court to testify, then we damn well better be there. We need to be able to anticipate when we have to go to court, and we need the court to call us quickly so we don't have to sit there all day—very basic things. We've had excellent support from probation in all the courts we service. If we need information or if we recommend that a batterer needs to be taken back to court, the response from probation is great. In some of the courts, once it gets above that level and gets back to court, there are still problems, but usually because a judge just doesn't understand."

Charlotte Watson feels that judges must be better educated about domestic violence in order for them to change certain ingrained attitudes about men who batter. "In some courts," Watson says, "judges are not taking domestic violence seriously. They're not giving the men any kind of sentence, not finding them guilty. There needs to be a systemwide agreement that this is going to happen. When you start having one piece of the system fall down, every program becomes useless. We need some real direction from high up that tells the court to act in a certain consistent way with some discretion. There also needs to be an accountability for judges who do not adhere."

While it is crucial to remember that victim safety must come before anything else, what is also crucial to remember is that these men are criminals who break the law. It makes no difference who or what they are in other areas of their lives.

Identifying the victim of this crime is usually not difficult, since she has bruises that indicate she has been assaulted, or she has psychological symptoms because she has been terrorized, threatened, or intimidated. Identifying the men who commit these crimes is often extremely difficult.

The situations that Trisha Mian has witnessed as an advocate for battered women at Massachusetts General Hospital are usually the end result of years of manipulation and control of battered women by their batterers. Trisha considers that the most dangerous situation is the one in which the batterer brings his injured wife or girlfriend for treatment, or shows up while she is recuperating in hospital to wheedle his way back into her life, only to continue what will be an escalated and more deadly series of assaults.

"Most of these men are sociopathic and charming," Trisha maintains, "so when they come here with flowers and candy, promising it won't happen again, the woman wants to believe him because she loves the good part of this man."

Trisha can cite numerous examples of women who sought treatment for serious medical injuries and who, after they recovered, simply resumed their relationships with their assailants. "After all," Trisha admits, "we're not privy to the history of intimacy, memories, and emotions."

According to Jennifer Robertson, who runs the AWAKE program at Children's Hospital in Boston, the process from the victim's first encounter with her abuser to the moment that she enters the AWAKE program with her children follows a very precise pattern of events. It is a formula used effectively by the batterer.

On the basis of her years of experience in dealing with the battered woman, Robertson can describe how the relationship between the couple began and then continued until it degenerated to the point where the woman and her children found themselves in a life-threatening situation.

"The abuser," Robertson says, "begins by asking questions that seem normal on any first date—when was the last time she was involved in a relationship and why it broke up, what her family is like—a whole series of intimate questions. One of the things we try to tell women is about this trust-building stage that perpetrators use."

According to Robertson, after the male abuser has asked a series of questions that include the woman's fears, desires, hopes, and dreams, he is then in a position to become the person that she had always hoped to meet.

"He becomes everything she wants in a man because he has learned enough to know when to praise her for her dreams, empathize for anything in her background that has been painful or has diminished her. He can do all the things she loves to do, take her to all the places she loves to go, eat the foods she prefers, become the person she has always dreamed of meeting, the totally compatible lover. And for a while, this doesn't go away."

If a woman has finally found someone whom she totally loves and who appears to love her totally, while encouraging her to achieve more, making her secure and confident that she can succeed, there is every reason to believe that she has finally found the ideal man. Unless there are certain signs that begin to appear, some of which can be determined through the questionnaire compiled by Charlotte Klein and her Brigade, there is no reason to suspect that she has stumbled upon the typical batterer. After all, not every man on crutches who flags down a woman in a passing car on a lonely road at night is Ted Bundy.

"After the abuser has convinced her that he represents everything she wants," Robertson goes on, "that's the time when he can begin with some subtle control as in, 'I love you in that beige sweater, but you're so much more beautiful in blue. I wish you'd wear the blue one.' Or, 'You look beautiful in makeup, but you're far more beautiful without it.' " Robertson continues, "It's the same thing with her friends, when he tells her that he adores her friend so-and-so, but there's something about her that's a little quirky, and she seems a little different when she's with her; it's not a problem of course . . . But he's planting seeds of doubt. The woman naturally thinks that it takes so little to please this wonderful man that not wearing makeup or wearing a different color sweater or seeing her friend so-and-so less often is a small price to pay for complete happiness. After all, in most relationships, each person gives up something."

But this is not about giving up something to make the relationship work. As Robertson maintains, "This is about making the woman look less attractive to other people or eliminating her friends so she has less of a support system. This is about isolating this woman and making her totally dependent on this man so he has more and more power over her and she has fewer and fewer options."

This entire process that constitutes domestic violence, whether it is subtle or overt, is about control and power, the two driving forces that propel a man to batter a woman. Which only gets to the next series of very specific questions.

Who are these men who batter, and what are the common traits and characteristics that women can use to recognize them? In other words, who exactly is Prince Charming?

FOURTEEN

Prince Charming

THE BATTERER is often hard to recognize until it is too late. He can be the construction worker on the side of the highway or the family doctor who delivers the baby, treats the toddler for chicken pox, or signs a grandmother's death certificate. He can be the psychiatrist who councils the bulemic teenager, the family lawyer who handles the real estate closing, the postman, policeman, dentist, sports figure, actor, musician, writer. He can be the favorite high school teacher, the war hero, research scientist, weatherman, politician, or social worker. Whatever his vocation, his avocation is that he batters his intimate partner, most often with premeditation and control. Quite probably, if the batterer were not in control, he would also not limit his abuse to his wife or girlfriend. If provoked, he might also batter his secretary or coworkers for making mistakes on the job, a captain in a restaurant for giving him a lousy table, the neighborhood dry cleaner for not removing a spot on his suit, a driver on the road who cut him off, or a policeman who stopped him for speeding. If the batterer didn't measure his abuse, more women would have bruises and marks on those parts of their body not covered by clothing, more bumps and cuts on those parts of their head not covered by hair. In fact, if the batterer abused for any other reason than to gain power and control, more women would end up dead.

To those who meet the batterer briefly or who are super-ficially, professionally, or cordially involved, he is often per-ceived as polite, kind, understanding, and undemanding. After he has been either arrested or exposed for spousal assault, opinion about him doesn't change when he is often described by close friends or family members as "the last man on earth who would hurt his wife or children."

On the other hand, there are men on the wrong side of respectability and the law, convicted felons, rapists, thieves, murderers, or white-collar criminals, who have never bat-tered their wives or girlfriends. In those cases, it is safe to assume that while all batterers are criminals, not all criminals are batterers.

Charlotte Watson believes that one of the reasons the batterer is so misunderstood is that the people involved in developing theories have insufficient firsthand experience. According to Watson, domestic violence is not a new phe-nomenon, discovered in the last twenty or so years by social scientists or feminists. Domestic violence has always existed. "Back then," Watson says, "when it didn't have a name, domestic violence was simply called 'life.' "

Identifying the batterer is also difficult because society tends to separate men into two categories: men, and men who batter. In the same way, women are also separated into two categories: women, and women who are victims. "Every-thing we know about men who batter," Watson maintains, "we've learned from women who have lived through it. You don't go to social workers' school to learn how to deal with this problem. When you go through school, you come out thinking you've got the answers, and if the people you were trying to help would just get on the right plan, everything would be all right."

In 1966, William Ryan, a psychologist at Yale University, wrote a book entitled *Blaming the Victim*. In it, Ryan wrote that society found it easier to isolate the victim of domestic violence by defining specific traits, characteristics, and back-ground to explain why she was different from women who had never been abused. In his thesis, Ryan maintained that society created a "pariah syndrome" to assure the majority that domestic violence is an aberrational situation. After all, it was not uncommon for people to think that only a woman who was in some way damaged would remain in an abusive relationship.

Ryan went on to explain that it was easier for the government to invent a "human action program" than to embark upon a program that addressed a social condition in which domestic violence can and does affect anyone and everyone. By studying the problem from a distance, the government automatically isolated the majority of the population, creating that same pariah syndrome for batterers, which was just as comforting and just as wrong.

To create a safe distance from the threat of domestic violence, society constructs situations to predict where and when it occurs as well as formulates specific profiles of both perpetrators and victims. The reality is that most people are afraid to accept that domestic violence can and does transcend all social, economic, and religious sectors of society. There are very few individuals who are immune to or exempt from becoming either a victim or a batterer, and those who claim that they have never been in an abusive relationship might change their minds if they were to learn all the different forms that kind of relationship can take.

While Ryan's thesis was original, the pariah syndrome had been used by the public to placate themselves about other unpleasant social realities. It wasn't that long ago that people stopped hiding their own or a family member's addiction to alcohol. It took years before Alcoholics Anonymous became a socially accepted institution, credited publicly with a high cure rate for the disease. In fact, it wasn't that long ago that alcoholism wasn't even considered a disease, but rather an asocial or criminal condition, while alcoholics were perceived as Bowery bums instead of a cross-section of society.

Incest was also a subject treated with cautious distance, relegated to backwoods communities or the poor and uneducated, until the advent of confessional television talk shows on which celebrities as well as ordinary people came forward to share their experiences. More recently, at the beginning of the AIDS epidemic, the vast majority wanted to believe that HIV was limited to the homosexual community or to IV drug users; that comfortably excluded everybody else.

Expert opinion about the batterer varies, since each man exhibits a different reaction when he is confronted, arrested, or jailed. Identifying batterers, therefore, is a near-impossible task.

The batterer is found as frequently among the affluent, middle class, and educated as he is in neighborhoods where there are high crime rates, unstable family structures, poverty, and illiteracy. Just as profiles of victims create pariahs, categorizing abusers into specific socioeconomic groups leads to inaccurate conclusions about domestic violence in general and batterers in particular. While economic or social status does not eliminate certain men from becoming batterers, the techniques they use to control their partners can reflect their level of education or sophistication. In all cases, however, without exception, the batterer uses whatever means are within his social, financial, and emotional power to control his partner.

The batterers' intervention program in Lawrence, Massachusetts, run by Douglas Gaudette, lasts for thirty-one weeks and includes an initial assessment interview, a four-to-six-week orientation, and the twenty-four-week ongoing group. According to Gaudette, "Our experience is that most men spend at least ten months in the program."

There is a flat fee for participation in the program of $100 for the initial intake/assessment, which is non-negotiable. All other program costs are on a sliding scale, which ranges from $20 to $50 per group, depending on the economic situation of each batterer/participant. While failure to pay fees will result in termination from the program and a return to court, where the batterer could be remanded to jail, there is a consideration for men who are indigent. "They can do an equivalent amount of hours of community service," Gaudette explains, "to make up the difference."

The groups meet once a week for two hours and are

usually limited to fifteen participants with two counselors, usually a male and a female. Unlike other batterer intervention groups, this one, as Gaudette puts it, is not a "big fan of role playing." According to Gaudette, the men are broken up in groups of three; one man tells his story of abuse while the other two listen and then report back to the group what they heard. "It's interesting when they begin to realize how someone minimalizes or trivializes his abuse or blames the victim," says Gaudette. "This exercise teaches the men to listen so they can understand that their stories really are quite similar."

"The methods that men use to maintain power and control differ the same way that people have different defense mechanisms to protect their egos from intrusion," Gaudette explains. "People exert power and control based upon what works for them. If the batterer happens to be fairly sophisticated and has the means to manipulate subtly, that's what he'll use. If he doesn't have that level of sophistication, he'll be more crude about it. But the driving force is still the same, even with those batterers who are intellectually superior, since they're also functioning on a low emotional level. In every case, it's just a matter of ability."

If the batterer is employed, whether he earns a low or middle income, he might divert paychecks or simply quit his job, forcing his partner and children to go on public assistance. If he is rich, the abuser does the same thing on a larger scale by cutting off charge accounts, memberships to country clubs, emptying bank accounts, and threatening his wife with a long, drawn-out divorce case that she knows he can finance. Rich, middle class, or poor, the batterer aims to make it as difficult as possible for his victim to survive without him.

Judge Virginia Knaplund hears many cases of domestic violence. "Those men who are functioning on a higher intellectual level," Judge Knaplund explains, "we can safely assume are more affluent. They are the ones who will go about controlling their partners in a more methodical and subtle way, while others, less sophisticated and successful, will achieve the same results by functioning more viscerally. Logically, the batterer is usually married or living with a woman who understands how he communicates, either with words or with actions. His techniques of control, therefore, depend only on what will make an impression on his partner, since she knows how to identify his desires, intentions, and threats. Whatever the method that he chooses, however, power and control are not necessarily cognitive entities, which makes it so important that all batterers be made to understand why they batter, while victims—all victims—must understand why they stay."

While Judge Knaplund acknowledges the different techniques the batterer uses for control, she also perceives a difference in the victim's reactions. "The blue-collar wife may accept the beating as something that binds her inexplicably to her partner," Knaplund claims, "while she may also be unaware that she has other options. There are many cases in Scarsdale where, if a man assaults his wife, he goes to a psychiatrist; if he does the same thing in Mount Vernon, he'll probably spend the night in jail."

The batterer is usually not psychotic, pathological, or sadistic, nor does he batter his partner either because he enjoys it or because she has done something to merit the abuse. He batters because he can, without the threat of reprisal or judicial repercussion, as would be the case if he battered a stranger at random during a robbery or a neighbor to settle a score.

District Attorney Janine Ferris Pirro makes this observation: "In New York State, most often, if a woman is beaten, threatened, or brutalized by her partner, she has limited recourse in the criminal justice system. If that same person, however, called his neighbor an S.O.B., he could go to jail for fifteen days on a disorderly conduct charge. There's a basic inequity that still exists in our criminal justice system."

In the experience of District Attorney Elizabeth Loewy, the more affluent and well connected the abuser, the more outraged he is that the state is getting involved in what he considers to be his private life. "We get letters all the time from friends and contacts of the affluent batterer," she says, "telling us who they are dealing with, et cetera, allusions to important friends in high places. In fact, we even get letters from their victims complaining that if we're supposed to be their lawyers, acting on their behalf, we should listen to what they want and drop the case. We try to explain that we represent the people of the state of New York, and although we try to give them some control, unlike in stranger crime we also try to find out their reasons for wanting the case dropped."

The batterer knows the rules. He is very aware that assaulting strangers carries a price that is immediate and high —a price society does not automatically impose upon him for assaulting his wife or girlfriend. It is not surprising, therefore, that in almost every instance, the batterer refuses to consider his behavior objectionable. In fact, a typical reaction when he finds himself confronted by the legal system for having battered his partner is anger and disbelief. The batterer justifies his use of escalating methods of abuse and violence as not only his right, but his responsibility as "head of household" to keep his wife and children "in line."

"When you talk to batterers," Douglas Gaudette explains, "they tell you what their limits are. Some only slap, some push, others draw the line at kicking, still others brag that they would never use a closed fist or a weapon or strangle her, so they know exactly what they're doing."

Charlotte Watson grew up in a small town in Texas where, "on a dare," she says, she spent several years as a police officer. "Every time I went in to make an arrest in a situation of domestic assault," she says, "the batterer was always amazed that I could actually come into his home and arrest him." "You can't arrest me, officer," the batterer protested; "she's my wife; this is my house."

The batterer who enjoys a good reputation within the community presents an even greater risk for his victim, because friends and neighbors often conclude that his wife or partner is exaggerating when she reports physical abuse. Although most criminals who are convicted of any violent crime feel they have been victimized either by the system or by society, batterers are particularly insistent about their victimization.

Then there are those batterers who simply assume that the police are men and therefore understand their rage and frustration against their wives or girlfriends. Unfortunately, in some cases, they are correct. Gaudette offers an example: "We had a man in our program whose parting words to his wife, as she was being removed to the hospital after a severe beating, were, 'This time you're being carried out on a stretcher; next time you'll be in a body bag.' " The police who arrived with the ambulance and were witness to that remark never charged the batterer with attempted murder. This once again raises the question, when does privacy end and public scrutiny begin?

There are other examples of denial that the batterer employs, some that are so ingrained in his psyche that often he has grown to believe them himself. For example, some batterers actually claim that they don't believe in ever hitting a woman, since as children they witnessed their fathers beating their mothers. They might also claim that their fathers always taught them never to hit a woman. Charlotte Watson explains how the batterer justifies beating up his partner when it supposedly goes against his moral code to beat up a woman. "They're not beating up women," Watson says; "they're beating up the bitch who burned the toast and made him late for the office, or the whore who wore the short skirt to work."

Watson goes on to explain that this technique is similar to the way American soldiers killed civilians in Vietnam against whom they had nothing. "They called them names," Watson explains, "gooks, Charlies, et cetera. It's the same principle of calling a woman a name that dehumanizes her until she loses her identity. She's honey, baby, sweetie when she does what he wants, and she's the whore, bitch, slut when she doesn't."

In 1976, David Adams founded an organization called Emerge in Boston, Massachusetts. It was the first program of

its kind, whose purpose was to provide an alternative to violence for men who were identified as batterers (either by
due process of law or through referrals by family therapists)
or who came on their own after they were given ultimatums
by their partners, either to attend counseling sessions or
move out. Emerge, considered the prototype, was mostly created by and composed of radical profeminist men who believed that in order to eliminate men's violence, changes
had to be made in what they considered to be an institutionalized and inherently sexist society.

David Adams contends that there are other cases, batterers who tend to categorize their violence as self-defense,
which is a common manipulation pattern of the abusive
man, to project blame for his violence onto the victim. Statements like "She drove me to it" or "She knows how to
push my buttons" or "She provoked me" are all common
rationalizations. "The abusive man presents himself as the
victim of his partner," Adams explains, "and of the system
in general, which he believes favors women."

Charlotte Watson can cite hundreds of examples of
women who all tell the same story after they were beaten
by husbands or boyfriends. "Batterers always think they're
justified," Watson agrees; "they all say the same thing:
'Honey, I wouldn't have done it if you hadn't provoked me,'
or, 'Look what you made me do.'" Watson suggests that
instead of having groups for men after they become batterers, there should be accountability groups for all men before
they become violent. "In fact," she adds with a trace of irony,
"maybe instead of having batterers' groups, we should have
'lousy wives' groups' so women can learn how not to provoke
these men."

Prince Charming is manipulative. As Jennifer Robertson, the director of the AWAKE program in Boston, pointed
out when she discussed the various techniques the batterer
uses, he conducts his own survey, a series of question-and-
answer sessions to learn which woman is controllable and fits
his specific needs.

Regardless of his education, intelligence, or sophistication, the batterer is an expert at knowing precisely who is best suited to his needs and where to strike at that person to get the best results for control: how to destroy her self-esteem, how to rob her of any joy or pleasure that might translate into her gaining or regaining her independence. As Robertson contends, before he wheedles his way into any new partner's life, the batterer, by doing his homework, has already learned his victim's weaknesses as well as developed an accurate method for ultimately using them against her.

Not every man who takes an interest in a woman, however, or who shares similar tastes, ambitions, and goals, is necessarily a batterer. There are women who have the good fortune to find and fall in love with the ideal partner. While nothing is ever guaranteed, there are certain behavior patterns that can be considered potential warning signals for those men who are ersatz Prince Charmings. For instance, the following questions can help determine if a woman is involved with an abusive man:

> What is his attitude toward women?
> How does he treat his mother and sister?
> How does he work with female colleagues or a female boss?
> Has he always refused to work for a woman?
> Does he make jokes about women in positions of power?
> How does he treat his partner's women friends?
> Does he understand that they are as important to her as he is?
> Does his partner understand that herself?
> What is his attitude toward the female anatomy?
> Does he respect his partner's professional work, or does he denigrate it or meddle or encourage his partner to quit?
> Does he tell his partner that he doesn't want her working, that it is an insult to his manhood, that he is capable of taking care of her without her help?
> Does he insist that all her leisure time be spent on his interests?

How much time does he invest in her interests?

Does he remember things she said that are important
   to her?

Is he possessive and jealous?

Does he accuse her of having affairs?

Does he require that she account for every minute of
   her time and every dollar that she spends?

Does he insist that she turn over her paycheck to him
   so that he controls all the money?

Does he accept her male friends?

Is his reaction violent when he doesn't get his own
   way?

According to David Adams, approximately one-third of
the men currently enrolled at Emerge are professionals who
are respected in their jobs and within their community and
church. "The basic problem," Adams suggests, "is that while
some abusers bear some resemblance to those traits and
characteristics that society has constructed of the batterer,
most of the men we see do not, which means they are the
type of batterers who present the greatest danger to their
victims because they pass unnoticed, often as pillars of the
community."

Douglas Gaudette makes the point that there are some
traits that all batterers share, but they may share those traits
with other men who aren't batterers. "I have a hard time
with any profile," Gaudette elaborates, "because it tends to
exclude people who need to be in there. I also have a hard
time drawing profiles of batterers because the only men
we've got that kind of information on are the ones who have
already been identified, accused, and convicted of spousal
abuse, or they wouldn't be in our program." About the only
aspect of this crime that everyone seems to agree on is that
when it comes to domestic violence, the contradictions are
endless.

Legally, when a man has been identified as a batterer, it
is usually because he has physically assaulted his partner.
Identifying a man as a batterer who uses more subtle means

of control presents enormous social as well as legal dilem-
mas. While it is complicated enough to find the right
method, moment, and means of intervening when physical
abuse happens in the privacy of any home, even more complicated a problem is how to combat emotional or psychological abuse that is not covered under the criminal justice
system. To confuse the issue even further, society sets boundaries that can be ambiguous.

In most cases of domestic violence, psychological abuse
is almost always a prerequisite to what finishes in violent
assault. In that regard, there are certain techniques batterers
use that usually end in physical violence. The following are
examples compiled by Common Purpose, a batterers' treatment program run by Mitchell Rottenberg in Quincy, Massachusetts, and connected to the Quincy Criminal Courts, to
determine typical abusive behavior that does not necessarily
fall under criminal assault. Common Purpose uses these examples to assess the danger level of the batterer as well as to
understand the general relationship he has with his victim.

Before the violence begins, a common feature of most
abusive households is secrecy. The batterer is able to control
his partner by keeping her isolated from outside influences,
which include friends and family. As a consequence, the
victim not only appears withdrawn but also chooses to isolate
herself, feeling shame and a lack of self-esteem because she
is unable to control her own life. As long as the victim remains under the batterer's control, the abuse usually doesn't
escalate into violence. When physical violence begins, it is
most often because the batterer is forced to step up his
controlling behavior to keep his partner "in line."

Isolation of the victim can be achieved also by accusing
her of infidelity, as well as of neglecting the children. What
these techniques accomplish is that the victim usually, for
the sake of maintaining peace at home, curtails her activities
and limits her contacts with friends, family, and coworkers.
Again, if the victim rebels, the batterer will control her behavior with harsher measures.

Common Purpose has also compiled a set of conditions

when certain personality traits or addictions of the batterer indicate a potential for lethal violence.

Batterers who tend toward extreme jealousy and possessiveness are especially dangerous. Isolating the victim from all outside contact is a key trait of a possessive batterer who believes that his partner doesn't have the right to end a relationship until he is ready to end it. The batterer who falls into this category may appear to be obsessed with his partner or suffer from a fear of abandonment, but these are only excuses for what is potentially a lethal outcome.

When the batterer has access to or actually possesses weapons or has used weapons in the past, he should be considered capable of committing murder. Verbal reference to a weapon should be considered as a direct threat, and no less dangerous than actually pointing a gun at the victim.

If a batterer has a history of substance abuse, he is considered an increased risk to the victim. A prior record of substance abuse should be considered potentially lethal, since such men are "recovering" rather than "cured" of drug or alcohol addictions. While not every substance abuser is a batterer, every batterer with an alcohol or drug addiction should be considered even more dangerous, since drugs and alcohol lower his level of inhibition.

If a batterer threatens to kill his partner or her children, or to commit suicide, his threats should, in all cases, be taken seriously. A high proportion of lethal assaults are preceded by lethal threats. Batterers do not commonly kill themselves without first attempting to kill at least one family member.

Batterers who have committed any previous sexual assaults against their victims are almost twice as likely to commit a dangerous or lethal act of violence than those who have not.

A significant proportion of murders and attempted murders of intimate partners are preceded by stalking, reading mail, listening in on phone calls, or other acts of monitoring or surveillance. Turning up unexpectedly, or "just by coincidence," at places where the victim is should also be considered an implied threat. Surveillance can also be carried out by friends of the batterer or by people whom he has hired.

A pattern of increased violence, in both frequency and severity, is a clear danger sign. Each time the batterer commits a more serious act without significant consequences, he feels emboldened to take the next step up the ladder.

Attempts to terrorize the victim, often associated with previous incidents of surveillance and escalation, are clear warning signs. Killing pets, describing violent fantasies in gory detail, cutting out newspaper articles about killings and leaving them around the house, and holding the victim from an upper-story window are all common examples of these tactics. The batterer may deliberately act crazy or unpredictable as a ploy to terrorize the victim.

Statistically, the best indicator of future violence is past violence. A batterer who has been violent often, two to three times a month, or has been severely violent, so that his victim required hospitalization, is at high risk to commit a final or lethal act in the future.

Evidence of hatred of women by a male batterer has been linked to a propensity to commit murder or other dangerous assaults against his partner. This extreme misogyny can produce violent statements that are made against women as a group, such as, "If I don't kill you, I'll kill someone else, because some bitch is gonna pay for what you've done."

Certain mental health problems are linked to increased likelihood to commit a lethal assault. The signs are delusional fears and severe depression caused by a major loss, such as the loss of a job or the death of a parent.

When it comes to accusations of infidelity, most abusive men who become obsessively jealous will monitor their partner's activity, a practice that escalates when the victim leaves or attempts to end the relationship. According to a study conducted by Daniel Jay Sonkin and Lenore Walker and published in their book *The Male Batterer, a Treatment Approach* in 1985, "following the victim, interrogating her children, eavesdropping on telephone conversations, and making frequent telephone calls to monitor her activities is a sign of pathological jealousy that is not evident in all men who abuse their partners. The presence of this kind of behavior, however, should be seen as a significant indicator of potential homicidality. Closely related to this extreme possessiveness is the abuser's unwillingness to accept the end of the relationship and as a consequence his loss of control over his partner." Walker and Sonkin conclude in their thesis that "women who do leave this kind of abuser are more likely to be murdered."

Yet, after having written many books on the subject strongly linking certain harassing and abusing acts to potential homicides, Lenore Walker agreed to work as a consultant for the defense in the O. J. Simpson trial.

Interviewed by Larry King after she went public with the information that she had been hired to work for Simpson, Walker explained: "You cannot say because anyone batters a woman, that person would kill them. You have to have evidence."

In response to King's direct question concerning Simpson's stalking of his ex-wife, which, according to Walker's book, could indicate a potentially lethal situation, she replied, "There is no profile of a batterer . . . We say to women if that's the kind of behavior that's going on, you better get some protection because the situation reaches a lethal level of danger. We still couldn't say that person would kill."

While Lenore Walker could not predict definitively which batterer will become a murderer, what studies in her books indicate is that women who are ultimately murdered by their partners have usually suffered days, weeks, months, or years of physical or emotional abuse.

Most experts agree that the batterer is capable of distinguishing between right and wrong, moral and immoral behavior. It is simply that old habits take a painfully long time to die. Society has been giving the "king of the castle" wide latitude to act like a lunatic as long as he confines his kicks and punches to his wife or girlfriend. Often, the same man who beats up his partner is an otherwise decent and charitable human being, politically outraged concerning human rights abuses in foreign countries, or someone who, in his past, has personally struggled with civil rights reform at home. There is nothing necessarily wrong with the thought process of the batterer, except that somewhere in his mind he still considers it his male right to use whatever means necessary to maintain his historical position of power.

FIFTEEN

A Window of Safety

OVER THE YEARS, the system has tried everything to stop men from battering. Men have been sent to therapy, educational groups, and jail. Nothing has proved successful over the long term because of a dearth of comprehensive follow-up programs. This lack of long-term education is also to blame for not changing behavior patterns in individual men, as well as not setting social limits for little boys so they can learn how to behave with the opposite sex, how to deal with their anger, and how to solve disputes or even differences of opinion before they escalate into violence.

Overheard in New York City on a subway train, two young men were talking matter-of-factly, not at all boasting or bragging, when young man number one said, "You know, I had to get my girl in line the other day." Young man number two answered, "Yeah, I know what you mean; I have to do that too once in a while."

Instead of commiserating, young man number two should have responded, "What do you mean, get her in line? If you do that kind of thing, I can't hang out with you anymore."

The philosophy of the program that Phyllis Frank runs in Rockland County is similar to that of Emerge. Frank says, "The only way to stop domestic violence is to make it as uncomfortable as possible for men to continue the abuse.

Society must begin to look at domestic violence with dis-
dain.''

District Attorney Janine Ferris Pirro points out that
there have been several long-term social programs that have
proven successful in a relatively short period of time. ''What
we've done with drinking and driving, and smoking in public
places,'' Pirro says, ''has made a huge change in a social
problem in a very short period of time. And we accomplished
this primarily because people took individual stands on the
issue and put pressure on others within the group to go
along with those changes. Since we're all social creatures,
barring the exceptions, who are sociopaths, and since the
batterer isn't a sociopath, he, like the rest of us, needs group
approval. When the group forbids certain kinds of behavior,
even the batterer will comply, perhaps less out of moral
conviction than a need to be accepted.''

Judge Knaplund adds, ''While we can't abandon the
legal response and responsibility, neither will work until
there are social limits placed on this issue, not until friends
and neighbors refuse to tolerate that behavior, which includes jokes about women and pornography. In certain social and economic circles, I firmly believe that there are men
who would like to stop battering but they're afraid they'd be
in a minority and therefore ostracized. We have to turn peer
pressure around and put it where it belongs, which means if
a man knows that he's going to jail for the night or the
weekend and he knows when he comes out that his friends
won't feel sorry for him or treat him like a hero, only then
will jail have more meaning.''

According to David Adams, there have been many men
who have passed through the doors of Emerge in the nineteen years that he has been running the organization who
can't believe that they could have been chastised or arrested
for such a ''minor thing'' as wife battering. ''Whether these
guys are mandated by the courts or come voluntarily to save
their relationships,'' Adams relates, ''so few are prepared to
accept the responsibility that what they have done is criminal. The problem with this attitude is that it isn't limited to

those men who participate in a batterers' group, but rather, it's an attitude that permeates society at large."

What is interesting about observing a group session of batterers is that hardly any man participating in a program, regardless of what had been his specific offense, will ever characterize himself as a man who beats his wife or girl-friend. The propensity to minimize his problem of abuse is comparable to an alcoholic's denial of his patterns of drinking. In each case, the batterer and the alcoholic compare their abuse or their drinking to the worst-case scenario. In the case of the alcoholic, it would be to a "Bowery bum"; in the case of the batterer, it would be to a man who murdered his partner.

In order for a man to qualify for admission into a batterers' intervention program, there are specific criteria.

Lucy Friedman runs Victim Services in New York City and, under its auspices, a batterers' treatment program that is connected to the courts. She explains, "Any man who is referred by the court after he has been judged guilty of spousal abuse cannot have psychiatric, drug, or alcohol problems unless they've already initiated treatment before they enter our program." Also, according to the rules in New York State, defendants with three or more bench warrants (for not appearing in court or for violating an order of protection) are also not accepted in the program, nor are those men whose battering convictions constitute felony convictions.

The rules are dangerous, since often the men excluded need to be monitored as much as or more than those who commit more minor offenses. If the usual batterers' intervention programs are reluctant to take such cases, additional programs should be created that separate substance abusers and felons from the others.

The batterers' treatment program in New York under the auspices of Victim Services is run by Warren Price, an expert in domestic violence and the male batterer. The program, which was just extended from ten weeks to six months, functions directly in conjunction with the New York City

Department of Probation as well as with the courts. When a man is judged guilty of spousal assault and remanded into the program instead of serving time in jail, he can be eligible for an adjournment in contemplation of dismissal (ACD) if he follows the conditions of his parole. Another advantage of this program and of others like it is that the batterer is assured that, if he complies and attends the sessions for the time prescribed by the court, and behaves himself so that there are no further complaints sworn against him for violence, his arrest record for that particular offense can be expunged.

As for payment, there is a sliding fee schedule, from $20 to $50 for each session, for each batterer. As in the program in Lawrence, if a man is indigent, the fee is waived under the condition that he perform a certain number of hours of community service in lieu of monetary payment.

In every batterers' treatment program throughout the country, participants who are given that opportunity instead of jail are made to understand that the reason is not that the crime is viewed as less serious than stranger assault, but, rather, the special relationship they have with their victim.

The Quincy court, in this particular case, maintains that under certain circumstances, depending on the seriousness of the crime and whether the perpetrator was a first-time offender, it is more effective not to incarcerate the batterer. In those cases, the judge determines that remanding him into a program prevents his family from being penalized further when he is unable to work and support them. These are the cases that justify adopting the policies used in the Ontario experiment, in which victims are consulted as to the extent and method of punishing their assailants. Curiously, despite the possibility of avoiding incarceration, there are some men who prefer jail over any treatment program. "These are the men who are so full of rage," Gaudette explains, "and in so much denial that they refuse to be placed in any 'fucking program.' " They would rather do six months in jail than a year or two of probation.

Brian Kean is a young practicing physician who has been in the program in Lawrence for six months. In Brian's case, he was not remanded there through the courts but went on his own volition after his wife threatened to leave him if he didn't get some kind of help. According to Brian's pregnant wife, Bonnie, he has battered and psychologically abused her for five out of the six years they have been married. As of last week, however, Bonnie decided that she wanted to separate, despite Brian's participation in the program, because, in her own words, "I've got a lot of memories that just won't heal." Brian is angry. "We had a deal," he says. "I promised to do this program and she promised to stay."

Douglas Gaudette interprets Bonnie's decision and Brian's reaction differently. "Brian is under the delusion that he is owed a reward for not being violent, that going to group is such a terrible sacrifice for him that Bonnie owes him not only to keep her promise but also to show him how grateful she is for his effort."

Brian's attitude of entitlement is another example of the batterer feeling victimized by his partner and by the system. When asked, Brian clearly states that he is being held accountable for something that he intuitively believed was allowed. "My job as a man to run my home is no different than my obligation to earn a living, file income taxes, and fulfill my responsibility to protect my wife."

The stories vary and the details of abuse are all different, as are the techniques of the batterer and the reactions of his victim. What is not different in almost every case is the way the batterer assesses the judicial system, as well as his perception of himself as a victim, his attitude toward women, and his perception of how, if ever, he ended up on the wrong side of the law.

The most effective course of treatment, according to experts, is to remand the batterer into an alternative-to-violence treatment program under the auspices of the judicial system as a condition of his parole or probation. Yet even with those compulsory programs, which in some instances include concurrent jail time, the belief is that the batterer will never be cured. Why, then, are batterers' programs so highly recommended?

While the purpose of any batterers' treatment program is to force the batterer to take responsibility for his violent actions, the primary consideration is to provide a window of safety for the victim. The theory is that the time the batterer is in the program is a block of time the victim can use to make an escape plan or explore her options. Or, if the victim needs ongoing care, most programs will put her in touch with social, legal, or medical services available to her, as well as advocates who can help her rebuild her life. In most cases, the victim will even be warned that any short-term changes that are evident in the batterer's behavior should not create the illusion that he is really changing, but that rather, in all probability, he will revert to his previous violent behavior after he completes the program. The most positive result of the program, for those batterers who will never change, is that, at least during the time they are participating, an impression has been made. Suddenly, these men realize, often for the first time in their lives, that society can and will respond to unacceptable behavior, even within the privacy of their own homes.

While it is rare, a small percentage of batterers do change, after participating in a program for one or two years, by learning new behavior. Still, people like Douglas Gaudette, Phyllis Frank, and Judge Virginia Knaplund insist that batterers' intervention programs will begin to show higher rates of success only when society changes its view concerning domestic violence.

Generally, the approach to any permanent change in batterers' behavior is the same as the approach to sex offenders. Sex offenders who are remanded to prison are also required to attend structured support groups while incarcerated, which last usually for a year. If the offender is released before five years, courts will also insist that he attend treatment programs on the outside for a time equal to his jail sentence. Sex offenders are made to understand that they will never be cured but that, in order not to reoffend, they must adhere to a "safety plan" that will make them aware for the rest of their lives that at any time they could slip back into sexually abusive behavior.

Batterers are also taught a safety plan in every intervention program, which helps them to recognize symptoms of impending violent behavior. Those circumstantial cues are sweaty palms, increased heart rate, heavy breathing, clenching fists, pacing, grinding teeth. The men are taught to pause and be aware of what is happening to their bodies at the moment they are in the middle of an exchange with their partners. They are also taught at that moment to step back and take what is called a "time-out," a pause for reflection as well as time to gather control. During that time-out, the rules are that they can't drink, drive, or take drugs. What is most frequently recommended is that they take a walk around the block or retreat into another room before they resume any conversation or contact with their partners.

District Attorney Janine Ferris Pirro explains, "In those cases where the abuser has not reoffended, it's not that the violence has disappeared, but rather that he's learned techniques to control his anger and refrain from lashing out physically."

Mitchell Rottenberg, who is the director of Common Purpose in Quincy, Massachusetts, agrees: "The batterer's behavior patterns can be changed by monitoring him and teaching him alternative ways to control himself, but overall I think that treatment of men who batter is in its infancy, similar to how sex offenders were treated fifteen or twenty years ago."

While most batterers' treatment programs are offered as part of the conditions of parole after a man has already been convicted of domestic abuse, Phyllis Frank explains that at the Rockland County program she has directed for the past ten years, that is not the case. "Never in lieu of jail," Frank maintains adamantly. "If a man is going to jail, he doesn't come here. This is a program designed for men who, before we existed, violated an order of protection and were only warned never to do that again. Our program was set up in lieu of *nothing*. Before we existed, nothing happened to the hundreds and thousands of men who committed a crime so heinous that if the victim was a stranger, they would have been tossed in jail for a very long time.''

Fernando Mederes is a doctoral candidate in clinical psychology at Harvard University, with a subspecialty in domestic violence. He is also a counselor at Common Purpose. Mederes believes that not only in situations of extreme violence, but even in circumstances of social mores and customs, the batterer is treated differently than perpetrators of felonies or misdemeanors in stranger crime. According to Mederes, who agrees with Phyllis Frank, that attitude means that all alternative-to-violence programs are an improvement in a system that did virtually nothing unless the victim was grievously injured or murdered.

''My argument would be that we need to be very blunt about this,'' Mederes begins. ''If someone was walking down the street naked in Boston, there would be a response in a variety of ways. Somebody would call the police, an ambulance would be called in, and I'm sure the police or the ambulance personnel would give the guy what we call in this state a 'pink slip,' which is an involuntary-commitment paper. The point is that it's not all right to walk down the street naked, even if it's summertime, because it's in violation of a rule that everyone agrees with and accepts, which is defined in the law as disturbing the peace. Hopefully, we'll get to the same place as it concerns domestic violence, where if we know that someone is being battered, it will be considered a violation of a rule that everyone agrees with, which is legally defined as criminal assault. In the consciousness of people, if there's a brawl going on in a private home and someone knocks on the door and the woman answers and says that she doesn't need or want the police, that there's nothing going on, and even if her teeth are missing and she's bleeding, the police or anybody else is going to back away. As it stands now, it's taboo to interfere, so it doesn't matter if there's a law on the books covering assault; it's somehow viewed as a different kind of assault when it hap-

pens in the privacy of someone's home. As for walking
naked, the law was generated because it offends the public,
so they're going to react. Domestic violence isn't even the
same thing as the civil rights movement, since integrating a
public school system is not the same as going into someone's
home to stop certain behavior. There must be long-term
education as well as short-term solutions, except the short
term is more critical since women are getting beaten, terrorized, and killed every day."

Judge Virginia Knaplund believes that all abusers violate
an invisible boundary that exists between all human beings.
"If he violates it once," Judge Knaplund explains, "it becomes a customary outlet for him, as opposed to other people, where that boundary is a given. For the batterer, it takes
a conscious and inordinate effort on his part not to cross
that line."

There are no uniform rules or format for batterers' intervention programs. On the basis of philosophy, funding,
the extent to which they are connected to the courts, and
the degree to which they have victim contact, each functions
differently. As a result, each also has varying degrees of success—measured solely by protecting victims and efficiency—
depending on the batterer's behavior during and after his
time in the program.

Specifically, some programs are less willing to accept
excuses if a man misses a meeting, while others will concentrate on the overall political and social problem of abuse,
while still others will focus on the batterer's monetary responsibility as a sign of commitment, while others have little
or no follow-up and contact with the victim and instead consider role playing as a viable substitute. Different as well in
each program is the required length of time that the batterer
must participate, along with specific requirements under the
law in any particular state for expunging his criminal record.
Each program, therefore, compiles an individual set of statistics to indicate the rate of recidivism, on the basis of its
own research and statistics; this ultimately produces many
different results throughout the country.

The main goal of the batterers' program at the Lawrence Mental Health Center is victim safety. Working with men and monitoring their activities is achieved not only by dealing with them in group situations but, more crucial, by having regular contact with their victims. The other policies of the program are to maintain close contact and frequent dialogue with the criminal justice system, human service providers, and shelters and to teach offenders alternatives to coercive, dominating, and violent behavior in intimate relationships.

The program philosophy is as follows: violence is intentional; battering is a system of abusive behavior that is used to maintain control over one's partner; our culture has sanctioned men's use of violence to maintain dominance in relationships with wives/partners; individual men can change, or at least learn new behavior and techniques for nonviolent confrontations, and except in cases of self-defense, there are always alternatives to violence.

The program content is as follows: participants must take total responsibility for their behavior; confrontation of beliefs and attitudes is central to this work; tactics used to control must be eliminated for battering to cease; minimization and denial will be challenged by group facilitators; group facilitators will assist men to develop relationships with women based on equality by teaching skills and alternative behavior.

And finally: the program will not compete with shelter programs for funding; battered women's advocates should be involved in development of program policies related to partner safety; communication procedures with the shelter will be in place relative to partner safety; partners should be notified and offered detailed information about the offender; programs should not elicit information until women have had an opportunity to explore safety options.

Before any man is accepted into the program, a contract must be signed by him which states: he must follow all rules; acts of violence and violations of court orders will be reported to the courts; program participants must sign release-of-information and program-contract agreements. (That last point is also crucial, since it allows the program to have all police records and court transcripts concerning the batterer's history of abuse.)

Among the consequences of breach of that contract are: the participant will be suspended, and he will be reported to his probation officer; volunteers will not be treated differently than court-mandated participants; program staff will testify at revocation or review hearings regarding violation of program rules or a reoccurrence of violence.

Finally, concerning an assessment of lethality of each batterer: all past and present threats will be explored by program staff; fantasies of homicide or suicide will be thoroughly examined, and the participant will be monitored; men who are *obsessive* about their partners will be considered "red flag" cases.

The program in Lawrence is more severe than the programs in New York and Boston concerning men who miss meetings. The rules are that unless the participant has a written excuse from a doctor or a coroner (in the event of a death in the family), he is automatically remanded to jail and his eligibility to participate in the program is cancelled. Gaudette explains, "Our group is specifically for talking about issues of domestic violence, which means if any of these men commit a breaking-and-entering over the weekend, we tell them to deal with that in another area, just as we insist they deal with their drug and alcohol problems in another forum. They're only allowed to be here if they concentrate on domestic violence, attend the sessions, pay the sliding fee, or show up for their community service work. What we're trying to impress upon these men is that just because we don't deal with other crimes doesn't mean the system views domestic violence as a lesser crime. It's a crime like anything else."

Unlike the program in New York under the auspices of Victim Services, if men have a substance abuse problem, they are accepted in the batterers' program on the condition that they treat their drug or alcohol dependency simultaneously in another forum.

According to Gaudette, counselors will and have testified against the batterer for admissions he has made during group sessions. "We've called the police in during meetings and told them to lock a guy up," Gaudette says, "so we clearly take a very hard line that this behavior is not to be tolerated."

Ellen Ferland, who works with Douglas Gaudette, adds, "We're not providing therapy for these men; we're providing intervention to make them stop battering their partners, at least for the time that they're in our program. What we're aiming for is safety and not his marvelous insights into what makes him a batterer or the other problems he has in his life. If it happens, that's great, but that's not our goal. Our goal is to stop him from physically abusing his partner or violating an order of protection or whatever crime he has committed that landed him here for the time that he is here, so his victim can live peacefully, without fear. After that, he can work on other issues, and if he needs therapy for drugs, alcohol, or a lousy childhood, we'll recommend a therapist. Our program would be a success if these guys never abused their partners again but, instead, went out and robbed a bank."

Further, in the program in Lawrence, the courts make all records available for review and allow the counselors access to the batterer's full history of abuse, alcohol, drugs, and other criminal activity, which would include the batterer's propensity for or use of any weapons. "Without police records," Gaudette claims, "we would have to take the word of every batterer who comes into our program."

According to Gaudette, since the vast majority of these men claim that they are innocent, victimized by the system, and, in fact, victims themselves of violence at the hands of their partners, most of the time spent in session would be lost deciphering what exactly is the truth. Also, since victim safety is paramount, having the police report in hand means that the victim can be warned to take appropriate measures when, in the opinion of the counselors, the batterer's behavior shows signs of erupting into violence. "We have a basis for comparison," Gaudette explains, "so we can and will warn the victim of any secrets that the batterer is keeping that could affect her safety and well-being, as well as warning the batterer's probation officer."

The people at Lawrence maintain that the only way to assure victim safety is to monitor the batterer's behavior toward his partner for as long as he participates in the program. "We consider ourselves an extension of the court and the probation system," Gaudette says, "which is the reason why we'll report any noncompliance to probation. If, in the process, we help the batterer learn new, nonviolent behavior, that's an unexpected advantage, but we don't count on it, since we believe battering is behavior that can be managed but never cured."

By keeping in touch with the victim with the batterer's knowledge, the legal system not only is able to monitor the batterer's progress but also makes him aware, often for the first time in his life, that when it comes to abusing his family, there are no longer any secrets. The batterer is, therefore, forced to confront the harsh reality that his behavior in the privacy of his home will have a direct impact on his eligibility to stay out of jail. The victim is protected as well, even if the batterer believes she has turned him in, since he knows that from the moment he is brought into court and either remanded to jail or only into a batterers' intervention program, he is forever a name and number in a computer. He is made aware that even if his criminal record is expunged, as it concerns domestic violence, his movements are monitored, police will routinely check his house, and all orders of protection filed against him are listed with every police officer in the county.

Gaudette's program in Lawrence is one of the most efficient and successful and should serve as a model for programs in place throughout the country, all of which must be connected to *all* criminal and family courts. Yet even in Lawrence, Massachusetts, a small community where it is possible to bring all the systems together without enormous budgetary constraints, there are still problems when it comes to dealing with the victims of this crime. "We are often met with fierce resistance and denial on the part of the victim for many reasons," Gaudette admits.

Just as the batterer draws limits when it comes to abuse, the victim also sets standards for what she considers to be abuse that warrants outside intervention. There are some women who don't consider it abuse if they are only called names, others who don't think being pushed or shoved constitutes abuse, while others judge abuse by its frequency rather than its severity. In every case, it is a matter of threshold and degree, depending on the individual's cultural, emotional, and physical tolerance. Here again, the question of potential lethality comes into focus if authorities or agencies continue to view domestic violence as an individual issue confined to the privacy of the home or a tacit agreement between victim and batterer.

The issue of identifying abuse even by the victim herself is a problem that has its roots in what society considers appropriate male/female roles. Jonathan Cohen, from the Rockland County Batterers' Program, maintains that too many times victims of domestic abuse are encouraged by their priests, pastors, and rabbis to go home and try harder because *they're* not doing something right. "If there was an effective batterers' intervention program in every town in the country," Cohen says, "with a coordinated response within the judicial system and the social service sector, men's violence would still not end until we completely transformed Hollywood, Madison Avenue, and the entire political and economic system, which continues to reward—disproportionately—men over women. What we do is paint women in a victimlike state or in a state where they are easily preyed upon, and that's precisely what we need to change."

A direct fallout of society's reluctance to condemn certain abusive behavior that does not fall within the context of the criminal justice system is often the victim's being unsure if she is living in an abusive situation. What is needed is a more comprehensive definition of domestic violence that includes abuse that is not technically covered under any existing judicial system. As it stands now, society has created a

response to this crime that is based on the degree or severity
of the violence inflicted. Instead, society should recognize
that men who end up murdering their partners began by
"only" abusing them verbally.

SIXTEEN

The Tragic Genius
of Violence

A COUPLE NEWLY MARRIED went to a Thanksgiving dinner at the home of the bride's parents. Something happened during the course of the visit that displeased the groom; perhaps his new wife made a comment that embarrassed him or perhaps she wasn't paying enough attention to him. Instead of reacting quietly or not reacting at all, the man waited until they were outside the apartment house and standing near their car. There, he started to punch and kick his new wife, eventually pinning her down on the sidewalk, where he repeatedly smashed her head into the pavement. He probably would have killed her except that a couple happened along and stopped him.

For the rest of their ten-year marriage, the man never touched his wife again. Every time she disobeyed or displeased him, or when he wanted to control her behavior, all he needed to say were two words, "Remember Thanksgiving."

Domestic abuse isn't necessarily a lifetime of beatings. For some women, it is a life spent in fear of the men they love. Fernando Mederes calls these men "domestic terrorists."

"Even if they committed a physical act of violence only once," Mederes contends, "their form of abuse can be even worse because the techniques are so subtle."

Advocates for battered women maintain that abusive men do more than merely commit isolated acts of physical violence. Interviews of battered women have shown time and again that domestic violence is a "cohesive pattern of coercive controls that include verbal abuse, threats, psychological manipulation, sexual coercion, and control over economic resources." It is a definition that should be incorporated in the definition used by the American Medical Association.

Lydia Martinez, the policewoman and specialist in domestic violence who works out of the Chief of Patrol's Office in New York City, says, "Every woman must recognize that from the moment her partner calls her names, it's a major red signal that must be addressed. What the victim accepts, she condones, and that includes verbal as well as physical abuse. The more produced the level of power between two people, the more important it is to address unacceptable behavior, or that behavior becomes the norm."

Warren Price adds, "Emotional abuse isn't covered under our criminal justice system because our system was designed for one-time stranger crime."

Jonathan Cohen agrees and goes even further when he says, "Not only is [verbal abuse] as potentially lethal as physical abuse, but in fact, the most fundamental misunderstanding about battering is that it usually doesn't involve physical violence at all. Most men who batter are not physically violent each and every time, simply because they don't have to be. They're able to gain control over their partner by verbal abuse or financial deprivation."

One man in the Quincy group admitted that causing his partner emotional pain was easy; most of the time, he didn't have to move from his place in front of the television. "I just sit there," he explained, "and the abuse just blows out of my mouth."

To dispel the myth that all domestic violence is physical, it must be understood that men batter on a "need-to-batter" basis. If the batterer can control his partner with a small amount of coercion or force, there is no need for him to escalate that abuse until it is physical. The batterer's reasoning is not unlike advice given by physicians who caution that using antibiotics randomly to cure a sore throat renders them ineffective when they are needed to cure strep.

According to Judith Kahan, "By the time a woman arrives at a shelter with black-and-blue marks or fractures, she has no idea that she has been the victim of emotional abuse for months and sometimes even years. If women aren't able to identify emotional abuse when they're living with it and are its target, how are they supposed to help themselves to get out before they're killed?"

Kahan tells the story about the woman who arrived at her shelter, terrified of getting into a bathtub. "She couldn't explain why until we had talked about it for several weeks," Kahan explains, "and suddenly she remembered." According to the woman, every time she used to get into the bath, her husband would come into the bathroom and hold her head under the water until she almost drowned. It took a while for the woman to unlearn her conditioned terror of bathing.

If society is offended by a naked man strolling down the street even in the summertime, why isn't society equally offended or outraged by a man who abuses, intimidates, threatens, or terrorizes his partner psychologically? In the case of the naked man, he is arrested not because he is considered a potential rapist but because he is disturbing the peace, the sensibilities of the public at large. Since it has been proven that men who murder their partners have a history of prior abuse, beginning with verbal abuse, why should the police wait to intervene only after the batterer has physically assaulted or murdered?

The problem with the legal response to this crime is that there are so many obstacles to arresting a man who has physically abused his partner that intervening in cases of verbal abuse as a preventive measure is a distant dream. The problem of enforcing legal penalties on someone who does not actually break the law goes against everything that is held sacred in a democratic system. Yet there are ways to achieve this dream without compromising basic human rights.

Intervening in cases of verbal or psychological abuse between intimate partners should be done in the form of a warning, equal in severity to a citation for jaywalking, that obliges the abuser to appear in court and pay a fine. Even then, his name should be entered in the same computerized system that contains all names of batterers, including men who have participated in batterers' intervention programs and men accused and acquitted of battering who have attended educational programs.

Emotional or psychological abuse is a very sophisticated technique that can be more dangerous than a beating because it has the potential to go unpunished forever. Many of the experts cited above agree that it is a technique that some batterers are learning is as effective as using violence to control and coerce their partners, while remaining within the boundaries of legal behavior. "As the judicial system is taking this crime more seriously where there are more severe penalties," Judge Knaplund explains, "some batterers are becoming more savvy and sophisticated by using methods which keep them out of jail."

In reaction to these new techniques, according to Ellen Ferland, victims are more fearful, more terrorized, oppressed, and frustrated because there are no laws covering this particular type of abuse. Even more disturbing is that this type of abuse can be only an allusion to a one-time abusive incident, as in "Remember Thanksgiving." A gesture that evokes the memory of a single violent event can be sufficient for the batterer to get his message across.

A man once stabbed his partner during an argument. From that day on, he never touched her again. Whenever there was a conflict or disagreement, the man merely took out a pocketknife and cleaned his fingernails, whereupon she became instantly terrorized.

Fernando Mederes and Mitchell Rottenberg, both of Common Purpose, follow the basic principles not only of Emerge in Boston but also of the Duluth Domestic Violence Intervention Program in Minnesota, whose thesis is that abuse is ingrained, in one form or the other, in all men.

Rottenberg explains, "I don't say that abuse equals violence, because not all men are violent, but men act in ways which are more male, which is a male thing and which women recognize. A man doesn't have to be physically violent with his partner for her to know that he has that potential. Chances are she has seen other men who were imposing, dominating, threatening, intimidating, and abusive, so even if her current partner does nothing more than raise his voice, it might trigger something in her."

"Piggybacking" is an expression used frequently in group sessions with batterers at Common Purpose. According to Mederes and Rottenberg, it is a technique that the batterer uses so that an action or word will reverberate in his partner, making it unnecessary the next time to recreate that action or repeat that word; a look will suffice, or a gesture; or the way he stands, sits, or raises an arm or an eyebrow is enough to gain control of or instill fear in another person.

Fernando Mederes explains, "While I don't think all men are abusive, I do believe that all men piggyback. If a man is with a partner who's been abused before, just doing something that seems innocuous on the surface may have a very powerful effect on her."

This is what Machiavelli, on a more macro scale, called the "tragic genius of violence," the way one act of violence can reverberate within a system or in a person endlessly, making it so easy to evoke terror so subtly. It calls to mind the work of Ivan Pavlov, the Russian physiologist, whose experiments showed that dogs, by merely smelling or seeing food, produced a copious flow of gastric juices, proving his theory of conditioned reflexes.

David Adams and his colleagues at Emerge define domestic violence as any act that causes the victim to do something she does not want to do, prevents her from doing something she does want to do, or causes her in either case to be fearful of her partner. "There are so many cases that fit that definition," Adams explains, "that it has become almost impossible to separate controlling, or emotional intimidation, which is a subtle variation of that same violence, from physical assault, which is technically covered under the law."

Domestic violence can be a way of life for anyone—victim or batterer. While it takes only luck—bad luck—to get into an abusive relationship, it can take years of concerted effort to get out, either because the victim is unaware that she is living with a batterer or because society has not constructed sufficient barriers to protect her or extricate her from a situation from which she can't get out on her own.

Equality and freedom from harm are two of the most basic values found in any democratic society. Every individual has the right to control the money that he or she earns; to refuse sex at any time; to be free from threats and fear; to be safe from violence and other mistreatment; to leave a place or relationship at will; to receive assistance from social service agencies and the police if needed; to request that the court prosecute any criminal who inflicts harm upon them. While all of those points are supposedly foregone conclusions when it comes to protecting citizens in our society, they are not foregone conclusions when it comes to protecting victims of crimes that are committed by someone they know or have known intimately.

Ann Ring is a twenty-four-year-old African American woman who currently lives in a shelter in Brooklyn with her infant son, Jason. At the time of the interview, Ann had been running away from her baby's father for four months and in the shelter only for two weeks. Now that she is safely settled, she says she can smile again because she is no longer afraid of getting beaten or killed.

The violence began when she was four months pregnant and paying room and board to live with her boyfriend in his parents' house. "I was getting $150 a month in public assistance and paying them $125," Ann explains, "which only left me $25. Thank God I had food stamps."

Ann is no different from any other woman who falls in love and wants to make a relationship work, which sometimes includes being blind to her partner's faults and defects. What made Ann more vulnerable perhaps was that she was all alone in the world; her parents were both dead, and she had no skills or training to get a job. When she met Randy, all she wanted was a stable relationship and the permission to call his parents "Mom" and "Dad." "I explained to Randy's mother that I needed a mother," Ann says, "because my own mother died when I was very small and I wanted her to be the mother I never had." What Ann wanted more than anything else was to belong to a family.

"Randy started sleeping with a neighbor right after I got pregnant," Ann says, "and when I confronted him, he beat me in front of his parents." Randy's mother advised Ann not to provoke her son. Apparently, she had seen his temper before, when his ex-wife landed in the hospital with a broken jaw and his last girlfriend miscarried when he kicked her down a flight of stairs.

When Ann was five months pregnant, she went to the hospital for a sonogram and was questioned about the bruises all over her body. "I was afraid to tell them what happened because Randy threatened to kill me if I did," Ann admits. On one occasion when Randy beat Ann, she tried to use the phone to call the police but his mother stopped her. "When you're beaten by a man, your heart is in so much pain," Ann says, "it hurts more inside than a person feels on the outside." After a while, Ann just used to sit in the corner of her bed all day and all night, looking out the window and up at the sky. "My first black eye was in 1994," Ann says; "my first split lip was with him too. I never had anything like that before."

Two weeks after her baby was born, Randy came into the room and announced that he wanted to have sex. He wasn't interested when Ann told him that the doctor had advised her to wait six weeks until she healed after childbirth. "Randy turned on the radio really loud so his parents wouldn't hear anything upstairs. Then he took me and bent me over my dresser and sodomized me. I was screaming because it hurt so much, but he wouldn't stop. My son was in his crib in the same room and he started screaming too."

When Randy finished, he opened a drawer in the dresser and took out a gun that a friend had given him, held Ann's face to force open her mouth, and stuck the gun inside. "I thought I was going to die," Ann says. Laughing, Randy finally put the gun away, but not before he told her that he never intended to kill her since the city didn't give public assistance to a dead woman.

Ann Ring lives in a democratic system where freedom and equality are inalienable rights. Yet she found herself in a situation where she had lost control of her money, was forced to have sex, was never free from threats, violence, or mistreatment, and was unable to leave at will or enlist the police to help her. Why should Ann Ring have had to suffer as she did? What could have been done to protect her? What could Ann have done to protect herself?

Once again, the question asked was why Ann didn't just leave. Perhaps Ann should never have moved in with Randy and his parents; perhaps she should have left before she got pregnant; perhaps she should have learned how to type, finished high school, or become an astronaut; perhaps she should have known better; perhaps she should have escaped instead of spending her days and nights on the bed; perhaps she should have refused to hand over her public assistance; perhaps she should have told the truth about her bruises when she went to that hospital for a sonogram; perhaps she should have gotten an abortion and moved to Paris.

Or perhaps Randy should have been arrested when he broke his ex-wife's jaw or kicked his ex-girlfriend down a flight of stairs. Perhaps his parents should have made an effort to educate their son that beating women was not allowed. Perhaps Randy's mother should have warned Ann or called the police herself. Perhaps Randy could have found his inner child or come to grips with his own victimization as a drug-addicted African American male who lacked the skills to make a decent life for himself, Ann, and their son. Perhaps, then, none of this would have happened to Ann.

What remains baffling is why Randy, with all his problems, addictions, and poor job training, was allowed to batter not one but three women—at least those were the victims of whom his mother was aware—causing the death of an un-born child, and as of this writing is still living in the same semidetached house with his parents and the upstairs neighbor, who moved downstairs and is currently pregnant with his baby. Something is very wrong with the system.

Everyone says the woman should have left. Charlotte Watson recalls, "I grew up with a grandmother and mother who were hairdressers and I saw them change women's hair color to help them get out of town."

If the batterer is asked why his partner didn't leave rather than take all his abuse, his answer will vary according to his social and economic position.

The most prevalent answer among blue-collar workers is that the system protects women. According to John Fartucci, a construction worker who is currently in the Lawrence Mental Health Clinic program for batterers, "Women don't leave because they want to 'stick it to men,' because women are just as violent."

Gabriel Luckhouse, a chiropractor who is a participant in the batterers' program in Lawrence, sees it differently. "I think that the way male supremacy works gives us [men] a menu of attitudes, behaviors, and options which allow us to take care of all our rage. Battering a partner gets rid of a lot of rage that might have nothing to do with the woman, but because of this convenient and socially approved menu, it becomes an expression, a way to feel powerful, in control, important, and central."

Still other men who are extremely successful and affluent have other opinions as to why their partners put up with the abuse.

Caroline Schneider's husband, the New York lawyer, explains why she decided not to leave him. "My wife wouldn't leave no matter what happened because she's too used to her standard of living. What are necessities to my wife are luxuries to anybody else."

There are so many different scenarios and reasons given when it comes to crimes committed between people who are or have been intimate that the conclusion remains that there is no predicting who, where, what, how, or why this crime happens. The most logical answers to the "why" are: men batter because they can usually get away with it; women stay, regardless of their economic or social level, because the system gives them so few alternatives and options.

The law technically covers each crime that was committed against Ann Ring, as well as against Randy's previous partners. Yet crimes that are committed in the context of a relationship or within the privacy of the home make those laws that work for everyone else rife with exceptions when it comes to women battered by men they live with or love. The reality is that rather than a separate or abstract entity of codes, rules, and regulations, people make up the law. And while people tend to view the law as a list of absolutes, the law is nothing more than an encodement of relative values held by society.

Domestic violence is not taught within those families where fathers beat mothers and sons. Frequently, when those sons are big enough, they are the ones who plant themselves between their parents to protect their mothers from abuse. This kind of violence against women is woven into the fabric of society. While unlearning this kind of behavior is a painful and lengthy process, relearning new behavior is even more difficult.

SEVENTEEN

The Group

WHEN ASHER FRAM moved to Boston, according to what he told friends and family, it was the only way he could put the tragedy of Emily Goldenberg behind him and get on with his life. Through his father, Fram had contacts within the Orthodox Jewish business community in Boston, and before making the move, he was able to land a good job with a major investment company. It took only two days for him to decide on an apartment, an airy two-bedroom flat that had views of the Charles River. With the help of the daughter of family friends, it took only a month for Asher to furnish the apartment exactly to his taste and begin that new life he so desperately wanted and felt he deserved.

As Fram told his family, within six months he had more than he ever dreamed: a good job, an apartment, and a fiancée named Deborah, the same young woman who had helped him fix up his flat when he first arrived.

The wedding was held in a suburb of Boston, where the bride lived with her family. In fact, the couple planned to move there after their honeymoon. They both felt that living in a suburb close to Deborah's family would allow them to keep their jobs when they started a family, since Deborah's parents would be close by to help with the children. With tears in his eyes, Asher made a toast at his wedding, "To

Deborah, who brings me enough joy to forget my sorrow."
The problem was that old habits die hard.

When Douglas Gaudette first received the police report
on Asher Fram, he was surprised. "This was a guy with three
master's degrees, in business administration, accounting,
and business management, who worked for a prestigious
investment company where he earned a hefty six-figure
salary."

The other information that Gaudette had on Fram was
his statement when the police arrested him in front of a
bank building. Fram's story was that he had met his wife at
the bank to discuss a matter of estate planning when an
argument broke out. According to Fram, the argument escalated after Deborah threw a set of financial papers at him
and raced out of the bank. Fram followed her. Witnesses
reported that near the parking lot, more heated words were
exchanged, culminating in Fram pushing Deborah down in
the pine mulch and holding her there facedown with his
foot firmly placed on the small of her back. With a twisted
ankle, covered with pine bark, Deborah began screaming
and crying in pain. Two men who happened to be across the
street saw the scene and raced over to subdue Asher.

Fram's version of why the men came running over, however, was quite different. According to what Fram told
Gaudette, the men had interfered because his wife is attractive and was wearing tight-fitting white slacks. "They came
over to check her out," Fram told Gaudette.

"For some reason," Gaudette adds, "it never occurred
to him that they came over because he was beating the shit
out of her, kicking her in the ribs, and at one point, grabbing
her hair and slamming her head repeatedly on the ground."

After Fram was hauled into court and charged with assault, his lawyer managed to negotiate six months' participation in the batterers' intervention program at the Lawrence
Mental Health Center instead of jail time. According to
Gaudette, during the first intake meeting when Fram entered the program, he insisted that it was the first time the
police had ever been involved with him in any incident of

domestic violence. But Gaudette already had Fram's entire police report in hand, which told quite a different story of his pattern of abuse at home. "Wrong," Gaudette says simply. "The police were involved on four previous occasions, and we had copies of all the police reports, including the incident when Fram threw a chicken around the house because he wasn't greeted by anyone when he came home."

Douglas Gaudette confronted Fram with that particular incident, as well as the incident when the police were called by a neighbor who heard Deborah's screams after Fram slammed a car door on her finger, which resulted in a compound fracture. Taken verbatim from the record, Fram's response was, "I didn't consider either incident to be a case of domestic abuse."

"You need to really define abuse because these men do lie," Gaudette explains. "They are classic manipulators; they minimize, deny, and victim-blame. If we were to spend all day talking to these guys about whether or not they should be in the program, that's all we'd be doing. Our feeling is that if they insist they shouldn't be here, we agree and tell them that the alternative to being here is jail, so good-bye."

Douglas Gaudette has compiled a list of tactics and excuses used by batterers in his program, as well as certain responses that he has trained his counselors to give. The following are some examples:

Denial. The batterer refuses to admit violent behavior by offering excuses. "I didn't do anything." "She just bruises easy." "I had my fist out and she ran into it."

Minimalization. The batterer admits less than what actually happened, making the assault sound trivial. "I just gave her a little push." "It was only a love tap." "Her ribs are just a little bruised, not broken."

Response. The batterer is told that he has already been found guilty in a court of law, but if he insists, he could request another hearing with the judge.

Counselors also give the batterer a detailed account of the abuse provided by the victim, as well as any hospital and police reports.

Focusing on intentions. The batterer defends his violence by attributing positive reasons for his behavior. "I was just trying to keep her from hurting herself." "She was so hysterical and yelling nonstop, so I slapped her to calm her down."

Response. The counselors point out that terror, fear, distrust, pain, injury, and destruction are the effects of violence. Even if his intentions are good, violence is never justified nor is it ever legal.

Victim blaming. The most popular excuse is that the victim is such a terrible person that she deserved whatever she got. The offender hopes that deflecting the blame will focus on the victim's behavior rather than on his misconduct. "I found her with another man." "She's a drunk, drug addict, bad mother, thief." "She assaulted me."

Response. A woman doesn't have to be Betty Crocker in order to avoid a beating. People do not have to earn the right to live a life free of violence and fear. Spousal abuse itself is illegal, just as bank robbery is illegal even if the perpetrator is poor or the bank cheated him on a mortgage.

Loss of control. "I'm not really responsible for what happened; I exploded, but it wasn't really me." If the batterer believes that his explanation has been accepted, he might go on to say, "I lost it, and the next thing I remember she was down and bleeding and screaming," or, "I saw a white (blue, yellow, red) light and blacked out. When I came to, she was lying on the ground."

Response. If the batterer is convinced that he really has no control over his actions, he should surrender himself immediately to authorities, since the batterers' program is totally useless.

The following questions might also be asked of

the batterer: "Do you get violent in the same way when a stranger gets you really upset, or your boss, for instance?" In other words, reacting violently is not an automatic response.

Provocation. The batterer claims that the victim drove him over the edge, which means that he is not responsible for his actions. "She made me do it." "She knew it was coming." "She baited me."

Response. No one has the ability to make anyone violent. People can hurt, frustrate, and anger other people, but there are many alternative ways to respond that don't involve violence.

Lack of money and time. The batterer claims that he cannot attend treatment sessions because he is too busy with his work or that he is unable to pay the sliding scale fee that most batterers' programs charge. The batterer may also claim that the victim assures him that he is fine now and doesn't need to continue the program. Or he may explain that he has a new partner who agrees with him that his former partner was just "out to get him."

Response. Most treatment programs provide for any indigent batterer to do a certain number of hours of community service in lieu of paying any monetary sliding scale fee. Also, it is crucial for any counselor, court appointed or otherwise, to keep in constant contact with former or present partners to determine whether or not the batterer has committed any repeat violent episodes.

After Fram had been in the program for six weeks, one of the counselors who was running his particular group learned from Deborah, during one of the routine victim-contact sessions, that Fram, in a fit of temper, had slammed his fist into the wall right next to Deborah's face. Deborah was immediately sorry that she said anything when she realized that her husband was about to be remanded to jail, his probation and the program no longer an option since he had violated the conditions of his parole. Deborah, three months pregnant, pleaded with a counselor to spare him since he had suffered enough trauma in his life and was obviously feeling pressured since they were expecting their first child. "She was defending him," the counselor relates. "It was incredible, as if he wasn't responsible for his actions because *they* were expecting a baby. As for the trauma in his life, we all have trauma is what I told Deborah." Still, Fram was granted another chance.

Over the next several weeks, the counselor met on a dozen occasions with Deborah Fram, who acknowledged that the situation was not improving. Little by little, Deborah began telling the story of Emily Goldenberg's "accidental" death, a fact that legally had no bearing on Fram's sentencing in Massachusetts since he had never been indicted in New York. "But suddenly it all made sense," the counselor says. "The fact that this man had a history of deadly violence explained his current behavior. Needless to say, regardless of Deborah's version of the story which Fram had told her, and notwithstanding the judicial outcome of that prior case, we had our own opinion about what really happened back in Brooklyn."

The weekly intake group in Lawrence, according to Douglas Gaudette, is the most difficult and challenging, since the men are all "raw." Gaudette explains, "It is their first experience with a group, the first time they are forced to confront their own violence in a setting which is mandated by the courts in lieu of their going to jail."

The eleven men who are seated in a circle around the room are encouraged by Gaudette and Ferland, who run the meeting, to refer to their partners by name in an effort to make them real human beings instead of abstractions that merit neither respect nor nonviolent treatment. The meeting begins with the men taking turns to discuss the incident that finally brought them to the attention of the courts. They are made to understand, however, that the counselors at Lawrence automatically assume that there were many other physically or emotionally abusive incidents that preceded their arrests. The men are also told that in case they have any idea about lying, their police records have been made available to the Lawrence Mental Health Center. "In other words," Gaudette explains, "these men are warned not to fool around or try to invent stories, because we have the facts."

Each man in turn is made to give details of his last abusive incident. This exercise is called a "check-in," carried out in a similar fashion to that in Alcoholics Anonymous meetings, where people introduce themselves by saying, "Hello, I'm so-and-so, and I'm an alcoholic." In the case of Asher Fram, when his turn came, he did not check in with, "I'm Asher Fram and I'm here because I slammed my partner's face in pine bark, kicked her in the ribs, and slammed her head against the ground." Instead, Fram made a short speech.

"I love my wife," Fram began with tears in his eyes, "and I believe she loves me regardless of the incident which brought me here. My wife has a tendency not to listen to my advice; she thinks she knows about finances . . ." At that point, Fram was instructed to stick to the subject of the violence that he inflicted on his wife—regardless of the reason —which ultimately brought the cops who arrested him.

The men are also required to report on their average intake of alcohol or drugs the previous week. "The rule is," Gaudette says, "as a condition of their probation, that they cannot drink or take drugs while they're in the program."

Of the eleven men in that intake group with Fram, there is a middle-aged African American employed in a responsible position with the Internal Revenue Service. Elroy Richardson was remanded to the group because he swung at his partner with a knife. As he put it, "That's what landed me here, I got in trouble after that one."

"The reality," Gaudette says, "is that if he swung a knife at a stranger on the subway or on the street, he wouldn't have the option of attending a batterers' group once a week for six months."

Another participant in the group is Donald Packard, an

aspiring musician with a local rock band. Packard describes
an incident when he pushed his pregnant wife out of his way
when she tried to prevent him from going out. While Mrs.
Packard sustained minimal physical injuries and never
sought medical treatment, petition papers that she filed with
the court resulted in her getting an order of protection
against her husband. Apparently, Packard violated that order
when he returned that night and stood in the street outside
their house calling his wife names and threatening to kill her
entire family. In that case, a neighbor called the police, who
issued a citation charging Donald Packard with disorderly
conduct and harassment. Represented by an attorney, he
appeared in court and voluntarily agreed to participate in
the batterers' group in lieu of thirty days in the county jail.

An unemployed Hispanic man with an admitted alcohol
problem, Carmine Ferrer, reported that he had been sober
for nineteen months and regularly attended AA meetings
when he "lost it" because he suspected his wife of cheating
on him with his brother. The incident that landed him in
the group was that he apparently chased his wife out of the
house, brandishing a shotgun, firing at her while she ran for
her life. When asked by Gaudette during the intake meeting
if he thought that he had hit her at the time, Ferrer replies,
"I couldn't tell because it was dark, but later on when the
cops came, I learned that she wasn't injured."

After each man told his story, a debate followed, led by
Gaudette and Ferland, that focused on how to identify abuse
that is not physical. With the exception of Fram, who stead-
fastly maintained throughout that first intake session that he
had never abused Deborah or any other woman in his life,
the men were all trying to make a good impression. Articu-
late and animated during the discussion, they could all man-
age at least one story about how they degraded their partners
about their hair, weight, or intelligence, or preyed on their
weaknesses.

For example, one man knew that his wife prided herself
on her cooking. "I'd throw every single dinner she cooked
into the garbage," the man related. Another man admitted

playing "mind games" with his girlfriend, giving her the silent treatment, which caused her to ask what was wrong. "Eventually, I'd turn it around and lose my temper with her by accusing her of always starting the argument," he explained. Still another man admitted that he humiliated his wife in front of her friends, telling her to shut up or calling her stupid every time she opened her mouth to join in the conversation.

And finally, there was the small timid man, who looked as if he would be afraid of his own shadow, who related an incident where he greeted his wife with the words "Hi, gummy" after she had gone through hours of oral surgery to remove several front teeth. His version, which he insisted was the truth, was that he had intended only to reinforce how courageous she was for having undergone such extensive surgery. His attempt at complimenting his partner for her bravery ended at a nearby emergency room. Apparently, the woman suffered a gash on her forehead, which required stitches, after he clobbered her with a beer bottle when she got "hysterical" after he called her "gummy."

Curiously, each of the men in the group claimed that he had limits when it came to abuse. Some maintained that they have never or would never use a weapon, while others swear they would never punch their partner with a closed fist, never cause injuries that required stitches, or never throw food around the house. What became clear was that each man had, in fact, committed one or more of the acts listed above during his relationship or marriage. Another curious similarity between the men was that regardless of their education or economic level, each defined his partner's role as cleaning the house, caring for the children, and cooking the meals. It made little difference even in those cases where the woman worked outside the house and contributed to the support of the family. "According to these guys," Gaudette clarifies, "a woman's job is a woman's job, and the rest is secondary."

The men also all believed that "woman's liberation" or "equality," more than economic, was an "invention that contributed to the breakdown of the family," even though some of the men expressing those opinions also consider themselves to be politically liberal. When they were told that holding that particularly archaic view of the female sex puts them comfortably in bed with certain members of the Moral Majority, the men defended themselves by claiming that their opinions were less a political philosophy than a matter of nature, specifically, that men should enjoy more privileges than women. Or precisely, as Asher Fram explains, "It's not about politics, but human nature. God created all men equal."

"If you talk to batterers about attributes that they find attractive in a woman," Gaudette says, "you're able to sense from them that they're looking at someone with whom they can enjoy a relationship where they're in control. We also get this from victims, where having a man in charge is a familiar and comfortable way that she's learned to have a relationship."

At the end of the intake session, the men are asked, again going around in a circle, to offer their opinion on why they believe that battering a partner should not be considered as serious a crime as assaulting a stranger. Asher Fram offers the following insight: "Our parents tell us that we shouldn't hit people we love, and yet they hit us and then claim it's for our own good, like, if I didn't love you, I wouldn't hit you. Behavior is always a more powerful teacher than words. The message is, if it happens to me at home, perhaps it's for my own good and it's all right. Obviously, if that same kind of stuff happens to me on the street, there's something wrong if I don't fight back and defend myself. What happened between us at the bank was humiliating, but I shouldn't have reacted there, I should have waited until we got home."

During the next meeting that the counselor had with Deborah Fram, Deborah offered the following insight as to why her husband reacts violently when there is a disagreement. "When I was a little girl, I'd come home from school and report that some little boy pulled my hair or pushed me, and the message from my mother was that it was his way of showing affection. Every time Asher reacted violently or tried to explain something to me and it got out of hand, he would always tell me that if he didn't love me, he wouldn't bother, the same way my parents told me when they punished me for something."

Ellen Ferland believes that sports also has a lot to do with it—when coaches tell boys and girls not to run like a girl or throw a ball like a sissy. "Boys are taught that girls are inferior," Ferland maintains, "that they're objects, and it's not good to be one. Girls are taught in some ways that, based on what you get out of life, it's better to be a boy—they have permission to live more freely and do more things—that there are even more choices when it comes to getting a good job."

Men and women who deal either with the batterer or with his victim find that there are many different explanations given from each to explain *his* behavior. These differences account for a chasm within the ranks of experts when it comes to one standard explanation, which proves that each case of domestic violence is individual. For example, there are some experts in the field who claim that the batterer is a man who fears intimacy.

Fernando Mederes believes that battering occurs only within a sphere of intimacy. "To me, it's a way for a man to possess or control intimacy," Mederes says, "and that's a dangerous illusion, because no one can possess intimacy; it has to be consensual."

According to Douglas Gaudette, there are some "feel good" groups that have sprung up around the country that promote the notion that the batterer is searching for his inner child. The predecessor to the inner child theory is the claim of those people who say that the batterer batters because he was the victim of abuse himself while growing up or has a drug or alcohol problem that causes him to lose control. Douglas Gaudette takes a simple approach to any social, medical, or psychological excuse given on behalf of any batterer who enters his program.

"My approach to these men is that they have battered and abused their partners because they have chosen to do that," he says. "And I don't really care how or why they have chosen to do that. Whether it's because they were beaten as a child, or because they have problems with drugs or alcohol, it makes no difference to me. If they want to take care of that somewhere else, they're free to do that.

"We treat these men with dignity and respect, but we don't coddle them; we take this very seriously, and we're frightened of this new movement that claims batterers need to find and heal their inner child before they can have empathy for their partner. The answer to that is that it's against the law to punch out his partner, and he can go work with his inner child on his own time. These men are here because they broke the law, and this program is not a court of law here, so they can't argue with me that their attorneys shafted them, or they didn't realize this was going to happen. They either pleaded guilty or they were found guilty, and if they don't want to be here, they don't have to come. But if they don't come, they'll end up in jail, and I'll testify against them, and that's the way that works."

Patricia Martel runs a program for male batterers at the Fordham-Tremont Community Mental Health Center in the Bronx, a twenty-six-week program that is ordered by the courts as part of probation or parole for perpetrators of domestic abuse. Martel maintains that a batterer usually gets the message early in life that a woman's role is to nurture and provide services for her man; that a woman needs to be controlled and dominated; and that violence, intimidation, and withholding financial support are acceptable ways to get that; that it's perfectly acceptable to smack a woman when dinner isn't ready on time or if the house is dirty.

One of Martel's first rules is to tell all participants in her group right at the beginning, "Don't blame the woman or some deep-seated psychological problem for your behavior. You hit because you thought you could get away with it."

Michael Paymar, a training coordinator for the Domestic Violence Intervention Project in Duluth, Minnesota, says,

"We're trying to convey that these men are not sick or mentally ill, even if they need to work out some issues in therapy." According to Paymar, sexist perceptions of women and the association between masculinity and violence are the universal causes of domestic violence. "These men have made a clear choice to abuse because in ninety-eight percent of the cases, a batterer knows what he's doing."

Warren Price, who runs the batterers' treatment program in New York under the auspices of Victims Services, also has no sympathy for the batterer and what, if any, hardships he endured that cause him to be violent. "We educate batterers in our program," Price explains; "we don't use therapy, because to do that would mean the batterer is sick and needs to be healed. These men aren't sick. Battering isn't an illness. Battering is learned behavior. They chose to abuse, and what we do is try to get them to make other choices."

Jonathan Cohen, from the Rockland County Batterers' Intervention Program, which approaches the subject from a sociopolitical point of view rather than from either a criminal or a behavioral context, says, "Psychopathology has nothing to do with battering, since it's about oppression, rooted in what we would consider to be the fundamental cause of the problem, institutionalized sexism. From what we've learned, violence is systematically taught and trained to men along with the belief of male privilege. There are a few primary reasons why men batter. First and foremost is that men can—we are allowed to. And not only are we not punished historically for controlling our violent behavior, but we are rewarded, honored, and encouraged. The other factor is about male bonding and how we interact with each other and put women down, which again comes from all the systematized and culturally indoctrinated misogyny. Men have to commit themselves to holding other men accountable for their actions in this culture. Abusive men don't need psychotherapy to address their abuse; they need to be stopped, and the only way to stop them is to adjust a system in which they have a sense of what we're talking about. The system itself creates the violence; the culture creates the violence through our institutional setup, which we would call patriarchy, which creates the necessity for men to be violent against women in order to protect this disproportionate power."

Douglas Gaudette, Ellen Ferland, Fernando Mederes, Warren Price, Jonathan Cohen, Phyllis Frank, and Mitchell Rottenberg, in their dealings with victims of domestic violence, all maintain that it is the pressures of society and the inherent role of women, as society defines it, that cause most victims to return to their abusive partners with a sense of hope and guilt.

"For the first couple of times that women leave," Mederes explains, "they return by convincing themselves that the batterer was under pressure because of work or health or money or whatever."

Gaudette adds, "They also return because the batterer promises to come to batterers' meetings or go to church, all because he's a changed man, or at least that's what they want to believe."

Rottenberg says, "There's also pressure from the kids to take their daddy back home. It's hard to ignore a kid who says how much he loves and misses daddy."

"It's not only the kids but the victim herself sometimes loves this man," Ellen Ferland maintains. "What she doesn't love is the monster in him, so she convinces herself that the monster is gone."

"Other times," Warren Price explains, "she returns for more practical reasons. While she's given up hope that the monster will never again appear, she also knows that without him, she won't get child support and she won't be able to pay the rent."

Jonathan Cohen adds, "She also figures that if she doesn't take him back, he won't stop kicking her door in and the landlord will make good on his threat to evict her. So the alternative is, better to take the beatings rather than be on the street without enough money to feed the children or, worse, be forced to relinquish the children to foster care."

"At least if she's with the batterer in the same house," Phyllis Frank says, "she believes she can control the violence, or at least she knows what to expect, which makes the known fear better than the unknown fear of the street."

As it concerns domestic violence, any standard definition of what constitutes criminal behavior is viewed differently for a variety of reasons. Society blames the victim each time that question is asked, "Why doesn't she just leave?"

Society gives women false assurances and the wrong messages about how they can protect themselves against a violent intimate partner. Women are told that if they call the police, the police will protect them; if they get an order of protection, the batterer will stay away; if they go to a therapist, it will change the batterer's behavior or help her learn less provocative behavior. Every one of these messages is not only inaccurate but dangerous. The reality is that in the worst of circumstances, if a woman calls the police, the police don't always protect her—and how many women are killed with orders of protection in their house or on their bodies?

If existing laws don't protect women from physical abuse, how can women expect to be protected from emotional terror? Before laws can be adjusted, adapted, or changed to protect all victims of this crime, society must first learn how to identify all aspects of domestic violence. So far, that has not happened.

There are countless incidents that illustrate every type of violence between family members or intimate partners; countless arguments for changing the way domestic violence is viewed by the social service system or the public in general; countless variations on the type of violence in the home (to whom, how often, how severe); so many cases in the courts where victims have been wrongly prosecuted and batterers unjustly acquitted for crimes having to do with partner assault; countless examples of how one act of spousal abuse can cause death or injury to people other than the victim targeted by the abuser. Julio Gonzalez is an example of the last.

Julio Gonzalez had a tough life before he came to New York. Beaten and jailed by soldiers in his native Cuba, he arrived on the first *Mariel* boat lift, one of thousands whom Castro claimed were political prisoners, although the United States Department of State claimed they were criminals that the Cuban leader simply released from jails and set adrift in small rafts heading toward the Florida coast.

After arriving in Florida, Julio made his way to the Bronx, where he had several distant cousins who let him sleep on the floor in the front room of their already crowded tenement. Julio found a series of odd jobs as well as a girl-friend named Lydia Feliciano. After a few months, however, Lydia tired of Julio and his jealous rages and broke up with him. The problem was that Julio didn't want to break up. He still loved Lydia.

One night, Julio arrived unannounced and uninvited at the Happyland Social Club in the Bronx, where Lydia worked as a coatcheck girl. At first, Lydia politely asked Julio to leave, before she called Melvin, the bouncer, to escort Julio outside. Melvin did as he was told before he stepped back inside to tell Lydia that Julio wanted just one minute to tell her something. Lydia decided to hear what Julio had to say instead of risking an ugly scene. What Julio had to say was that he wasn't going to be coming around the club any-more to bother her because she wasn't going to be working there anymore. Indignant, Lydia told Julio that she would work anywhere she pleased and he could go straight to hell. She left Julio standing in the street as she raced back inside. It was crowded and cold, and there was already a line of people waiting to check their coats. Passing Melvin, Lydia told him to make sure Julio was gone.

Julio was gone, all right. He was already at the corner gas station on Southern Boulevard, where he bought a dol-lar's worth of gas in a plastic antifreeze container. From there, he went back to the Happyland Social Club. Spilling the gasoline on the floor just inside the front door, Julio lit two matches, setting the club ablaze.

Julio's target was Lydia, but somehow Lydia survived. Within five minutes, the fire that Julio lit swept through the wood structure, trapping, suffocating, and burning alive eighty-seven people. It was considered the worst single act of murder in the history of the United States before that terrorist bomb exploded in Oklahoma City. What it was never considered was just one more example of domestic violence.

In the United States, a blood test is required before a marriage license is issued, specific fines are set for various traffic violations, income tax returns are periodically audited, inoculation against contagious diseases is required before children can enter school, cars and trucks require inspection every few years, and there are innumerable other ordinary constraints and guidelines that people accept without debate or protest.

Why is there so much resistance and conflict about acknowledging, convicting, and sentencing perpetrators to prison?

EIGHTEEN

The Serial Killer

IN THE 1970s, the feminist movement rejuvenated and women began holding consciousness-raising meetings. "We'd sit around and talk about our lives and what it meant to grow up female," Charlotte Watson recalls, "and during those sessions, we learned that there were a number of women who were being battered."

According to Watson, that was the period when women began fleeing to shelters, where their stories were all the same. "They called the police," Watson continues; "the police ignored them, laughed at them, blamed them, or in the best of cases, advised the husband to take a walk around the block to cool off." As for those few brave women who dared to press charges against their partners, they found that prosecutors and judges sent them home to make up for the sake of the children.

If there was one positive result that emerged from long discussions and consciousness-raising groups, it was that women realized that domestic violence was not about men's anger. There were too many women who confirmed that their batterers were otherwise calm in situations outside of the home to uphold the premise that men who beat their partners did so in a moment of temporary rage. In fact, women reported that their partners' colleagues or friends often described them as patient, calm, and cool individuals, a mystifying description since they knew these men to be impatient, violent, and explosive.

Fernando Mederes grew up in an abusive home.

"I began working as a psychotherapist," Mederes begins, "and most of the people I saw were women, and quite a few talked about being battered or abused in other ways. It was interesting for me because instinctively I understood the situation and decided I wanted to work with the men to get to the core of the problem. The minute I began dealing with these men, I realized that I was looking at my own family. After my father's funeral, the men came over to give me very powerful hugs and tell me what a wonderful mentor my father was, how encouraging he was to all of them. I literally began to get dizzy; I felt as if I was in the wrong wake, because I didn't recognize the man they were extolling. My father was above all a psychological batterer. He controlled the family with his face; an expression was enough to make us all terrified. The point is that a stranger or even a close friend doesn't know the batterer in the same way as his victim knows him. He has a much different face to the outside world."

Charlotte Watson offers another explanation. "The batterer is a man who in other situations when he's angry doesn't punch people out," she says; "he's very much in control. In fact, he's even in control when it comes to his partner, since instead of slapping her in public, he'll wait until they get home to beat her up, or he'll beat her up in the car on the way home. So this isn't about poor impulse control or anger, since it's a very controlled act."

A dangerous aspect of this Jekyll-and-Hyde personality is that often it is reproduced in a courtroom setting, where the batterer can appear as a more credible witness than his partner, especially if he is professional, affluent, or perceived as a pillar of the community. Judge Knaplund explains, "Because most of these men are manipulative, they're forced to be charming, and as you go up the social ladder, the abuse is even more hidden. With money, these men are more generous to friends and family, so people are even more shocked when they learn that he's a batterer or a murderer."

In the late 1970s social scientists, including Lenore Walker, the architect of *The Battered Women's Syndrome* and *Learned Helplessness,* began compiling statistics on domestic violence. As a result, several different theories on the subject were presented. Determining that there was a communications problem between men and women, researchers suggested that women should learn to fight fairly so arguments wouldn't escalate into violent confrontations. On the basis of those theories along with her own work, Lenore Walker developed what she called the "cycle of violence wheel." Her thesis suggested that in any cycle of violence, there was a period in the relationship when the tension would build. Then it escalated into violent confrontation. Afterward followed what she called the "honeymoon phase," which included apologies by the batterer—before the tension would build once again, only to erupt in more violent behavior, to be followed by another honeymoon phase . . . and around and around and around.

On the basis of Walker's model, social workers, feminists, and therapists decided that the most urgent priority was to interrupt that tension-building phase in order to eliminate the violence that ensued. As a result, men were sent off to groups to learn how to deal with their feelings and express their anger in ways that didn't hurt people. Couples counseling and mediation became the mode as well, which, according to David Adams, put women in even greater life-threatening danger. "In any dual counseling and mediation program, it's assumed that there is an equal division of power in the relationship," Adams explains. "When there's violence on the part of one partner or the other, that power balance has shifted."

Judge Knaplund agrees, offering an interesting comparison that once again separates stranger crime from domestic violence. "When was the last time that a rapist was ordered to engage in therapy with his victim?" Knaplund asks, "or when is a mugger required to talk out his problems with his victim? Violence between people with a prior or ongoing relationship shouldn't be viewed as any different than what is already provided for under the statutes of criminal law."

Ellen Pence is a plumber by trade. She is also the founder of the Duluth Domestic Violence Intervention Project, which subscribes to the theory that society supports and encourages battering. Pence believes that every aspect of life is affected by hierarchical structures in which someone is "in charge" while others are the "subordinates." Pence's interest in and awareness of domestic violence was a direct result of her work as a plumber. After she finished repairing appliances or faucets, she would sit around the kitchen table and talk to the women, listening to their stories about the violence they suffered at the hands of their intimate partners.

Pence began to realize that Lenore Walker's cycle of violence wheel actually minimized what women went through during the aggression period in the cycle, since the model accounted only for physical violence. The women Pence talked to described incidents of verbal and psychological abuse that continued even when they were in the period that Walker described as the honeymoon phase. Pence also learned that the model didn't account for the fear that these women lived with every minute of their lives, regardless of where they or their batterers were in Walker's cycle. Further, Spence learned that when women thought about a honeymoon, they thought about a time when they felt really good about their partners and went off to some secluded place and made love. Contrary to what Walker suggested, Pence argued, "When a man has just beaten the shit out of his partner and wants to make love as part of the apology, women felt like they were being raped."

Again, Judge Knaplund equates those different responses during Walker's honeymoon phase to the social and economic level of the couple. "During that so-called honeymoon phase," Judge Knaplund suggests, "the Scarsdale woman may get a new Mercedes, while the Yonkers woman may get flowers, or perhaps the Bedford woman will get dinner at Lutèce, while the Mount Vernon woman may find her partner vacuuming the house." In every case, regardless of the reward, the batterer's goal is to entice, bribe, cajole, and seduce his partner into staying in the relationship.

While feminists, battered women, and their advocates began to understand the dynamics of the batterer, the rest of society still kept asking that same question, "Why doesn't she just leave?" Using her other theory, of learned helplessness, Lenore Walker answered that question as well. Ellen Pence disagreed.

According to Pence, the notion of learned helplessness not only trivializes the violence that the victim endures but ignores the threat of more brutal and escalated violence in retaliation for the victim attempting to escape her batterer. Pence believes that women who find themselves victims of an abusive partner did not necessarily begin life with low self-esteem or a sense of learned helplessness, as Lenore Walker maintained.

There is nothing mysterious about a woman feeling low self-esteem when she is in a situation where, because of economics or fear, she finds herself trapped and unable to escape her captor. The message being sent was that learned helplessness was something a woman acquired along with the beatings, as if that too were her fault. Rather, the reality was that any person, man or woman, who is forced into submission by constant terrorization, intimidation, and physical violence, naturally experiences low self-esteem brought on by the realization that he or she has remained in that situation. In the case of the battered woman, if she suffers from a psychological problem or deficiency (rather than learned helplessness), it is that she hasn't learned to acknowledge her partner's behavior as criminal.

On the basis of her twenty years of experience dealing with battered women and their abusers, Ellen Ferland offers what she maintains is the only valid example of learned helplessness.

"A child came to me for therapy," Ferland begins. "She came from a family where her father beat her mother and

the children, where her sisters were beaten by their boyfriends, and where, after the father died, her brother took
over the job of beating his mother and siblings. This child
walked around with a sign on her back that her brother had
put there which said, 'Kick me, I'm stupid.' Will this child go
on to become a battered woman? The answer is yes."

In the beginning, Ellen Ferland describes how the child
would look into a mirror and see nothing, until after four
years of therapy, she began to see her own reflection. "That's
an example of learned helplessness," Ferland maintains,
"not women who are in relationships and can't get out. In
those cases, learned helplessness implies they have relin-
quished their options as well as their feelings."

In the course of her research in Duluth, Ellen Pence
also found what she considered the most lethal catch-22 in
Walker's theory of learned helplessness, evident when a
woman did try to defend herself against her abuser and, as a
result, found herself facing the judicial system. According to
Pence, it was just one more example of the inequity of the
legal system as it concerned domestic violence and the perpetrators of that crime. "On one hand, Walker's theory of
learned helplessness has been somewhat accepted as a legal
defense when a battered woman kills her batterer, as it is
covered under the battered woman's syndrome," Pence explains. "Yet, on the other hand, how can a woman claim
learned helplessness or the battered woman syndrome if,
instead of being helpless, she actually fights back and gets
angry enough to kill or seriously injure her batterer? After
all, that's precisely the woman who's going to be facing the
judicial system, not the woman who was paralyzed by fear. In
fact, the woman suffering from what the law considers
learned helplessness or the battered woman's syndrome by
definition should end up as the victim, and her batterer
should face the judicial system after being charged with her
murder."

As a result of research conducted in Duluth by interviewing women whose lives had been directly affected by
domestic violence, Ellen Pence developed what she called

the "power and control" wheel to replace Walker's cycle of violence wheel. In Pence's model, power and control were at the hub of the wheel in every case of domestic violence. Whenever the batterer perceived that his partner was resisting his authority, he would step up whatever control he was using—economic, emotional (harassment), or verbal, or intimidation or threats—all escalating until the final result ended in physical abuse. According to Pence, it was just as subtle a technique of control as when the batterer presented himself as the perfect mate for any unsuspecting woman, and more subtle than the discrepancy between the batterer's public versus private image, which further endangered his partner's chances for escape. The conclusion that Pence drew was that it was just another example of victim blaming, which resulted, time and again, in the batterer either getting a minimum sentence or no sentence at all.

It takes only one case of domestic violence that the press determines merits public notice to make society aware that despite laws and consciousness-raising movements, the past is never really gone. Despite all that we learn and hear about domestic violence, regardless of the details of any particular case, that same infernal question is still asked over and over again, "Why didn't she just leave?"

The Steinberg/Nussbaum case riveted world attention not only because the ultimate victim of that violent relationship was the couple's illegally adopted child, Lisa, but also because the people involved were professional, educated, and lived in an upper-middle-class neighborhood far from any urban ghetto. The conclusion that the public should have drawn from that case was that domestic violence can and does happen anywhere and to anyone, putting children as well as adults at risk.

In the case of Hedda Nussbaum and Joel Steinberg, however, neither they nor their situation fit into what William Ryan described in his book *Blaming the Victim* as the pariah syndrome. Joel Steinberg was a lawyer, while Hedda Nussbaum, his live-in lover for seventeen years, was a children's book editor. Their home was an apartment in a landmark brownstone building in New York's Greenwich Village where Mark Twain once lived.

After the murder, one of the questions that everyone kept asking was, "How could he beat her?" What that question really asked was, "How could someone *like him* beat her?" The other question that people kept asking was, "Why did Hedda put up with it when she had an education and a job and wasn't even married to him?" That question was actually an insinuation that, obviously, Hedda must have been mentally incompetent, deranged, or masochistic. In fact, there were some people—educated, liberal, intellectual people who lived in their neighborhood—who told several reporters that the couple's relationship was "some kind of a sexual sadomasochistic game." It was a judgment that echoed what District Attorney Janine Ferris Pirro said about how society judges this kind of crime. "Some people believe," Pirro said, "that battered women think sex is better after a beating."

Neither question that was asked concerning Steinberg or Nussbaum, however, had anything to do with the crime of domestic violence or the reasons that men batter women or the reasons that women stay. Each question related to the social, economic, and intellectual credentials of the perpetrator and his victim.

In the end, when Joel Steinberg was finally arrested for the murder of little Lisa, society was finally able to find an appropriate variation for both questions when they asked, "How could Hedda Nussbaum have allowed Joel Steinberg to beat Lisa to death?"

First of all, the characterization of the batterer and the victim as educated professionals and therefore exempt from being either victim or perpetrator is an example of how society misunderstands the dynamics of those involved in any abusive relationship. As we know, not all batterers are racial minorities, uneducated, or poor. If the batterer can be a gainfully employed professional, so can the victim. Just because a woman is educated, employed, or financially independent, that doesn't mean that she doesn't want to find a partner and enter into a relationship, nor does it mean that she isn't vulnerable, or immune from making mistakes or choosing badly. One does not preclude the other. Second, putting the onus and responsibility on Nussbaum is an instance of victim blaming at its most virulent.

Hedda Nussbaum may have been a well-respected children's book editor, but she was also a battered woman who had been beaten physically and mentally to a veritable pulp. Joel Steinberg may have been active in the civil rights movement, but to Hedda, he was the man she loved and trusted the most, her most intimate friend. He was also the man who abused, battered, and controlled her in a daily situation of escalating violence from which she was unable to escape. Under those circumstances, how could society expect Hedda Nussbaum, in her diminished state, to achieve what the police, social workers, doctors, lawyers, and the courts were unable to accomplish?

The answer to how Hedda could have "allowed" Lisa to be beaten to death is that she didn't. There had been child protection workers in the house, policemen with guns, schoolteachers who saw the child every single day who knew or suspected that she was being abused. Yet nobody did anything to break the cycle of violence in the Steinberg/Nussbaum house. If all of those systems and professionals couldn't provide protection, how could society expect a woman who was barely alive to make rational decisions?

There were many people who argued that Hedda Nussbaum should not be viewed as the quintessential battered woman, because that does a disservice to other women, whose children were neither harmed nor killed as a result of violence inflicted on them by their mother's partner. To take that position is dangerous and damaging, but above all, it is counterproductive. Hedda Nussbaum may not be the most popular battered woman, but she is the most typical.

Until society grasps the concept that the battered woman is unable, whether physically or mentally, to extricate herself to save either her own life or the lives of her children, she will continue to be blamed, while her batterer will continue to go unpunished.

Lisa Steinberg (Launders) is an example of the failure of the police to insist, gain access to a house, and arrest without fear of subsequent individual legal action taken against them. The death of Lisa is a reason for must-arrest laws, nondiscretionary arrest laws, cameras in police cars, a computerized system that identifies batterers, different laws for misdemeanors and felonies as they pertain to domestic violence, incarceration without bail for all batterers until their court hearings, and routine contact between teachers and social service workers when schoolchildren appear to be living in violent situations.

Hedda Nussbaum stands as the justification for mandated reporting of abuse when there are minor children living in the home. She is the reason why programs such as AWAKE should be implemented throughout the country, to reach battered women through their children. Equally important, Hedda reminds every one of us that we are as guilty as the breakdown of any system if we know someone, intimately or vaguely, who is living in a home where there is violence and we don't react and embark on a rescue mission. And not one of us can afford to consider that rescue mission to be an intrusion into the private life of any citizen.

Joel Steinberg, the batterer and murderer, is an example of why cooperation, communication, and change throughout all systems are critical if these kinds of criminals are to be stopped.

Newsweek magazine called the Steinberg/Nussbaum tragedy a "chilling tale of drug abuse, systematic beatings and a life of squalor hidden behind a middle-class facade," painting a portrait of victim and abuser as anything but ordinary. What was so profoundly misunderstood was that the "chilling" aspect of the crime was that it was so ordinary.

On February 24, 1995, Asher Fram and Deborah Garner Fram left Logan International Airport in Boston for a vacation in Bermuda. It was meant to be a reconciliation trip to try and make a new beginning to what had been a short but troubled marriage.

On February 26, 1995, Deborah Garner Fram was pronounced dead on arrival at a hospital in Hamilton, Bermuda.

According to the chief medical examiner, Deborah suffered massive internal injuries and hemorrhaging resulting from a ruptured spleen, crushed chest and skull. According to witnesses who happened to be in the driveway of their hotel when the murder occurred, a young woman clad only in her underwear ran screaming from one of the hotel bungalows. In pursuit was a man on a moped whom people described as "clean-cut, white, and well dressed."

The woman stumbled and fell several yards before the end of the driveway, which was when the moped struck her once, sending her flying six feet through the air, landing facedown on the stump of a tree. Lying bloodied and unconscious, she was struck again by the moped, which screeched forward and ran over her crumpled body.

The victim's husband, Asher Fram, was arrested and convicted of murder. He is currently serving a twenty-five-year prison sentence in Bermuda.

AFTERWORD

LET THIS SERVE as a reminder to everyone that the O. J. Simpson double murder trial was about domestic violence. In case anyone has forgotten, the trial of O. J. Simpson, admitted wife beater and acquitted murderer, should have told the story of how Nicole Brown Simpson lived in constant fear of being beaten, terrorized, harrassed, stalked, and murdered by the man who was ultimately accused of killing her. "He's going to kill me one day," she said, "and he's going to get away with it because he's O. J. Simpson."

Now, in the dazed aftermath of the verdict, the greatest tragedy is that the core issue of domestic violence continues to be lost in a swirling and bitter discussion of race relations. In fact, domestic violence, which should have been the pivotal issue at this trial, was visible only for a moment, just long enough to give battered women hope that finally this crime would be put on trial on television throughout the country to show what can and does happen to women who live in this kind of hell.

Tragically, that never happened. The country was not suddenly made aware of the lethality of this crime, nor did this particular case provoke changes in the law so that every incident of domestic violence would be treated as a potential homicide, with every perpetrator considered a dangerous criminal. During the whole painful process of this trial the

most compelling motive for these murders remained buried
under legal technicalities, allegedly sloppy laboratory work,
and racist cops. Even now, after we have witnessed the ob-
scenities that have followed the Simpson acquittal, the most
plausible motive for the murder of Nicole Brown Simpson
and Ronald Goldman continues to be ignored.

And if people are not celebrating or profiting from this
tragedy, they are concentrating on the verdict and are blaming either the jurors or the Los Angeles Police Department
or the prosecution, or they are attacking the moral values in
a country where celebrities get special treatment and color
plays a part in all court cases, although the color that really
counted here was the green of money. The question, therefore, is, who exactly is to blame for this travesty of justice?
Who is responsible for the murders of Nicole Brown Simpson and Ronald Goldman? The list is long.

Society is to blame for the way it views women and especially for the way it deals with men who abuse and murder
women they know. Perhaps NBC should be offered a piece
of the blame for not firing O. J. Simpson as a sports commen-
tator after he was arrested for assaulting his wife. The Hertz
Corporation can also be blamed for judging that a convicted
wife batterer still makes a decent pitchman for rental cars.
And the Los Angeles Police Department, which arrived on
the scene back when Nicole had only been beaten and not
yet stabbed to death, and proceeded to slap the football
player lightly on the wrist instead of handcuffing him and
carting him off to jail, has earned its share of the shame. Let
us not forget, by the way, that it was members of that same
police department who came and went the night Nicole
made that harrowing call to 911, and that they did nothing to
make Simpson understand how horrifically, how criminally
wrong he was. And then there was the judge who sentenced
the *Naked Gun* star to community service and psychological
counseling that he could phone in. Which makes Simpson's
psychiatrist responsible as well for participating in those cel-
lular chats instead of realizing that while his patient may
have been too busy traveling all over the country or playing

golf to appear one hour a week in person, he was not busy enough to stop harrassing, stalking, terrorizing, beating, and eventually getting himself indicted for the murder of his ex-wife.

But the list does not end here.

Perhaps if everyone mentioned had reacted with appropriate outrage when O. J. Simpson was arrested the first time for spousal assault, the trial of the century would never have happened. All of us who wish that Nicole Brown Simpson had become a spokesperson for battered women instead of one of the well-known victims of this crime must carry the burden. As it stands now, given our system and our priorities, Nicole Brown Simpson didn't have a chance, and that makes every one of us responsible.

All that remains is shame—for all the mistakes, oversights, errors, and bad judgments that were made from the beginning when O. J. Simpson first raised his voice and hand to his wife. If only the police had taken action when they saw the condition of Nicole Brown Simpson's face and body. If only the first judge had considered spousal assault as serious a crime as stranger assault. If only that psychiatrist had refused to use a telephone to run a batterers' intervention program. If only the executives at NBC and Hertz had made it clear that wife battering was as serious an offense as drug abuse and fired O. J. Simpson. If only dogs could talk.

INDEX

abuse:
  child, *see* child abuse
  as ingrained in men, 236–37
  nonviolent, 61, 180, 196–97,
    206, 213, 231–38, 250–51,
    261
  problems with definition of,
    180, 196, 231, 233–38
  sexual, 105, 108, 167, 176,
    239–40
  see also battered women;
    batterers, battery; domestic
    violence
Adams, David, 209–10, 212,
    219–20, 237–38, 262
adjournment in contemplation
    of dismissal (ACD), 221
advocates for battered women,
    38, 120, 141
  arrest opposed by, 44, 45, 49
  battered women as viewed
    by, 144–47
  in court, 181
  empowerment and, 24–25,
    43–49
  hospital, 42, 47–48, 60, 63,
    72, 79, 88, 93–95, 97–100
  mandated reporting opposed
    by, 24, 43–49, 83
  victim's safety compromised
    by, 24

AIDS, 205
Alcoholics Anonymous, 204,
    249
alcoholism, 52, 115, 168, 204,
    214, 228
  battering and, 143–44, 153,
    220
American Bar Association,
    174
American Medical Association
    (AMA), 50, 66, 90, 174
  anti-domestic violence
    campaign begun by, 51
  Connecticut law and, 93
  domestic violence defined
    hy, 56, 234
  domestic violence statistics
    of, 51–52, 60
  failings of, 55–56, 58, 59
  guidelines of, 56, 59, 63, 91
  medical jargon and, 69
American Police Foundation,
    130
Amnesty International, 45, 46
anger, domestic violence and,
    260–61
arrest, 20, 208
  advocates' opposition to, 44,
    45, 49
  behavioral effects of, 44, 45,
    49, 132–33

as deterrent to further
violence, 131–33, 137
discretionary vs.
nondiscretionary laws
about, 137–40, 143, 146–
149
failure to, 13, 14, 15, 27, 127
false, 139, 148, 154
increase in, 93
in Minneapolis Experiment,
130–32
release on bail after, 99–100
Sherman's view of, 137, 146
in Thurman case, 13, 14,
26
when to, 25
assault, 21–25, 30, 72
best police responses to,
130–32, 134–36
early intervention in, 130
against intimates vs.
strangers, 18, 22, 25, 52,
120–21
judging victims of, 25
police decision making on
merits of case of, 126–27,
131
prevention of, 80
repetition of, 130
in Thurman case, 13, 15–16,
18
weapons in, 15, 51, 105, 115,
140
auto accidents, 51, 72
in Goldenberg case, 34–35,
37
AWAKE program, 111–14, 269

bail, 128–29
release on, 99–100, 103, 104,
150
Barre, Raymond, 22, 25
bathing, terror of, 235
Battered Woman, The (Walker),
17n–18n
battered women:
advocates for, *see* advocates
for battered women
AMA statistics on, 51–52

changing perception of,
144–47
characteristics of, 81
child abuse by, 86, 114
child abuse linked to, 105–
116
death of, *see* death of victim
emotional trauma of, 20, 24,
45, 52, 64, 65, 70
FBI statistics on, 150
fears of, 20, 41, 45, 50, 70,
85, 94–95, 108, 138
historical roots of, 119–20
hostages compared with, 45–
46
isolation of, 17, 200–201,
213, 214
Koop and, 40–41, 43, 50–
51
lying of, 137–39, 165
medical jargon and, 68–80
medical model and, 75–77,
79
Novello and, 43, 50–51
patient model and, 75
psychological views on, 53–
54
relevant questions about, 21,
22–23
research on, 53–54
as responsible for abuse, 41
rights of, 24–27, 48, 56, 57,
127, 141–42, 158, 159
sociologists' view of, 17
uniqueness of, 82
"Why doesn't she leave?"
question and, 16–22, 45,
47, 53, 183, 240–41, 256–
257
see also victims
*Battered Women's Syndrome and
Learned Helplessness, The*
(Walker), 262
batterers, battery, 21, 30, 195
acquittal of, 150
arrest of, *see* arrest
civil rights of, 28
Common Purpose's view of,
213–14

courts, *continued*
  batterer aided by, 19, 103,
    182–83
  communication and, 197–98
  contradictions in, 197
  escorts and, 194–95
  failure to report domestic
    violence and, 91–92
  Hughes case and, 145–46
  lack of family law experience
    and, 192–93
  Lawrence program and, 229
  lying in, 138
  testimony, police, 155–56
  testimony in, 87–88, 120
  in Thurman case, 13, 14, 26–
    27
  trauma in, 181
  unions and, 192
  see also specific courts
crime:
  domestic violence as, 18–33,
    41, 50, 52–53, 69–70, 72,
    86, 96, 120–21, 127, 128,
    144, 158–59, 164–65, 180–
    182, 208, 225, 262–63
  quantitative approach to, 117
  stranger, *see* stranger crime
  victim's part in, 21–22, 52–
    53
  see also specific crimes
Crime and Punishment
    (Dostoevski), 120
Crime Prevention Survey, 118
Criminal Court, 121, 123, 124–
    125, 194, 197
Criminal Justice Agency (CJA),
    194
Cummings, Cheryl, 167–71
custody, *see* child custody
cycle of violence wheel, 262–66

death, of children, 105, 109
death of victim:
  Deborah Fram, 269–70
  Emily Goldenberg, 35–39,
    243, 248
  mandated recording and,
    48–49

death penalty, opposition to, 137
Deltufo, Alisa, 163–64
delusional fears, battering and,
    215
denial:
  batterer's use of, 209, 220,
    221, 245–46
  victim's use of, 231
depression, battering and, 215
Dialogue on Democracy
    program, 58
discrimination, domestic
    violence and, 149
divorce, 17, 19, 24
  battering as negotiation
    point in, 137
doctor-patient relationship:
  distance in, 66–68
  trust and communication in,
    76–77
domestic violence:
  Adams's definition of, 237–
    238
  AMA and, 51–52, 56, 60, 234
  in Colorado, 102
  in Connecticut, 91–93
  costs of, 60, 88–89
  as crime, 18–33, 41, 50, 52–
    53, 69–70, 72, 86, 96, 120–
    121, 127, 128, 144, 158–59,
    164–65, 180–82, 208, 225,
    262–63
  emotional trauma of, 20, 24,
    45, 52, 64, 65, 70
  as learned abuse, 164
  long-term programs for
    solving of, 30
  low priority of, 117–18
  medical system and, *see*
    medical system
  as pariah syndrome, 204
  police response to, *see* police
  preventive medicine and, 80
  public health impact of, 51–
    52
  public reluctance in
    condemnation of, 29–30,
    218–20, 230–32, 254–59,
    272–73